the **digital photographer's** handbook

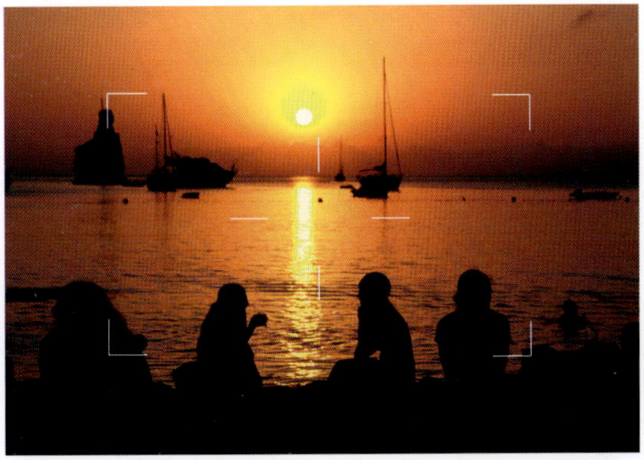

# travel

RotoVision

A RotoVision Book
Published and distributed by RotoVision SA,
Route Suisse 9, CH-1295 Mies
Switzerland

RotoVision SA, Sales, Editorial & Production Office
Sheridan House, 112/116a Western Road
Hove, East Sussex BN3 1DD, UK

Tel: +44 (0)1273 72 72 68
Fax: +44 (0)1273 72 72 69
Email: sales@rotovision.com
Website: www.rotovision.com



10 9 8 7 6 5 4 3 2 1

ISBN 2-88046-685-7

Designed by S2 Creative Solutions

Originated by Hong Kong Scanner Arts
Printed in China by Midas Printing International

the **digital photographer's** handbook

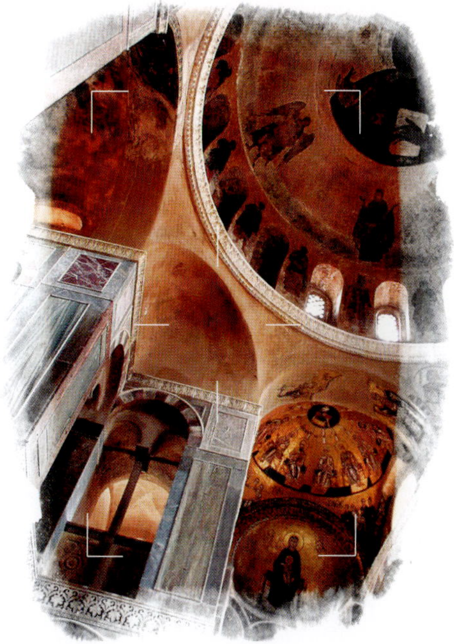

# travel

Simon Joinson

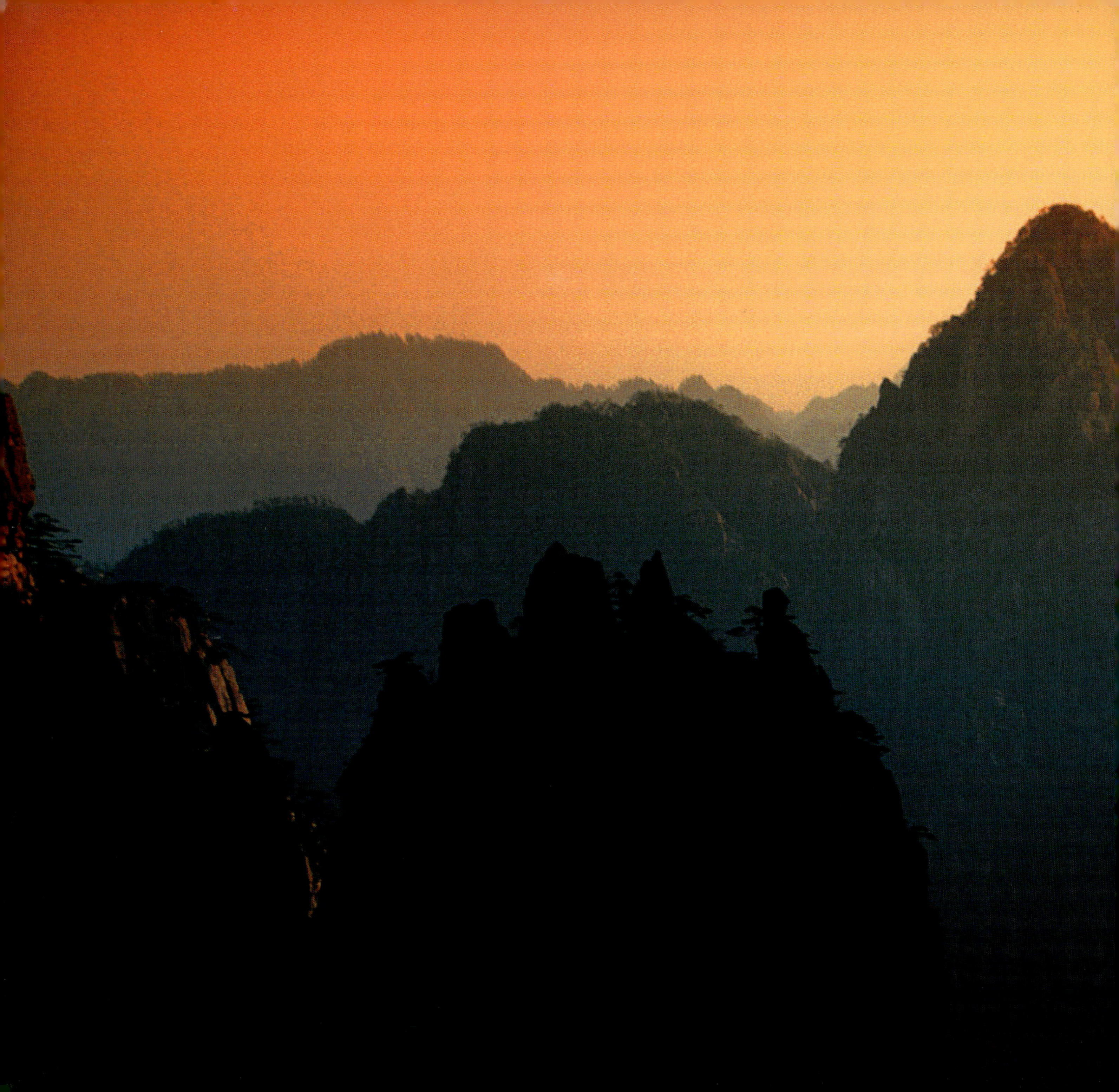

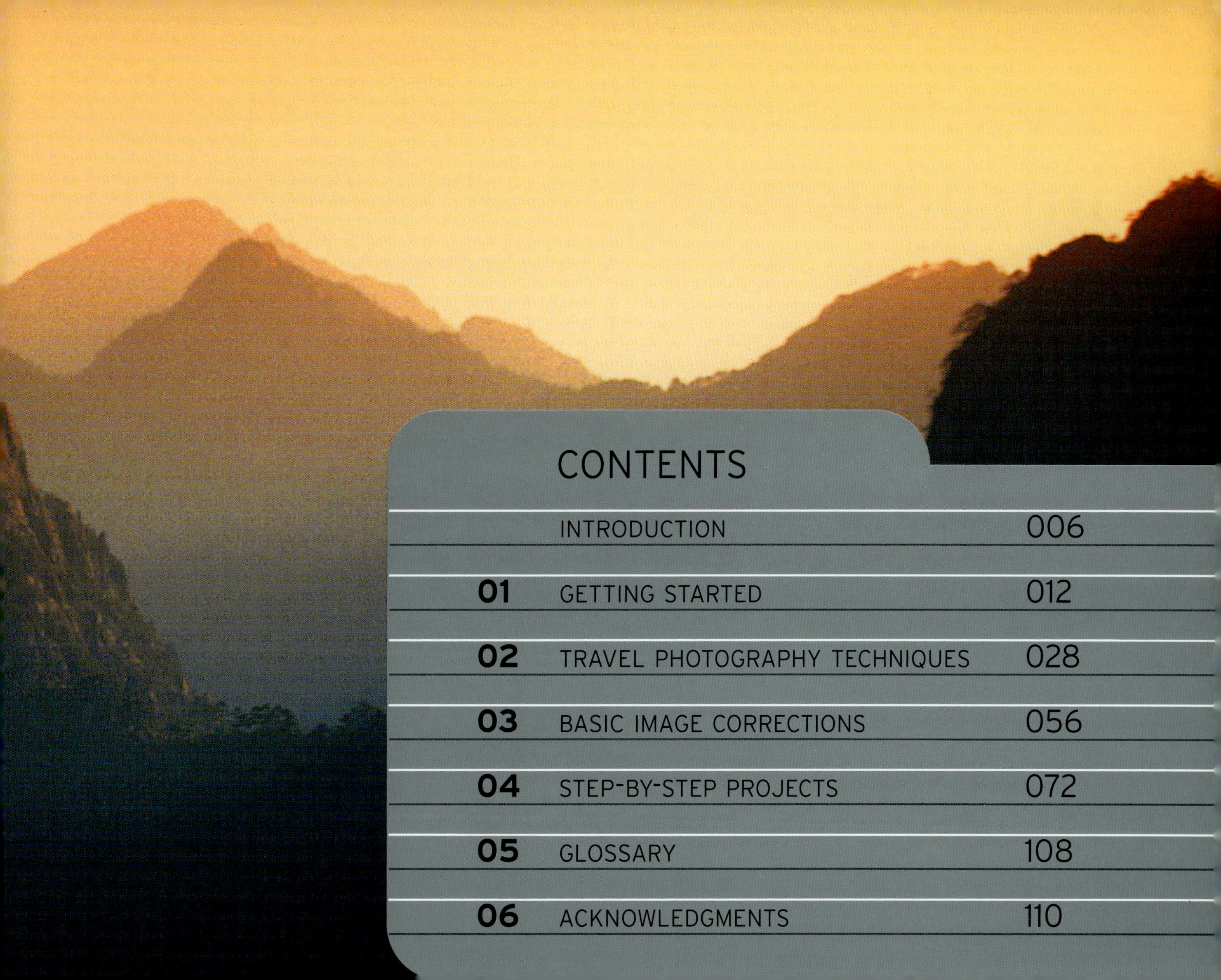

# CONTENTS

# Introduction

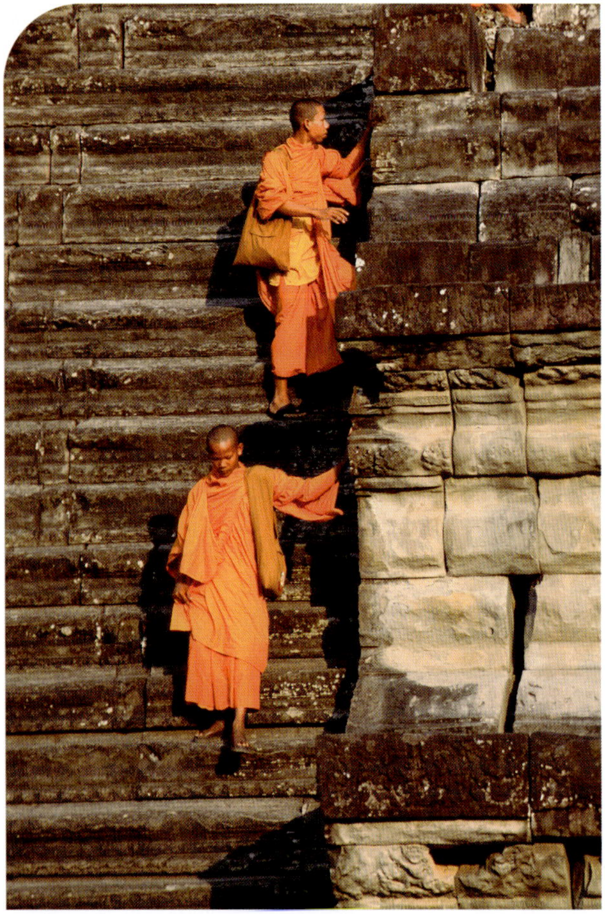

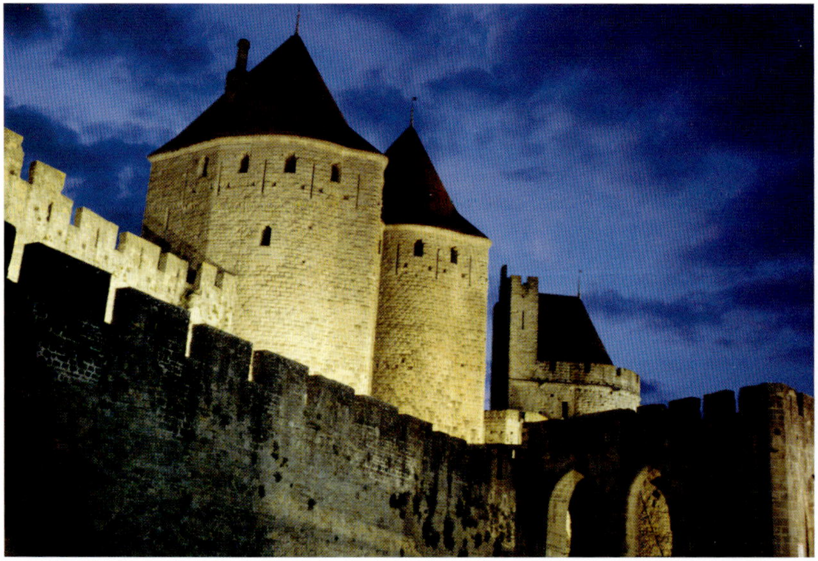

Travel photography is unusual in that it can – and does – encompass all styles and disciplines of photography.

It is about achieving a practical balance between carrying too much equipment and not carrying enough; being secure with your equipment and actually bringing out your camera to take pictures. Travel photography is just as much about carrying heavy equipment in difficult conditions and getting into the right place at the right time as it is about composition and exposure. It is about dealing with the familiar – your equipment – in an unfamiliar environment and still performing as well – technically and creatively – as you would back home. But travel photography is also incredibly rewarding and often leads you to do and see more, and meet and speak to more local people than you ever would do if you were just on holiday.

The first part of this book deals with traditional photographic skills, all of which

▲ Monks climbing down the steep steps of the central sanctuary, Angkor Wat, Cambodia

▲ Floodlit Citadel of Carcassone, France

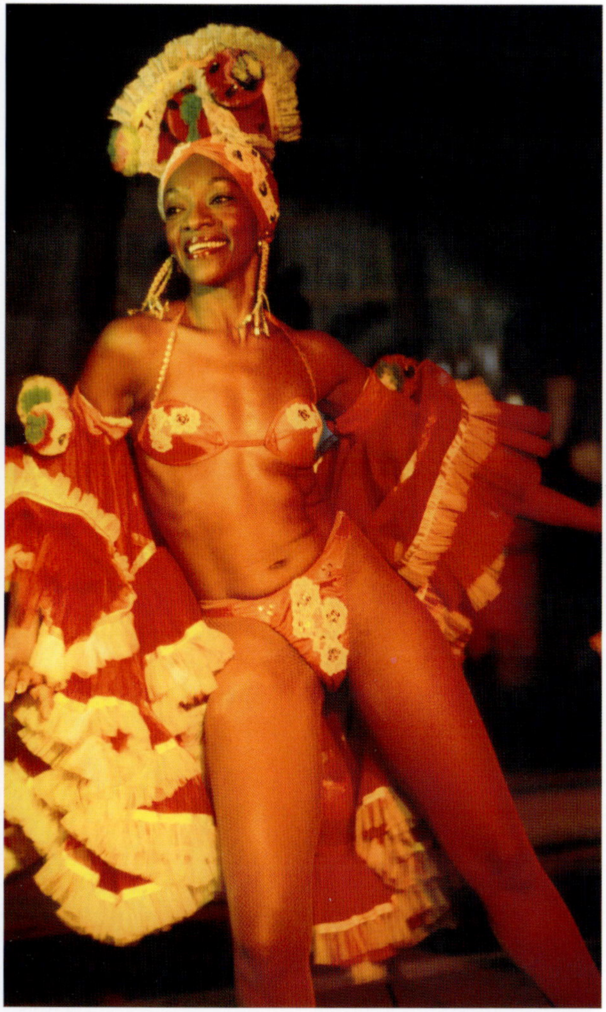

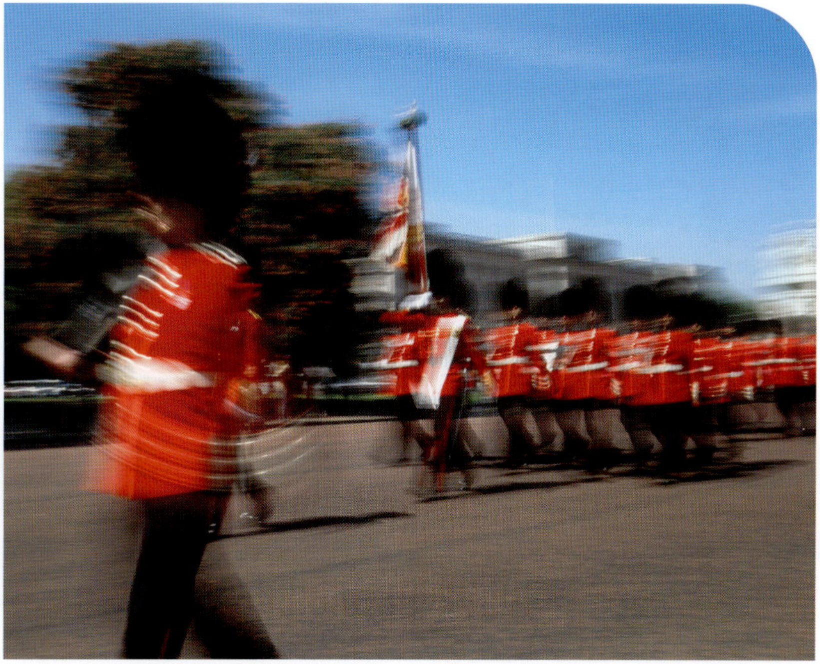

are still required even in this age of post-processing and manipulation. Sure, you can slap your pictures through a program like Photoshop and fix all sorts of composition, exposure or lighting errors, but you really can't turn a pig's ear into a silk purse. You can't introduce 'quality' where it never was, and it is better to use your computer skills for creative enhancements rather than spending time trying to fix problems caused by poor photography.

That said, there is a huge disparity between shooting digitally - or for digital processing - than shooting on film. With conventional photography, the creative process more or less finishes the moment you press the shutter, certainly for color work. With digital, the actual moment of the exposure is only the start of the process. Armed with this knowledge you can begin to shoot in a very different way. If a scene is spoilt by a couple of tourists on the horizon, you can shoot anyway,

▲ Cabaret Dancer, Varadero, Cuba

▲ Changing of the guard, Buckingham Palace, London, England

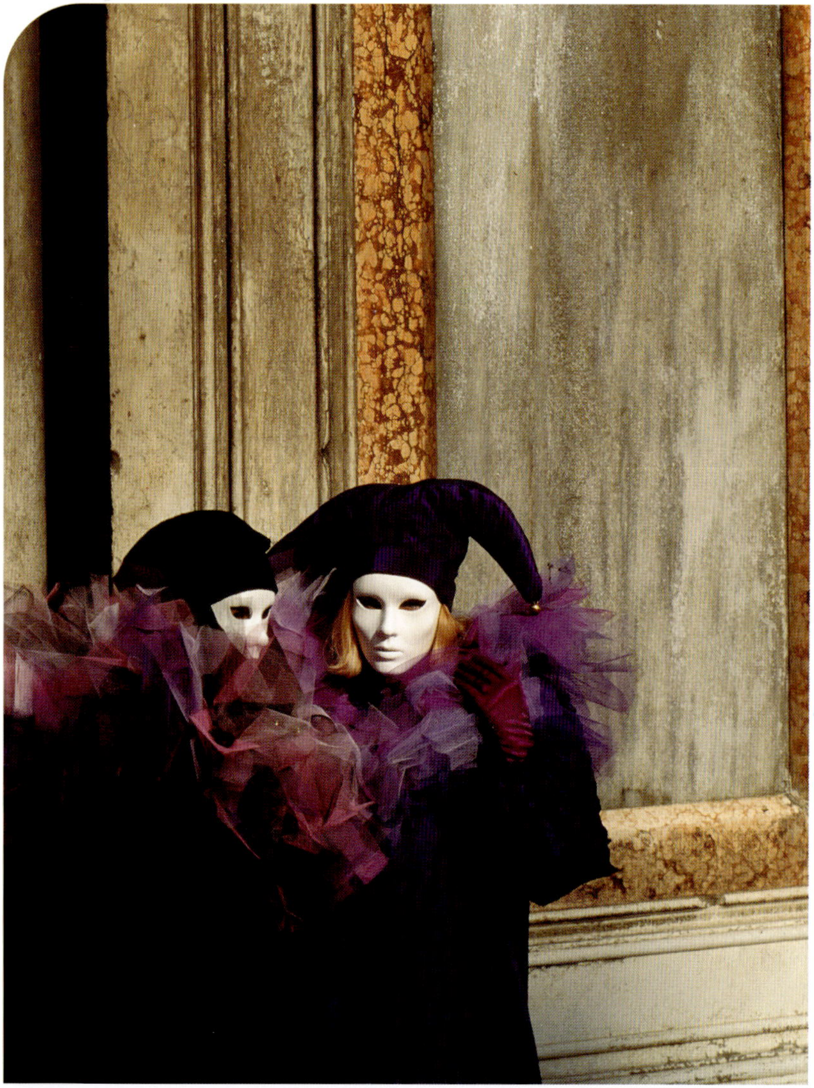

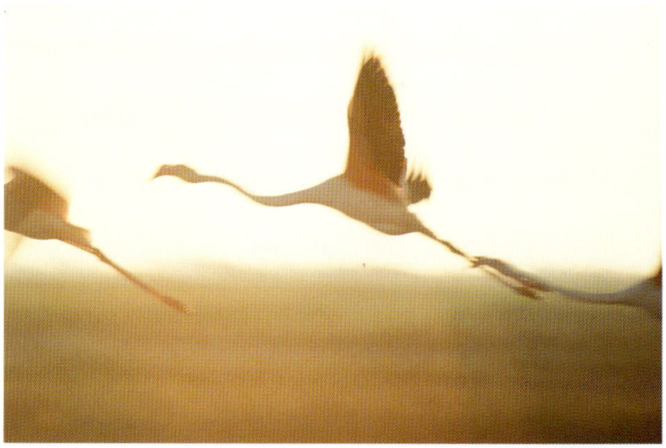

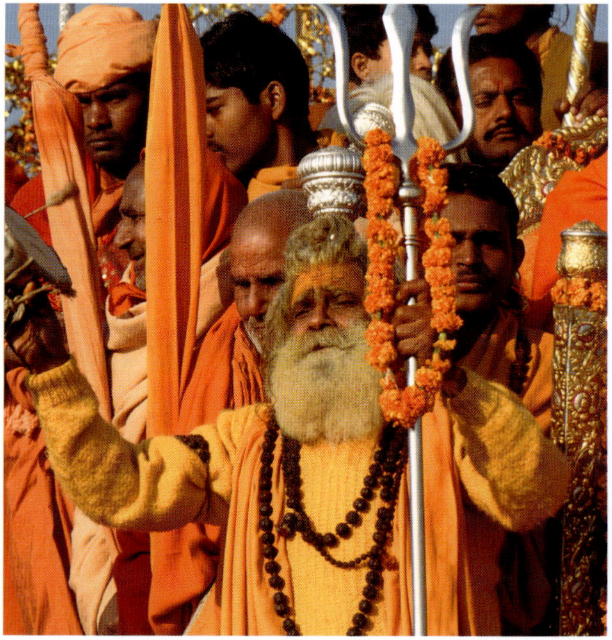

▲ Venice Carnival,
Venice, Italy

▲ **top:** Flamingos in the Camargue, France

▲ **above:** Holy Man, Allahabad, India

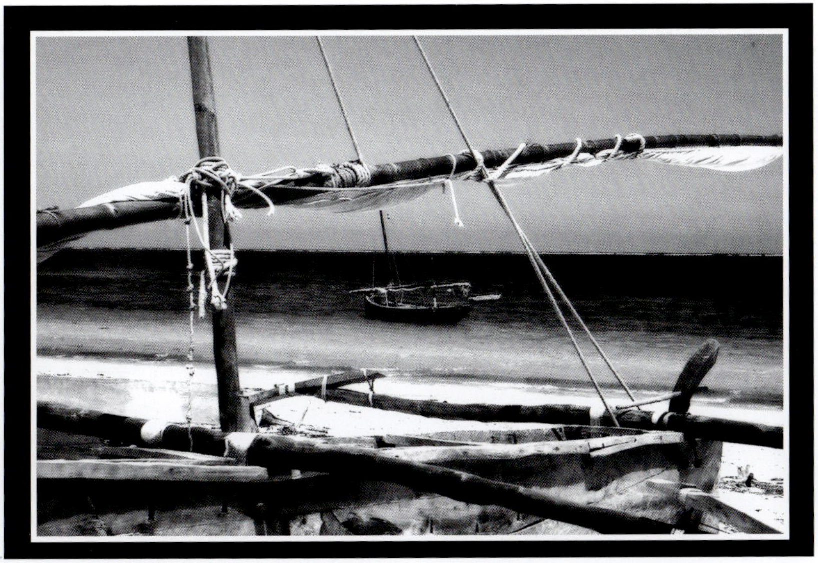

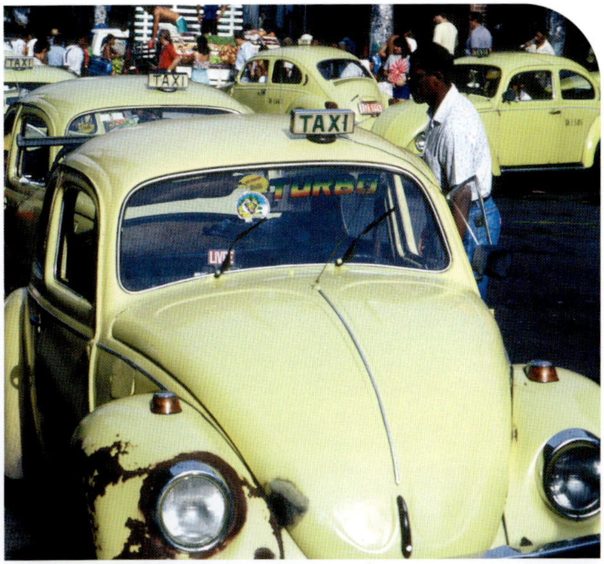


safe in the knowledge that any 'blemish' can be removed in a few minutes once you get home. Where traditional travel photographers would rise every day for a week to get the perfect sunset, we can simply take the picture and worry about minor problems later. This means it is more than possible to combine a normal family vacation with some serious photography without missing out on all the fun.

The latter half of this book deals in depth with some common post-processing tasks, from adding a more impactful sky by removing people from pictures, to basic color and contrast corrections. I've generally used Adobe Photoshop for all the step-by-step projects, simply because that is the application I use most of the time. Wherever possible, however, I've not used any tools that are unique to Photoshop; most of the projects will be easily adaptable to Paint Shop Pro, Photoshop Elements, Photo Paint and other similar applications.

So, whether you are travelling somewhere exotic or simply on a day trip to the seaside, with the advice and techniques described in these pages you should be able to return from your journey with pictures you can be proud of and which you will still be enjoying in many, many years to come.

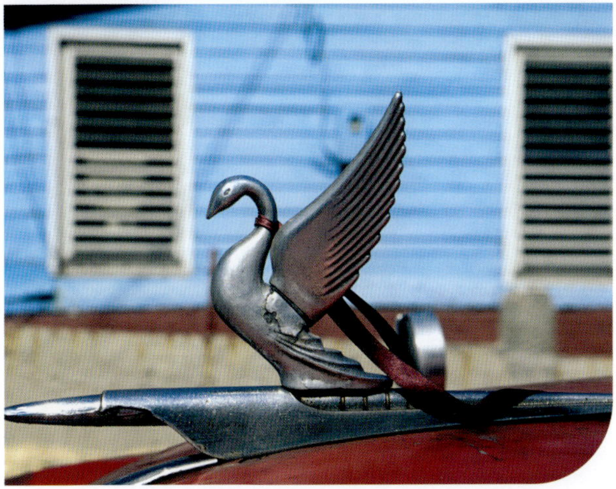

▲ **top: page 96**
Black-and-white

▲ **above:**
Old American car,
Varadero, Cuba

▲ **top: page 66**
Levels

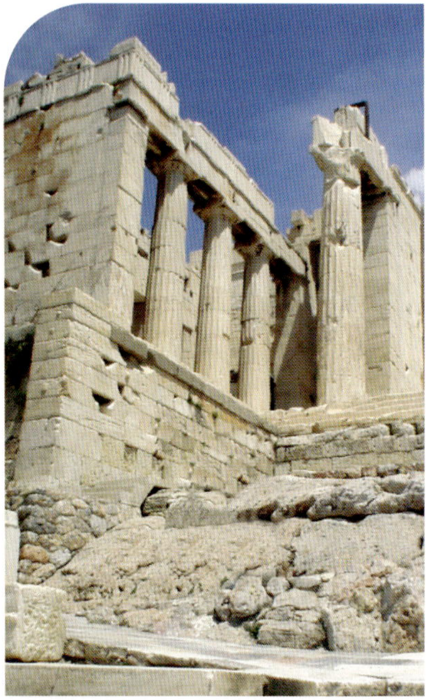

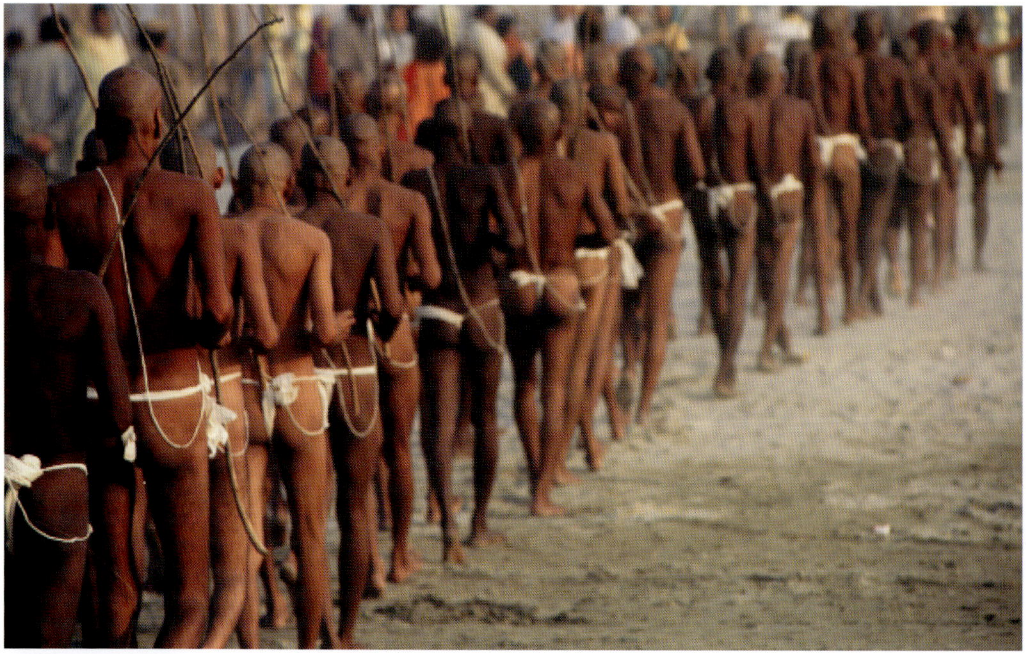

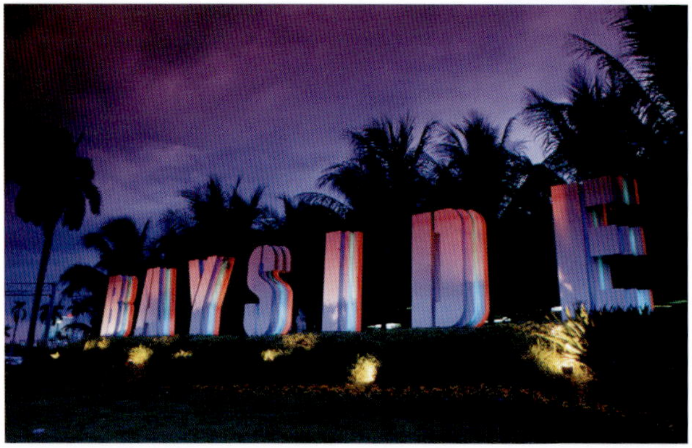


Whatever you do, keep your camera with you at all times; most of the techniques I've included don't require that you carry a huge professional camera, indeed many are designed to overcome the limitations of compact 'auto-only' digital cameras. Take lots of pictures, keep practising and, above all, have some fun.

**▲ top: page 74**
Removing elements

**▲ above: page 42**
Shooting at night

▲ Initiates into a holy order, Allahabad, India

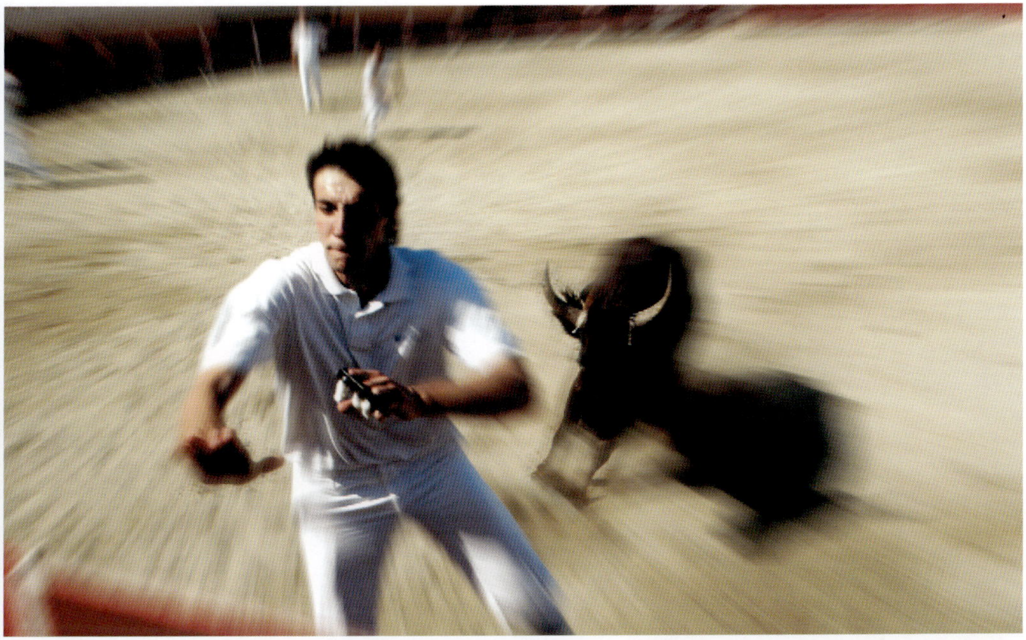

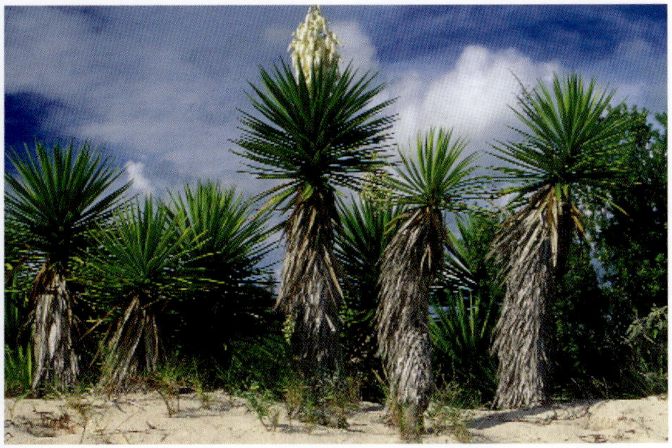

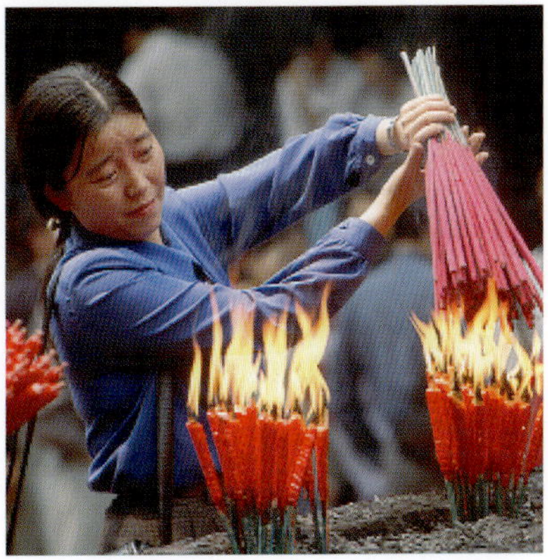

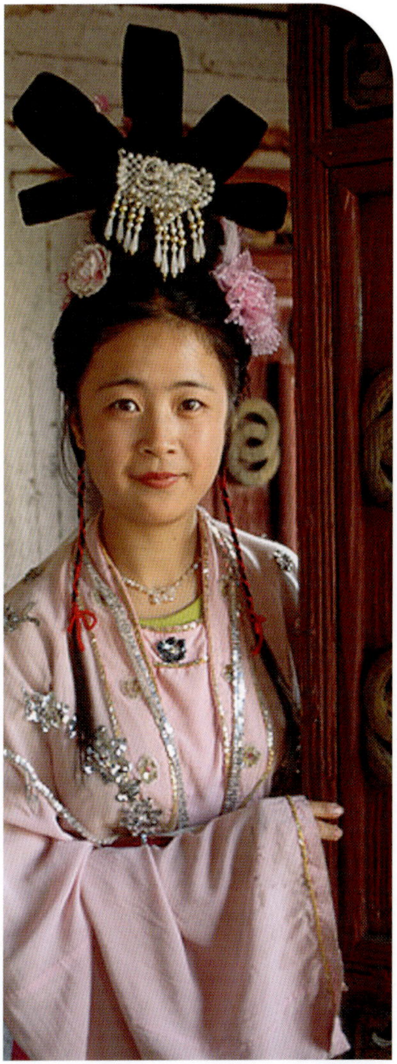

▲ **top: page 60**
Softening and blurring

▲ **above: page 58**
Basic corrections

▲ **top: page 90**
Motion blurring

▲ **above: page 62**
Woman making offerings at a temple, Leshan, Sichuan Province, China

▲ **above: page 62**
Cropping

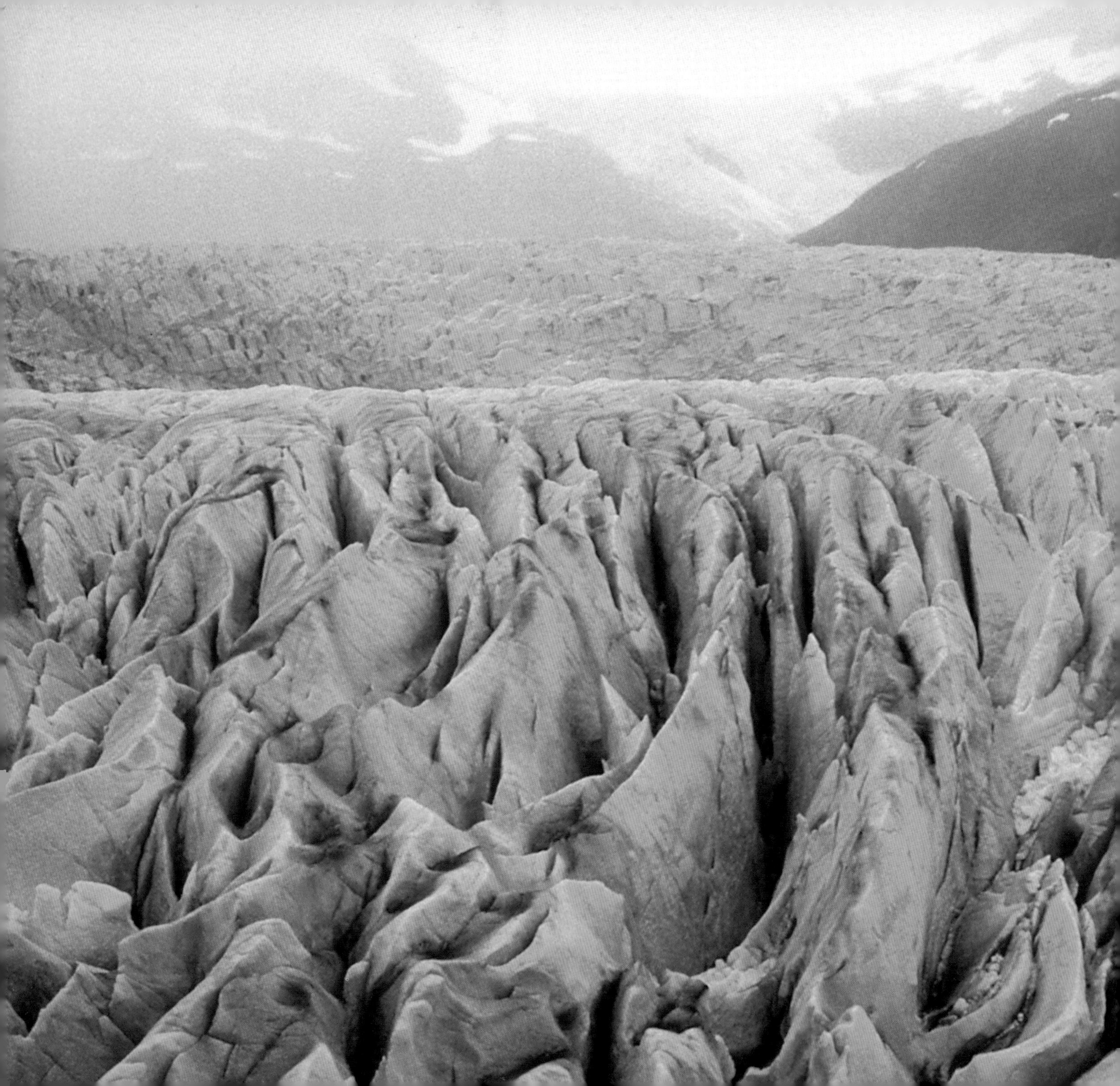

CHAPTER ONE

# GETTING STARTED

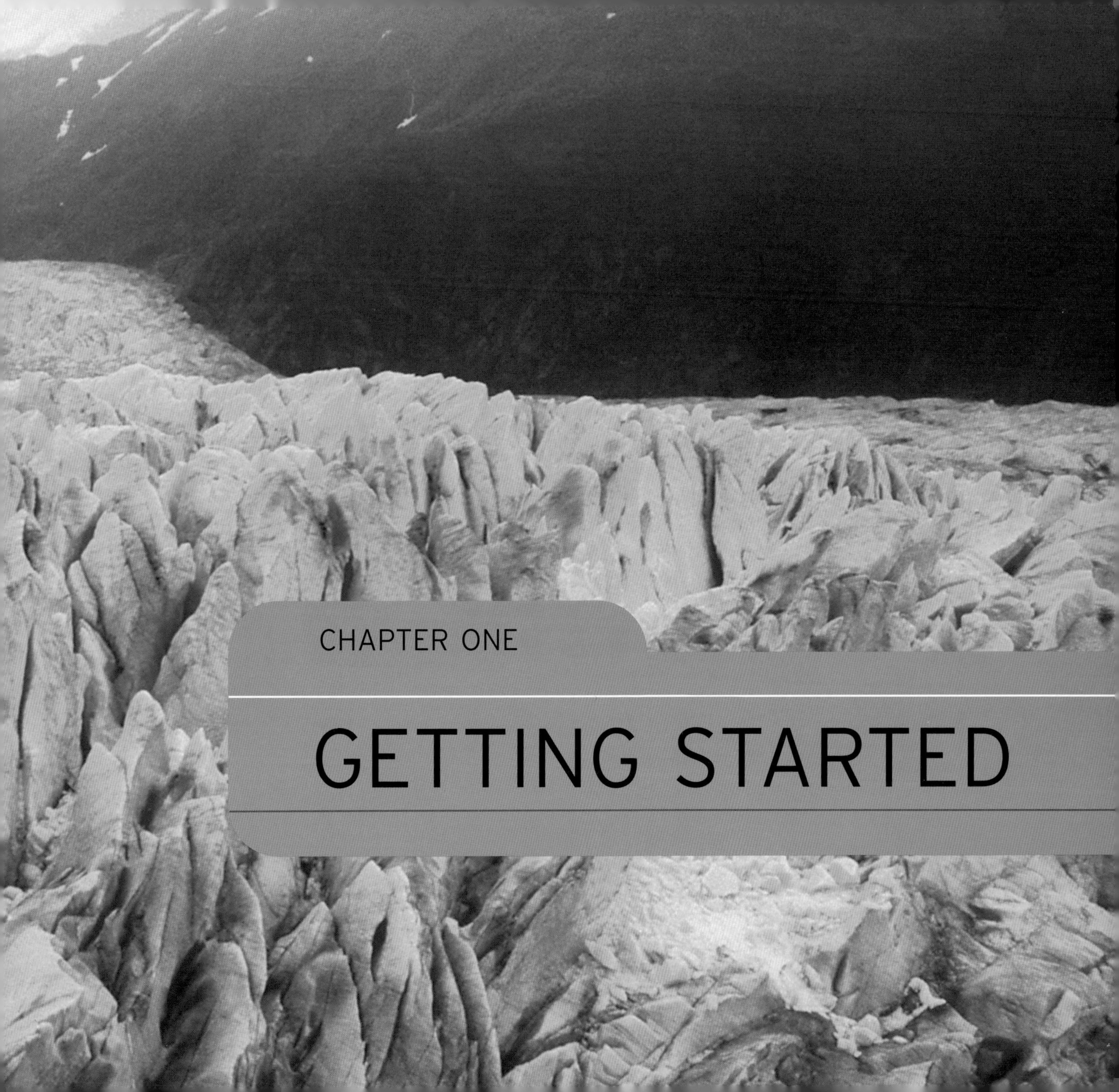

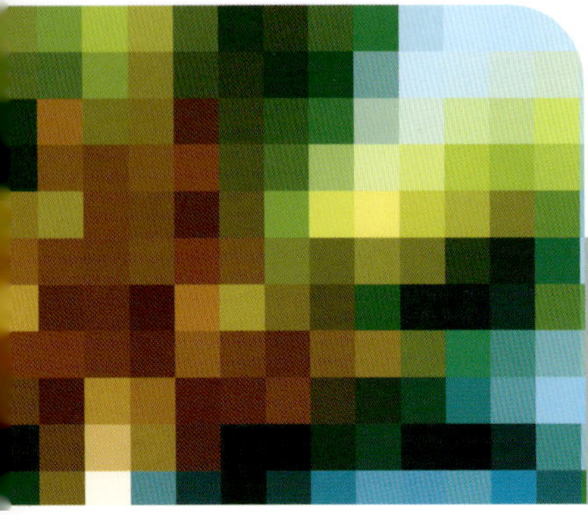

# The digital image

Shooting digitally or scanning existing photographs opens up a whole new world of creative possibilities. To get the most out of the hardware and software available, it helps to understand the basic theory behind digital images.

A digital image, no matter how it is generated, is made up of a grid of tiny squares called **pixels** (from picture elements). In the process of digitization, the scene (when using a digital camera) or photograph (when using a scanner) is captured using this grid, with the color from the original assigned to each corresponding pixel. The more pixels used, the more detail is captured and the sharper the image appears. The number of pixels in an image is a measure of its resolution – the higher the pixel count, the higher the resolution of the image.

The resolution also defines how large an image can be printed at 'photographic-quality' which, roughly translated, means without the pixels being visible in the print at normal viewing distance. If you can see the pixels, the image looks 'blocky'.

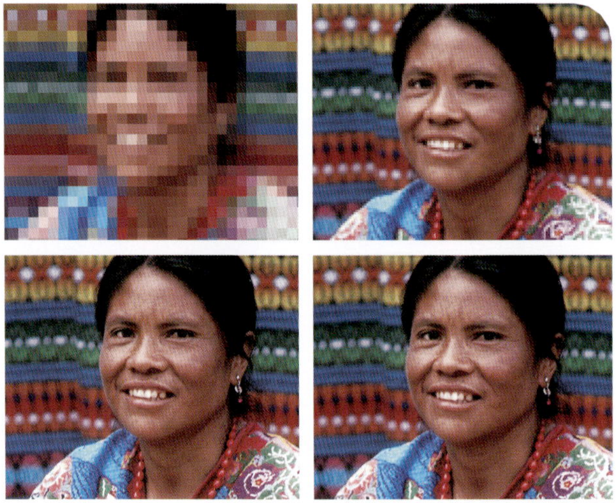

**At the heart of the digital image lies the pixel. The more pixels there are in an image, the more detail captured and the 'sharper' the result appears. These four shots show the effect of increasing resolution (clockwise from top left):**

**50x38 (1900) pixels**
**240x180 (43,200) pixels**
**640x480 (307,000) pixels**
**1200x1600 (1.92 million) pixels**

**How many pixels do I need?**

Resolution is one of the most important concepts in digital photography. It defines the quality of the image (in terms of the level of detail captured) and limits the size that you can print the results. The rough rule with resolution is that – within limits – you can't have too much. A truly photographic-quality print at 16x20" needs at least 3200 by 4000 (12.8 million) pixels – more than any consumer-level scanner or camera can produce. Most digital imaging is therefore something of a compromise. If you never print above 10x8" you needn't worry too much.

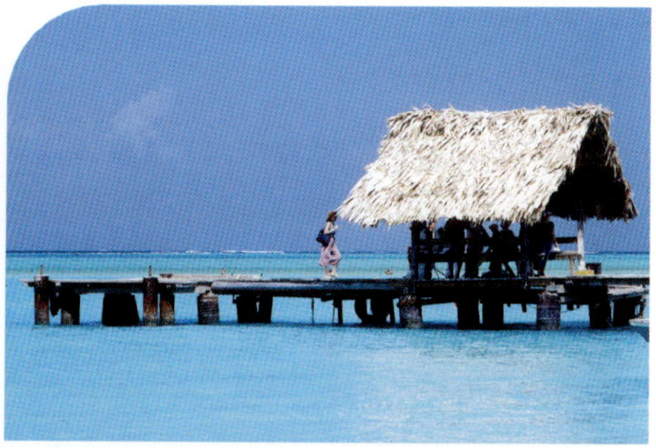
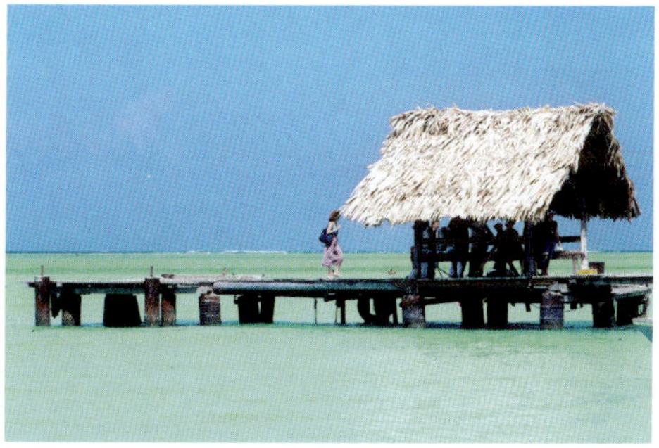
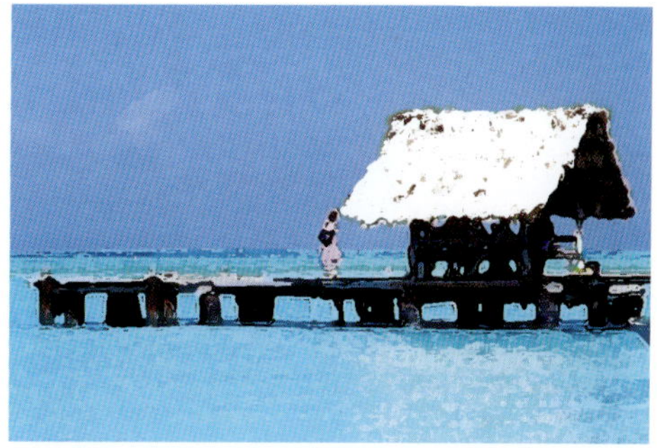
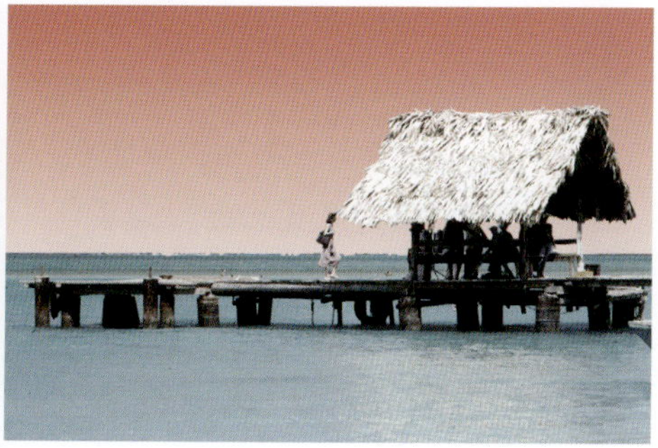
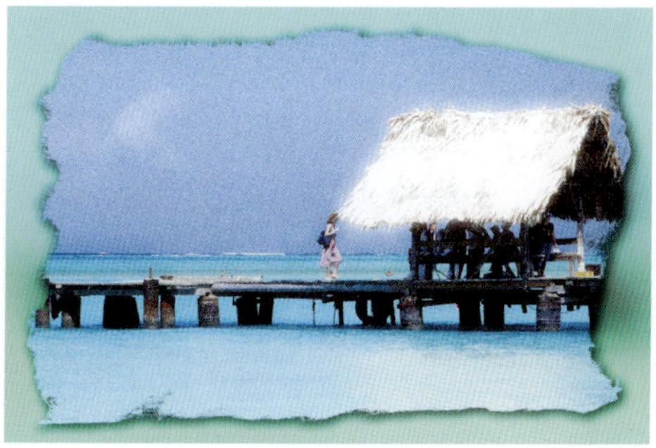
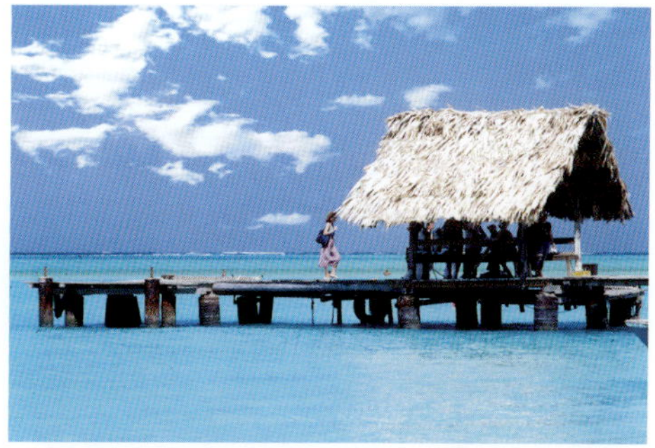

**Shooting for digital manipulation**

When the digital photographer presses the shutter, it is only the start of the creative process. Once the image is captured, we can reframe, remove unwanted elements, change colours and replace backgrounds.

So it is important to think ahead when shooting and look for the creative possibilities in even the most uninspiring shot. Carry your digital camera with you at all times and take as many pictures as you can – you've no film to waste.

The beauty of digital photography is the versatility of the software and the almost infinite possibilities on offer.

Whereas the traditional darkroom requires skill and dedication, digitally, you will be able to create amazing images within minutes. With practice and experimentation, it really is possible to transform the most mundane photograph into – if not a masterpiece – something worth printing.

The pictures on this page show the results of half an hour playing with the original digital camera shot (top left) in Photoshop, using quite basic techniques.

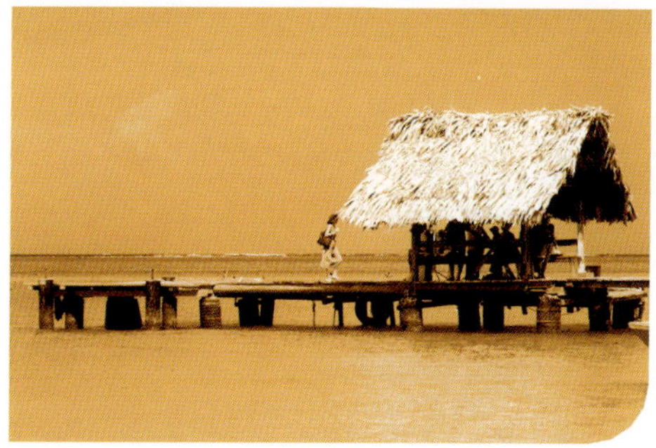

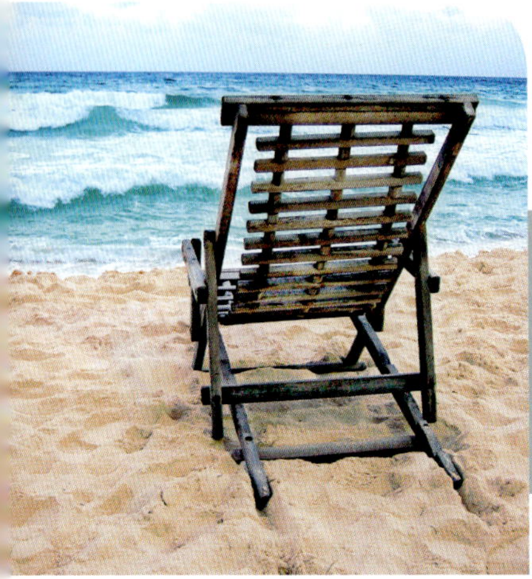

# The digital process

The basic digital photography process consists of three distinct stages: input, processing and output. The processing stage is usually performed by computer, but some digital camera systems allow computerless printing via a direct connection to the printer.

## input

The photograph is shot on film, whereupon it is processed and film scanned. Alternatively, prints are produced and scanned.

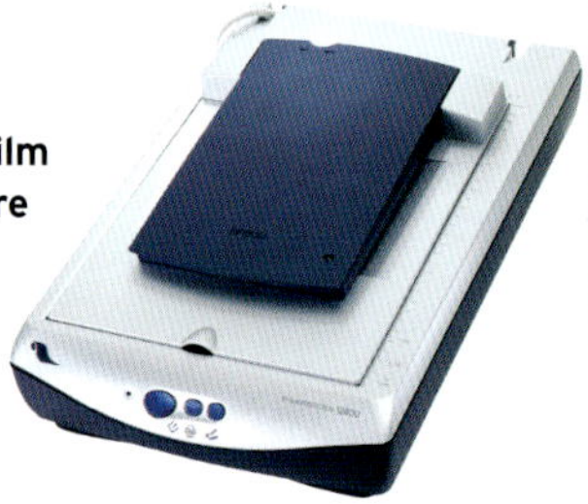

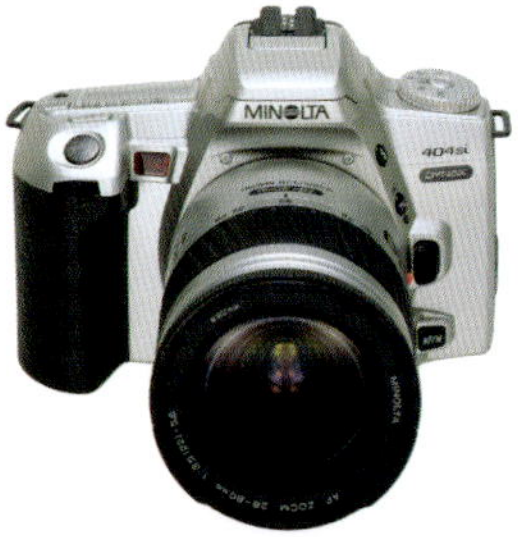

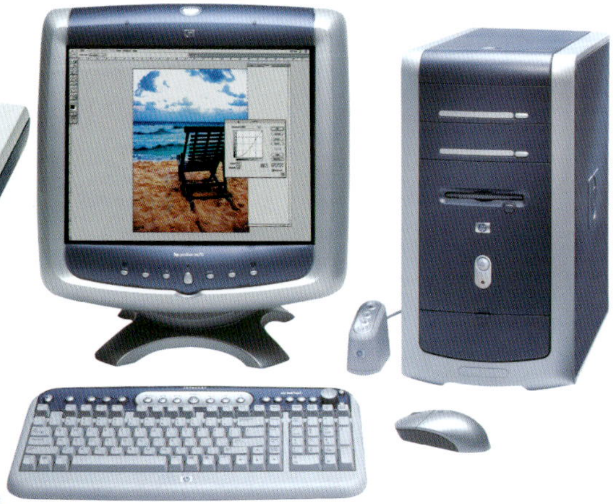

The digital camera captures digital photos, bypassing the scanning stage. The images are transferred to the PC via a direct connection or a separate card reader.

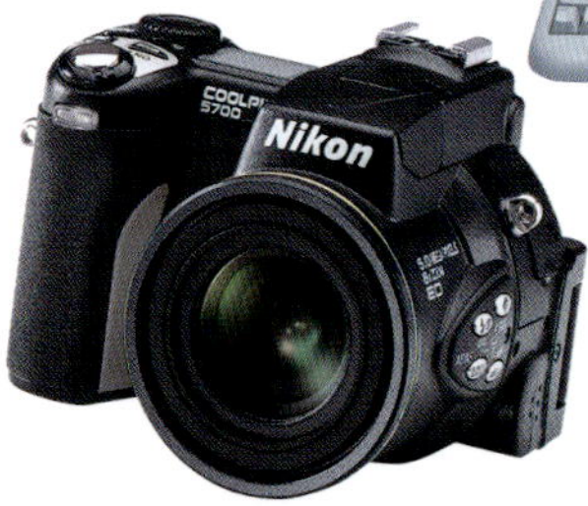

## process

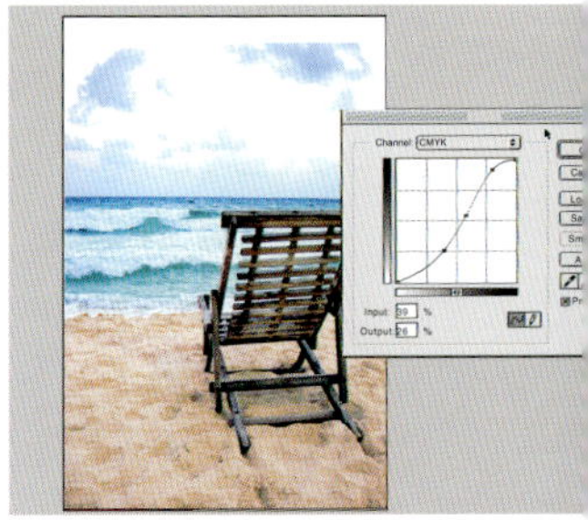

The processing stage can be as simple as opening the files and printing them, or it can involve a complicated series of corrections and manipulations.

### Calibration

Accurate color can be a real problem for digital systems, and monitor calibration is a vital part of ensuring consistent color throughout. Photoshop itself has extensive color-control and calibration features.

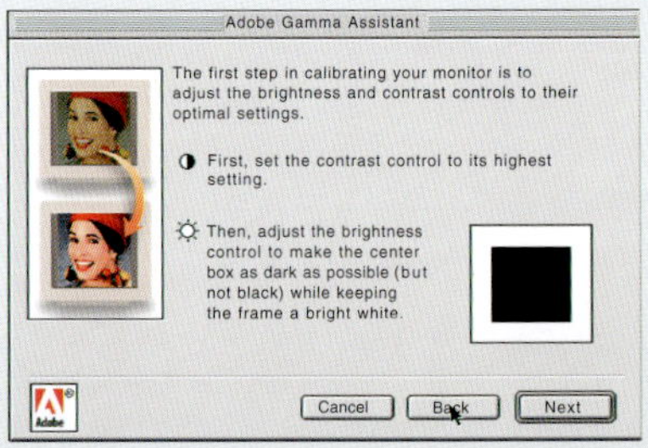

## output

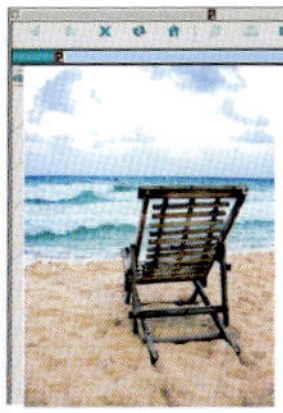

**In the broadest sense, output includes emailing photos or posting them on the web, or simply copying them onto a form of storage (such as CD-ROM) for archiving or distribution.**

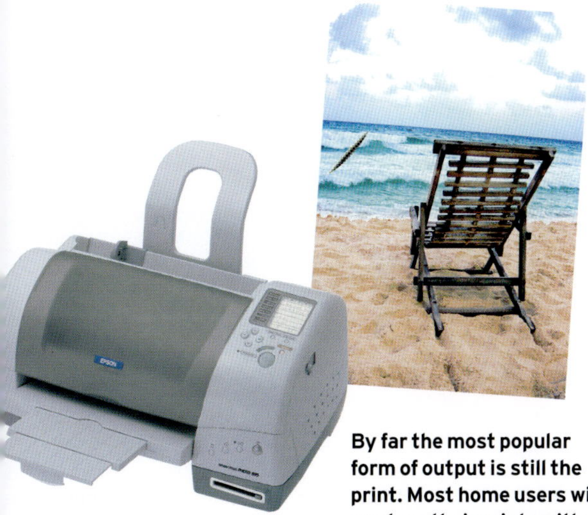

**By far the most popular form of output is still the print. Most home users will produce their prints with a color inkjet printer, some of which can easily rival conventional 'wet' photographic processes for quality.**

While there is a massive range of hardware and software on the market, there are only a few basic principles to understand.

Digital images are simply photographs in a form that the computer can understand - they can be described using numbers alone.

The digitization process splits the photograph into a grid of pixels, and the position and color of each of these pixels can be described numerically, a process known as 'bitmapping'. The size of the bitmap - how many pixels it contains - determines the resolution of the image and how much detail it contains.

In 24-bit color images (such as those created by digital cameras and scanners), the color of each pixel is defined as a mix of different proportions of red, green and blue (known in image editing as color channels). Each color channel can have one of 256 discrete values, from 0 to 255. The final image can thus have a maximum of 256x256x256 (16.7 million) different colors within it. Applications such as Photoshop allow you to alter the color values of each pixel individually or en masse. Thus, if you use Photoshop's color balance tools to change the overall color of a photograph, you simply alter the red, green and blue values of every pixel in the image by the same amount.

The computer monitor also uses red, green and blue dots to create a visual representation of your digital image on screen. Monitors work in exactly the same way as televisions, although they are higher resolution (the dots are smaller and more densely packed) as they need to be able to display readable text at small sizes.

The output stage of the digital-imaging process (which actually includes displaying it on screen) usually takes the form of a print on paper. Color printers use cyan, magenta, yellow and black inks to recreate each pixel in the image (you cannot use red, green and blue inks; see page 26 for more on this). The process of converting what you see on screen to what you get in print is where color accuracy problems are most likely to occur.

**Mac or PC?**

Although both Apple Macintosh and IBM PC (Windows) systems are perfectly capable of digital photography work, there are differences. Macs are generally considered easier to use and offer better system-level color management, but Windows PCs are cheaper, much more widely used and have a much wider range of general-purpose software available. If you are totally new to computers and are only really interested in digital imaging, I would go for a Mac; everyone else will probably be better off with a Windows machine.

**navigator**
The digital camera p18
Scanners p22
Color printing p26

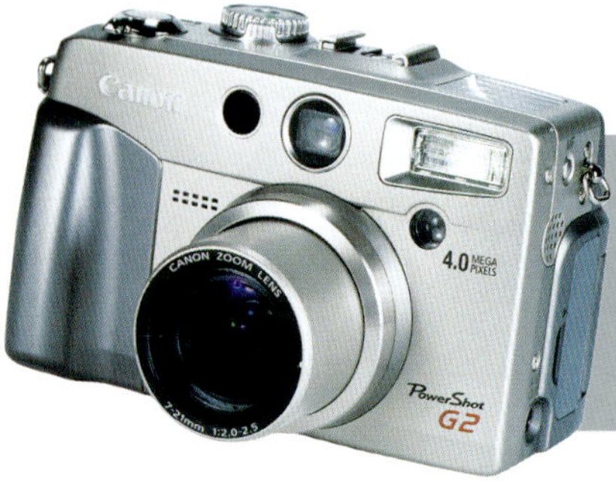


# The digital camera

**Unheard of a few years ago, the digital camera is fast replacing its film predecessor for both professional and amateur use. The latest models offer a huge range of photographic features, and they often sport a decent lens too.**

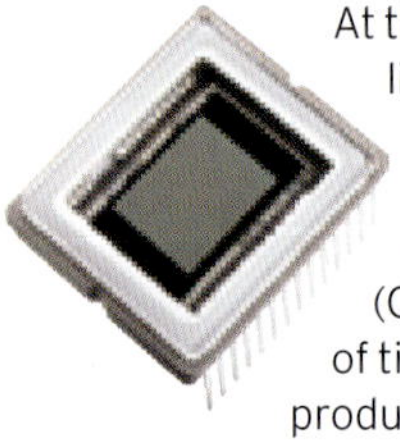

At the heart of every digital camera lies a sensor that converts light into an electrical signal. The most common type of sensor is the Charge-Coupled Device (CCD). The CCD is made up of a grid of tiny photodiodes, each of which produces a signal whose strength depends on the amount of light falling onto it. Each photodiode together with its lens and associated circuitry is known as a pixel (from picture element). When you take a picture, the electrical signal from every pixel is recorded, processed and assigned a value between 0 (darkest) and 255 (brightest).

Since CCDs record only levels of brightness, they are actually color blind. To add color information from the scene captured, the sensor sits behind a mosaic of color filters, meaning each pixel records only red, green or blue light. Sophisticated in-camera processing then reconstructs the full color scene. Each pixel is assigned a color based on a mixture of red, green and blue light. Using 256 different levels of each of the three color components allows for over 16 million shades, more than enough to look 'photorealistic'. This is also known as 24-bit color (the R,G and B components each using eight bits of computer data).

The number of pixels on the sensor (and thus in the resultant digital image) defines the resolution of the camera. The first generation of consumer digicams offered images containing about 300,000 pixels, whereas 3, 4 and even 5 million pixel cameras are now common.

Digital camera resolutions are often quoted as the pixel dimensions of the final image, rather than the total number of pixels therein. Thus a 1200x1600 pixel image comes from a 2 million pixel (or 2 megapixel) camera.

Virtually all digital cameras save the information captured in a compressed form (using a file format called JPEG) onto a removable storage card. JPEG compression has a small effect on the quality of the image, but does allow ten to twenty times more photos to be stored on each of the cards. The saved photographs are transferred to a computer for manipulation, printing or sharing via the internet.

**Digital Video (DV) cameras now usually offer a stills facility, although it will not produce results as good as a dedicated digital stills unit.**

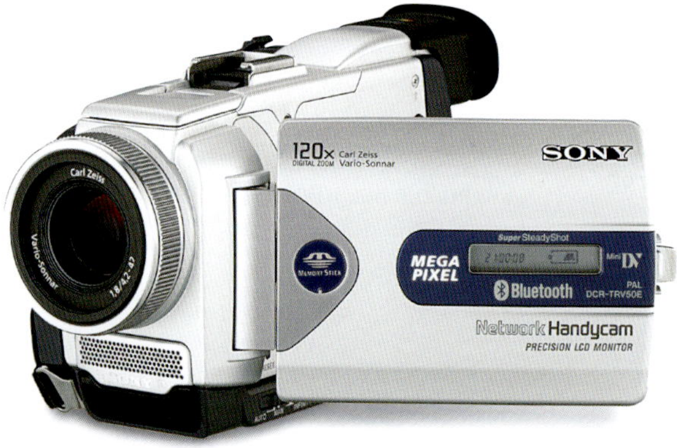


**typical digital cameras**

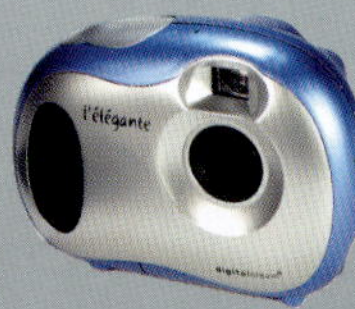

**webcams**
The least expensive digicams: 1 megapixel resolution, fixed lenses, no removable media.

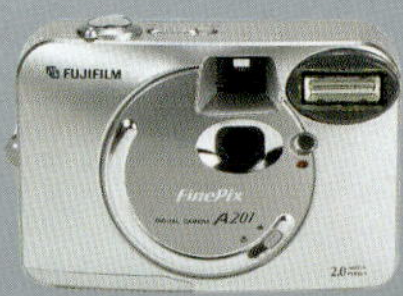


**entry level**
Ideal for beginners on a budget. Resolutions and specification vary, but zoom lenses and more than 1.5 megapixels are rare.

**Although digital cameras come in a variety of shapes and sizes, most share common functions and features.**

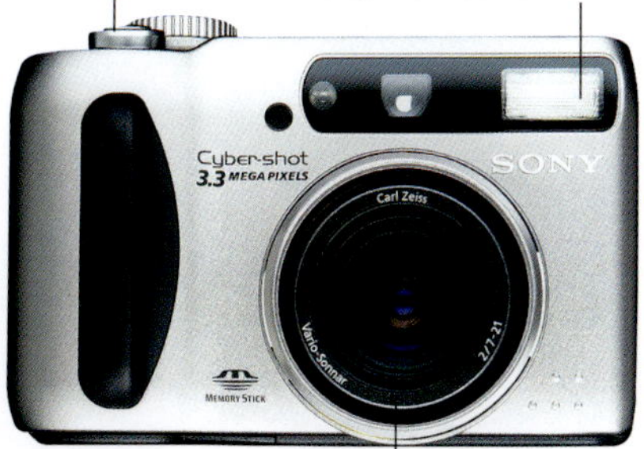


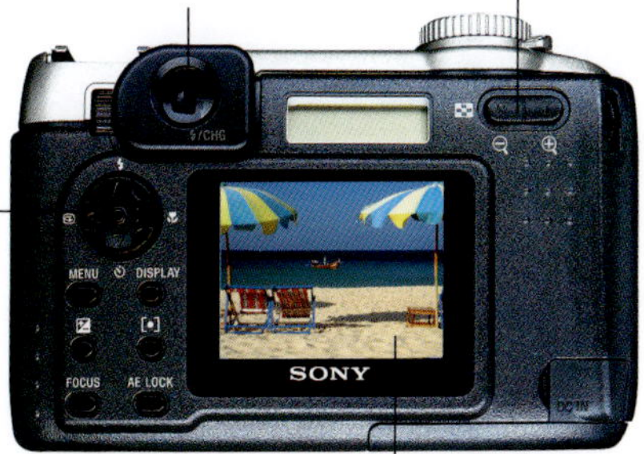


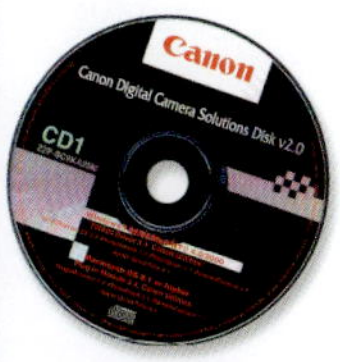

**Most cameras ship with a variety of transfer and image-enhancement utilities.**

## Camera features

Digital camera specification varies widely from very basic 'point-and-shoot' low-resolution beginners' cameras and webcams, to highly sophisticated photographic tools with all the features and functions of a top-level 35mm SLR.

All but the cheapest cameras have a small color LCD screen on the rear and a built-in flash. Photographic enthusiasts will be looking at the mid-to-high end of the range and should aim for at least 2 million pixels, a 3x wide-angle to short tele zoom and some exposure, focus and white-balance overrides.

## Image quality

For the photographic enthusiast, the quality of the final image is easily as important as design and specification. As well as resolution (which determines the amount of information captured), the performance of the camera's optics, exposure-, focus- and signal-processing systems, and the level of JPEG compression will all have an effect on the quality of the final image.

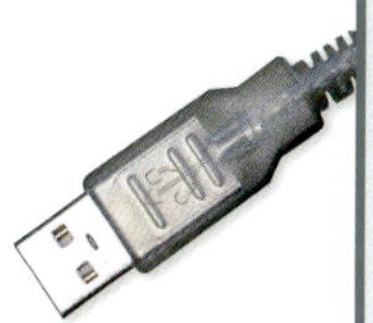

**Most digicams attach to the PC via a USB connection**

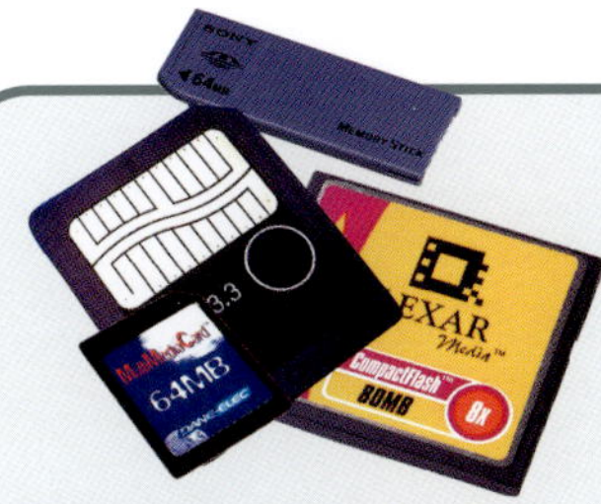

## Storage and transfer

There are four commonly used solid-state (flash) storage formats: SmartMedia, CompactFlash and Memory Stick (unique to Sony) and MultiMedia/SD. There is not much to choose between the formats, although CompactFlash is used by the majority of camera models.

Cards are available in capacities ranging from 2MB to around 256MB. The bigger the card, the more pictures you can take.

CompactFlash Type II compatibility allows the use of IBM's MicroDrive mini hard disks. These offer huge capacities at affordable prices, but are more fragile than their solid-state relatives.

Most cameras use a USB cable to connect to the host computer, although the use of a separate card reader' is an increasingly popular option.

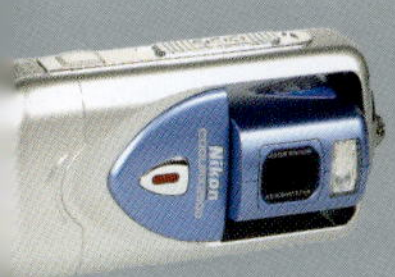

**mid-range**
The most popular type of digicam. From 1.3 to 3 megapixels, usually with a zoom lens and some level of control.

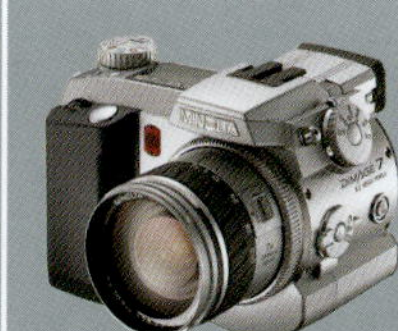

**high-end**
For the more serious photographer - higher resolutions (3 megapixels and over) and a full range of controls.

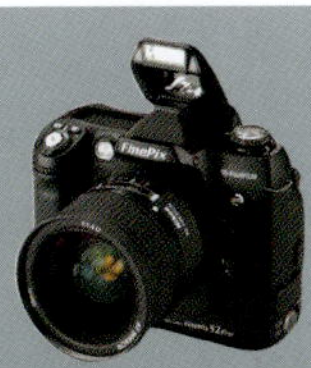

**digital SLRs**
The most expensive digicams: usually feature removable lenses and offer the ultimate quality.

# Lenses

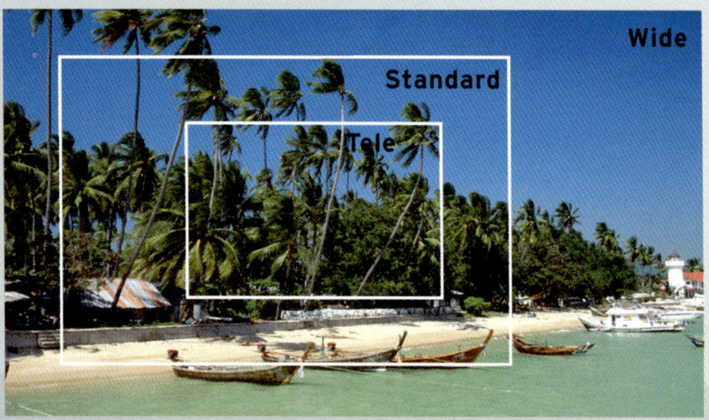


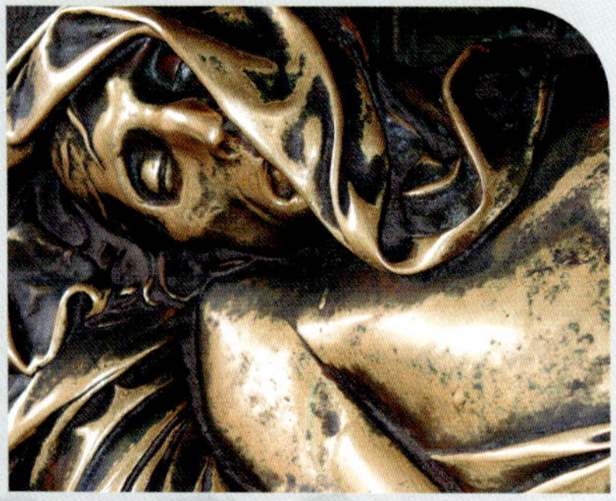

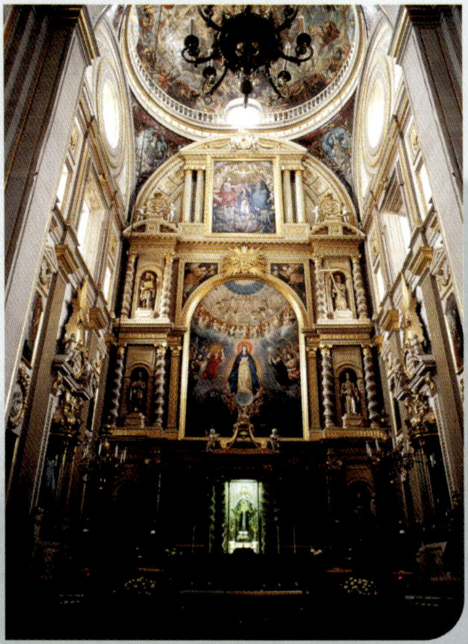

Most high-end digital cameras sport some kind of zoom lens. The zoom allows you to change your angle of view by pressing the wide or telephoto buttons on the camera. The range of the zoom – from wide-angle to tele – is usually quoted as either the 35mm lens equivalent (i.e. 34–102mm) or as a magnification range (i.e. 3x, where the telephoto is three times the focal length of the wide-angle). Some camera systems allow the addition of extra wide-angle or telephoto adaptors to extend the range.

Telephoto lenses are valuable tools for travel photography. Ideal for picking out details and isolating subjects, especially portraits, the tele lens brings its own unique feeling to scenic photographs. Also, when shooting with a long lens – use of a tripod is essential. Travel photography is perhaps more commonly associated with the wide-angle lens. A wide lens allows you to capture lots of the scene in front of you and to include plenty of sky and foreground. Wide-angle distortion can make objects nearer to the camera appear disproportionately large, whereas distant objects look even further away. Most zooms start at a focal length of around 35 or 38mm – not really wide enough for most landscapes. Look for a camera system that includes a wide-angle converter.

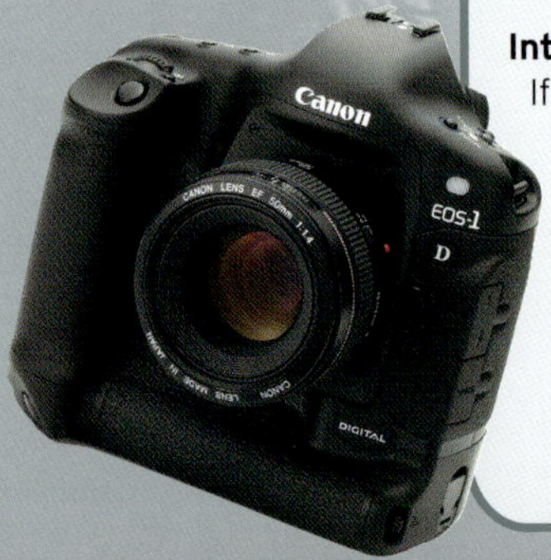


**Interchangeable lens digital SLRs**

If you feel restricted by the fixed zoom lens of a compact digital camera, you may be tempted to invest in a digital SLR camera with removable lenses. There are several reasons why this might not be sensible. Firstly, they are very expensive. Secondly, since the CCD inside the body is smaller than a 35mm frame, any lens used will see its effective focal length increased (by 50–100%), so true wide-angle photography is almost impossible. Initially, you would be better off investing in a good 35mm scanner and sticking with film.

**keep in mind**

Unless you have access to unlimited storage cards, the 'uncompressed' option is best left for once-in-a-lifetime shots. Most cameras have a 'high' JPEG setting, which allows ten times more pictures to fit onto each card with virtually negligible loss of detail.

**navigator**

Basic corrections p58
Cropping & rotating p62
The right lens p36

# Essential accessories

Most compact digital cameras are not hugely expandable, but there are still plenty of add-ons and extras you'll need to consider. Make sure you carry plenty of spare batteries. If your camera uses standard AA batteries, invest in a few sets of Nickel Metal Hydride (NiMH) cells. These rechargeable batteries offer by far the longest life and do not suffer from the memory problems associated with many other types.

After power, the most common problem faced by digicam owners is running out of storage space. Although expensive, extra storage cards are essential. Don't buy the largest possible cards – you will be a lot less unhappy if you lose or damage a relatively cheap card. If you are out on a long trip, it may be more cost-effective to buy a cheap laptop computer and transfer the images at the end of each day. Most laptops have a PCMCIA (PC card) slot and this can be used to copy images directly off the camera's cards using a cheap adaptor.

Other indispensable accessories include a sturdy tripod and a good, fully weatherproof case for the camera itself.

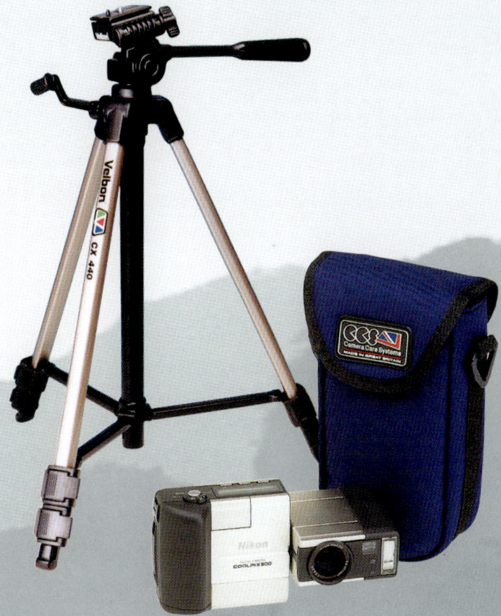


**Quality settings**

The images captured by a digital camera are usually saved using a file format called JPEG. JPEG files use compression to reduce the amount of disk space the picture takes up by 'throwing away' some picture detail. JPEG allows you to choose the level of compression; more compression equals lower quality, but smaller files. This is the basis for the quality settings on a digital camera. The 'high' setting is only compressed slightly, and the effect on the image is usually insignificant. Most high-end cameras offer an alternative to JPEG, usually saving the image as an uncompressed TIFF. Although this improves the quality slightly, it also produces enormous files.

**Uncompressed**

This TIFF image took up 5MB on the camera card. Despite the high quality, it is probably unsuitable for shooting in the field due to card space considerations. Using JPEG compression does not alter the resolution, it simply sacrifices some sharpness for the sake of file size.

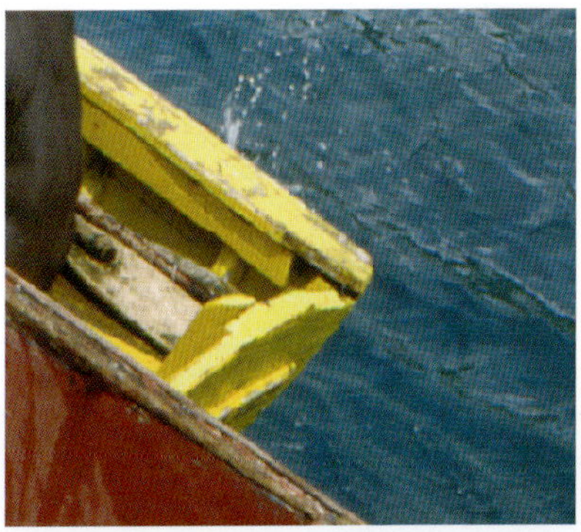

**Highly compressed**

This 'basic' quality JPEG took up only 200KB (0.2MB) of space on the camera card, but the loss of quality is obvious. By using a lower level of compression, you can produce manageable file sizes with a negligible loss of quality.

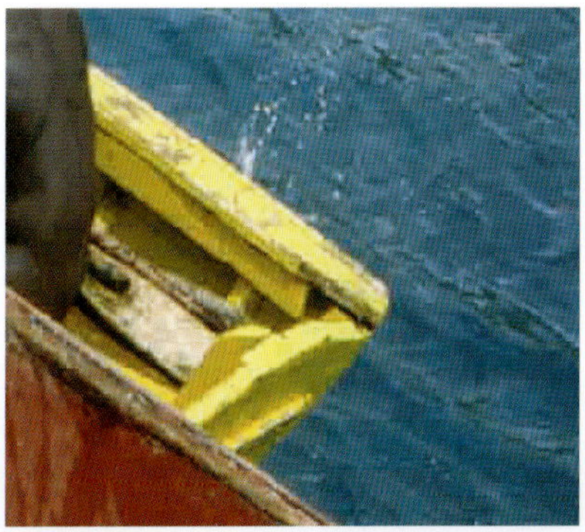

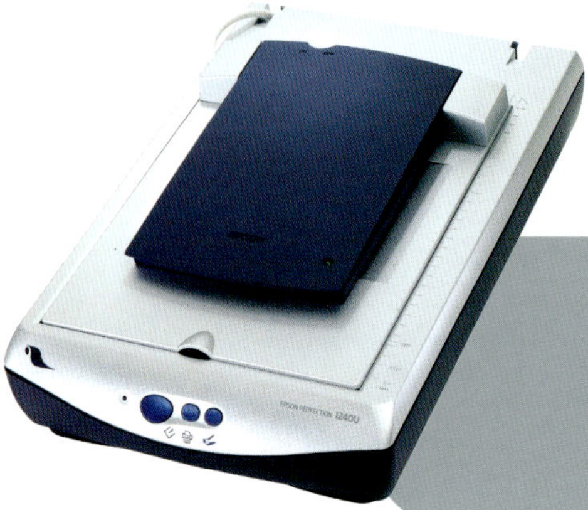

# Scanners

**Many photographers' first taste of digital comes in the shape of a scanner. Affordable and easy to use, scanners also have the distinct advantage of allowing you to use your existing camera gear, as well as working digitally with all the photos you've ever taken.**

Scanners use exactly the same technology as digital cameras, except that they move a narrow CCD sensor along a photograph, digitizing it one line at a time. This information is fed to the host computer where the scanner driver software processes it and constructs the digital image. Scanners attach to computers either via a USB or SCSI interface or, increasingly, via FireWire.

### Resolution

Scanner resolution is measured in dots per inch, since the absolute number of pixels will vary according to the physical size of the original. Thus a 600dpi scanner can produce a 600x600 (36,000) pixel image from a 1" square original, whilst the same scanner will produce a 4800x6000 (28.8 million) pixel image from an 8x10" original.

Flatbed scanners are used to digitize prints and other reflective originals of up to A4 size. The prints are placed face down on a glass plate and the lid closed before scanning. Some models are capable of scanning transparent media (films), usually via an optional transparency adaptor. Resolutions are usually from around 600dpi up to 2400dpi, and a wide range of models are available.

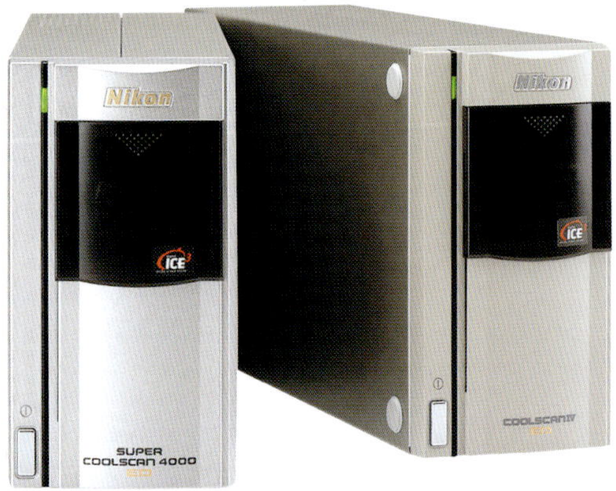


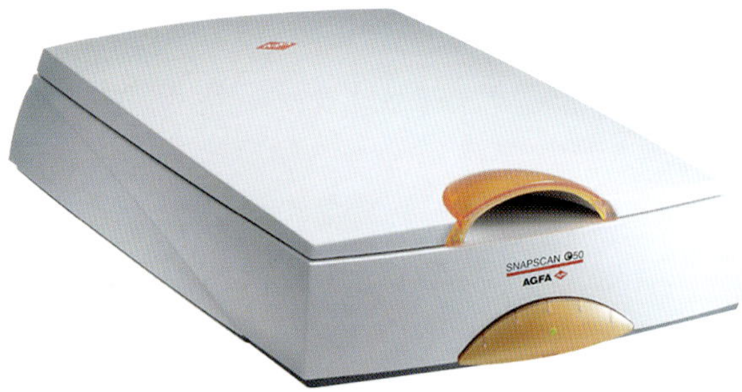


High-precision 35mm film scanners are capable of resolutions of up to 4000dpi. They can accept 35mm mounted slides and film strips, and many offer an optional APS adaptor. With fewer models to choose from, starting prices are quite high. Medium- and large-format film scanners are available, but are generally too expensive for nonprofessional use.

**flatbed scanner resolution**

Scanner resolution is sometimes quoted as a horizontal x vertical figure (i.e. 300x600 dpi). The first figure (horizontal) shows the density of pixels on the scanner CCD, whilst the second figure (vertical) is a measure of how far the CCD is moved between each 'line'. The horizontal figure is the truer measure of the 'optical' resolution of the scanner.

Most manufacturers also offer much higher resolutions as an option, but since these are generated using interpolation, the extra resolution is simply 'guesswork'.

## Scanner driver software

The software supplied with the scanner is nearly as important as the hardware in ensuring good-quality scans. The driver software usually comes as a 'plug-in' for Photoshop or similar applications, and is accessed via the Import command (usually found under the File menu). Some scanners also ship with stand-alone software. Driver software varies widely, but the basic process is invariably the same: prescan, adjust scan settings and scan. The prescan allows you to define the area of the original you want to scan. As well as settings such as resolution and magnification, most drivers allow you to adjust the color, exposure and contrast of the image based on the preview image. The controls generally mirror those found in Photoshop, with the better software offering full levels, curves, color balance and sharpening functions. Most also offer a fully automatic 'idiot-proof' mode.

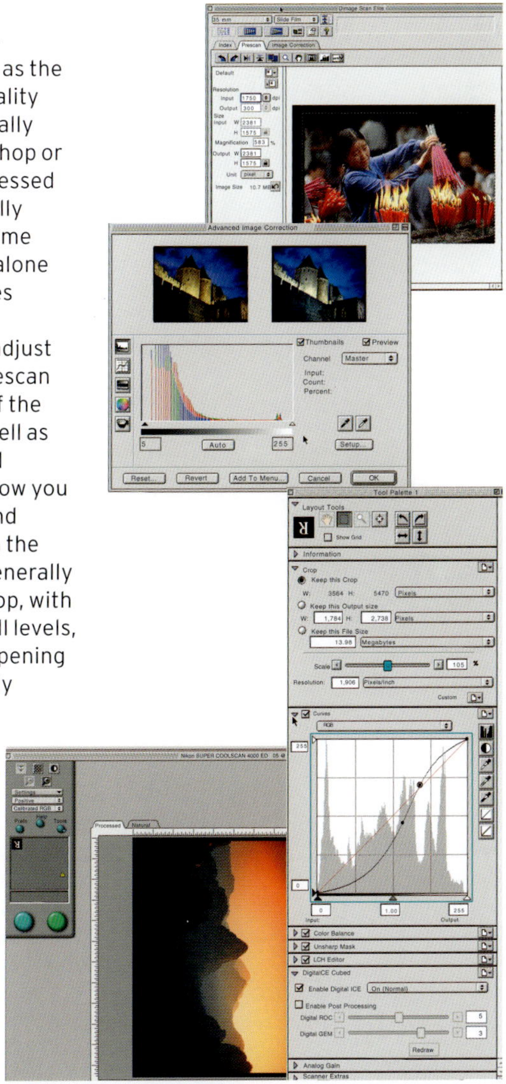

### Scanning tips

**■ Keep it flat**

The only way to get a sharp scan is to ensure the original is kept as flat as possible when scanning. This is especially true with flatbeds, where the weight of the lid alone may not be enough to hold things flat. For prints, try scanning with a large book on top of your original (leave the scanner lid open), and for films (using a transparency adaptor) a little Scotch tape will hold curly originals in place.

**■ Keep it clean**

Keep both originals and scanning equipment spotlessly clean. A can of compressed air and a lens cleaning cloth should be all you need. Some film scanners now offer a hardware and software dust-removal system - they actually work very well and are worth paying for.

**■ Prescan color adjustments**

Don't go mad! It is very easy to mess up when working with the low-resolution preview image and, generally, Photoshop's tools offer a finer level of control. Having said that, it is better to get the color, exposure and contrast more or less right at the time of scanning. Mastering driver software takes some time, so persevere.

**■ Resolution**

Try to scan at the correct resolution for your intended print size. Too high and you'll waste disk space and slow things down, too low and you'll get pixellated prints.

**navigator**
Fixing colors p68
Using curves p66
Basic corrections p58

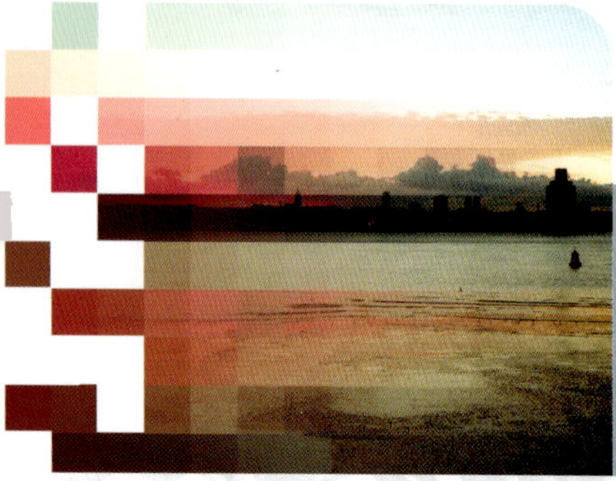

# Software tools

**The real power of digital imaging lies in the wealth of software tools available to subtly tweak or dramatically transform your photos in ways simply not offered by traditional methods.**

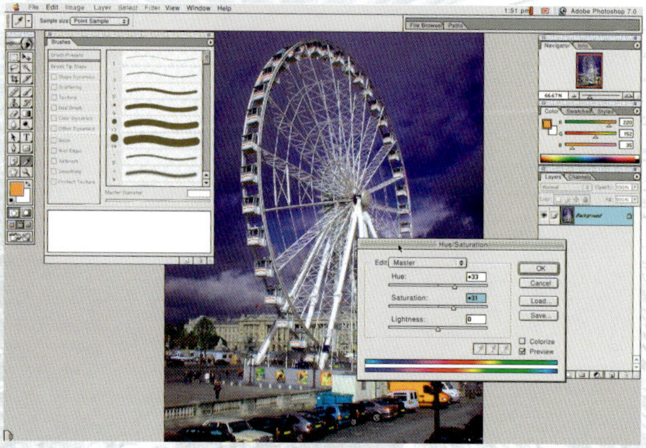

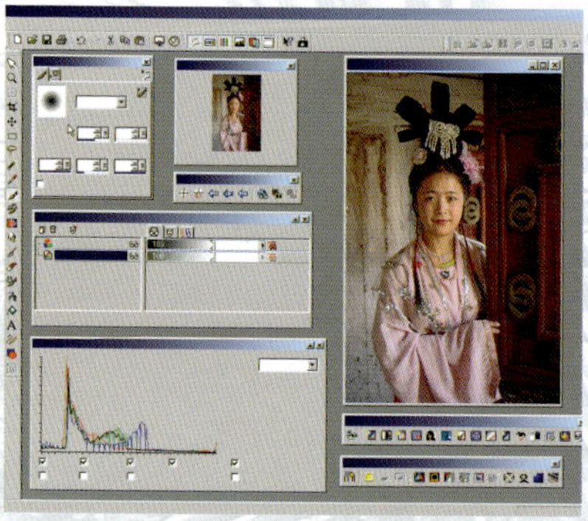

There are, broadly speaking, three different types of imaging software, although many products blur the boundaries, and a few defy classification.

The first, oldest group of products is that built on the Adobe Photoshop model (above): powerful, hands-on image editors with myriad correction, distortion and manipulation tools and a wide selection of effects filters. Virtually all the projects in this book were created using Photoshop 6.0. Photoshop is the undisputed king of the serious image editors but it is too expensive for many home users. Fortunately, some alternatives come close to offering all the features of Photoshop in affordable packages. Applications worth considering include Jasc Paint Shop Pro, Corel Photo Paint, Ulead PhotoImpact and Adobe Photoshop Elements.

A second group of photo-editing software has emerged since the arrival of affordable digital cameras and scanners. These 'project-led' programs are often very easy to use and tend to concentrate on making common tasks easy, one-click processes. The level of control and 'pixel-by-pixel' editing is limited but, as a user-friendly and affordable entry point, they are worth considering. Ultimately, however, most will tire of making calendars and birthday cards from their snaps and outgrow these applications. As their interest in the creative side of digital imaging develops, they will inevitably move on to more serious programs. The third type of software covers a wide range of products that perform one or more specific tasks. This includes 'funware' such as Kai's

**Photoshop versions**

There are currently three variants of Photoshop on sale; full Photoshop (currently on version 7.0), Photoshop LE (often given away free with scanners and digital cameras) and the relatively new Photoshop Elements. Full versions of Photoshop (any version from 5.0 onwards) offer the most powerful tools, whilst LE is crippled somewhat by its massively reduced feature set. Elements offers much of the power of Photoshop 6.0 in an easier to use, friendlier package.

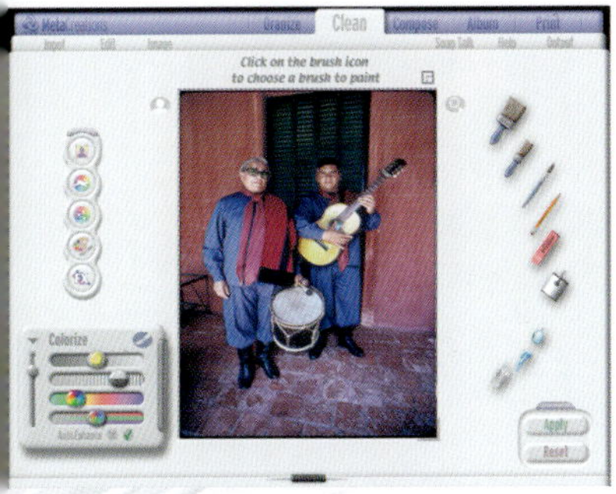

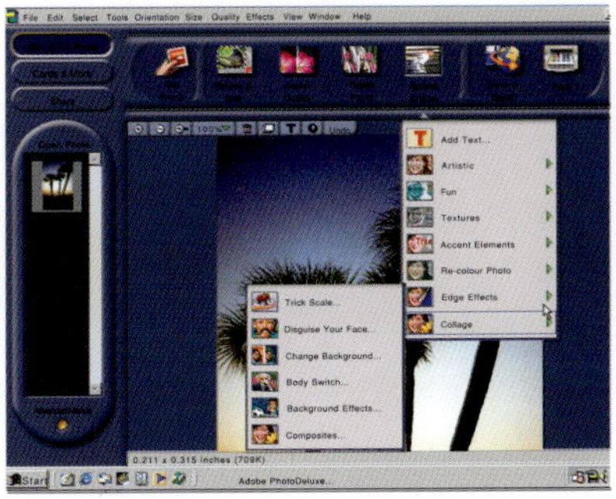

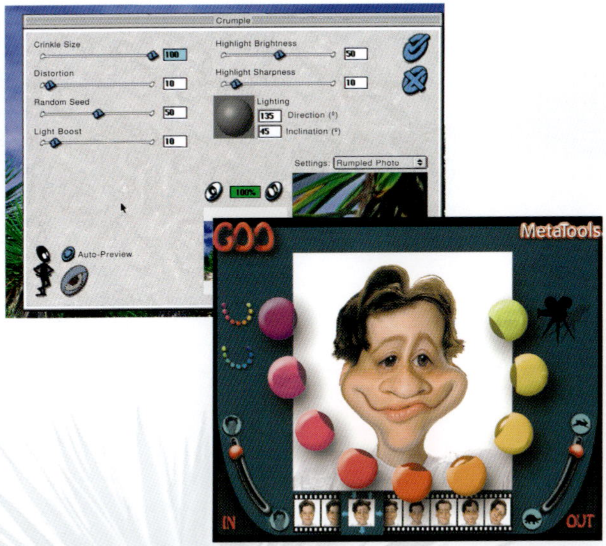


Super Goo, panorama creation software and template-based print programs (for creating cards for example). A separate group of 'mini applications' that run inside programs such as Photoshop (known as plug-ins) are available. These range from the useful to the frankly bizarre.

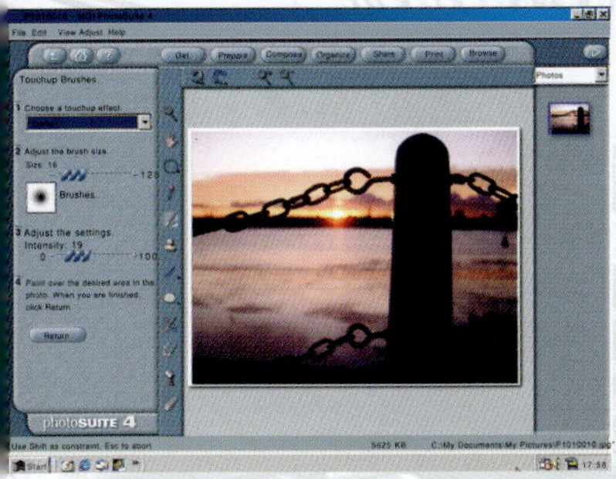

**Albums and image databases**

Keeping track of hundreds of digital images can be difficult. Applications such as Canto Cumulus offer ways to catalogue and classify your image library. As well as basic views of thumbnails, multiple text labels can be attached to each image to allow for complex searches. At the other end of the scale, inexpensive 'image browsers' allow you to view the contents of a folder of images as thumbnails.

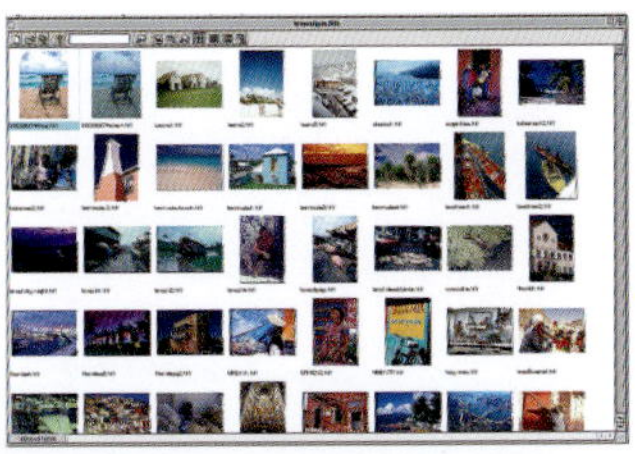

**Slideshows**

Sharing your images with other computer users is a very simple task. It is also possible to create self-running 'slideshows' with complex fades and dissolves between frames and text captions. Some image-editing applications offer this feature, or there are several stand-alone slideshow applications, the best of which is probably ScanSoft Kai's Photo Show.

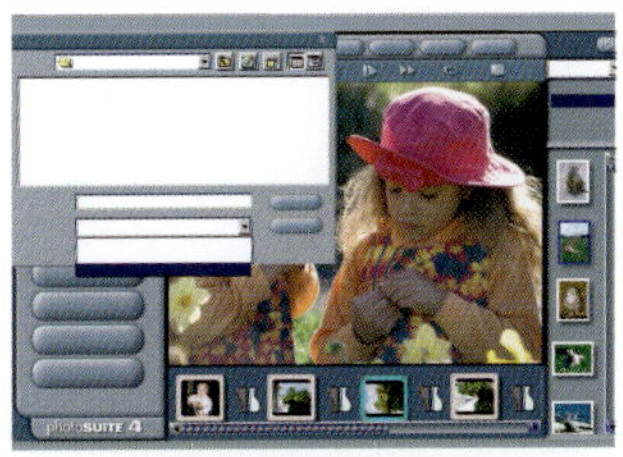

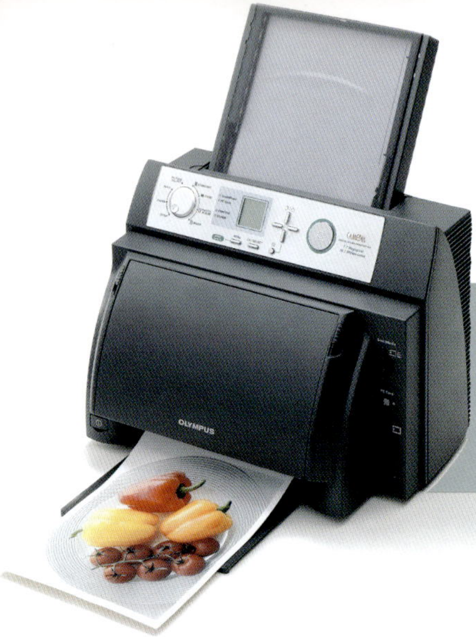

# Color printing

**The complexities of the printing process could easily fill a book on their own, but a basic understanding of how the systems work is important for getting the most out of your digital images in print.**

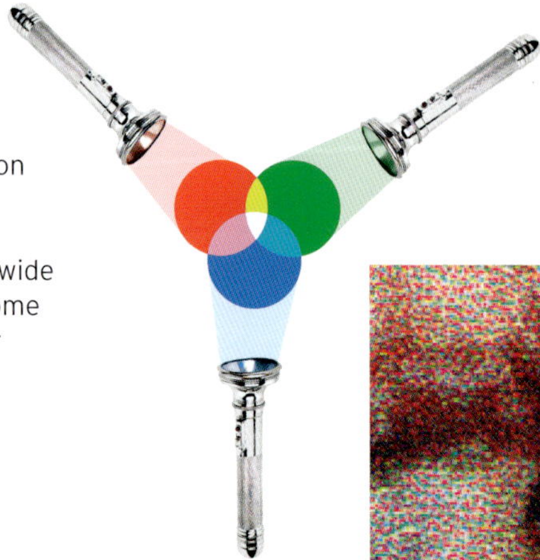

Digital cameras, scanners and monitors use a combination of red, green and blue light to create all the colors in the spectrum (RGB color). This is called an 'additive process' as the more color you add, the closer you get to white. A wide range of colors can be generated in this way, although some very dark tones can be difficult - a computer monitor, for example, will rarely display anything approaching a true black.

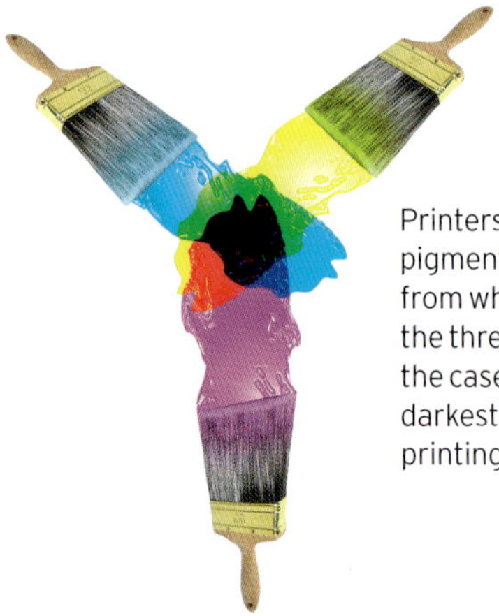

Printers use a combination of cyan, magenta and yellow pigments in a 'subtractive' process (adding pigments 'subtracts' from white, resulting in a darker color). In theory, 100% each of the three pigments should result in black, but as this is rarely the case, a fourth ink (black) is added to produce the very darkest tones. This CMYK (K for black) process is the basis for all printing, from books and newspapers to home inkjets.

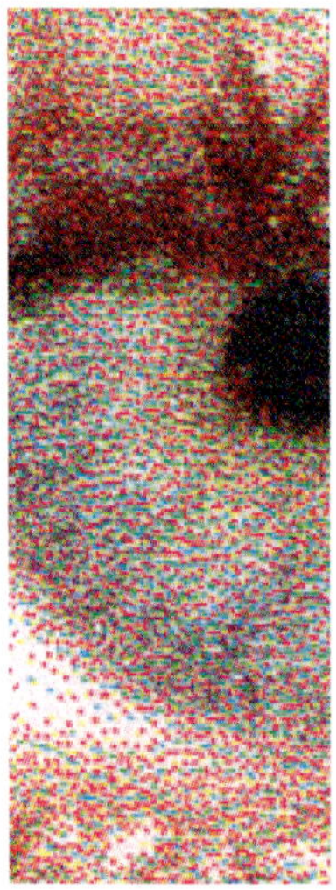

The four inks are laid down in patterns of tiny dots (the 'dots per inch', or dpi, mentioned in printer specification) using a 'dither pattern'. This process lets some of the paper show through, allowing pale tones to be recreated (the inks themselves can only be laid down at 100%). At normal viewing distance the dots themselves are invisible to the naked eye and the eye 'mixes' them to give the impression of a continuous range of tones.

Photo-quality inkjet printers add two extra inks (pale cyan and pale magenta) to reduce the visible graininess in pale pastel tones caused by the wide spaces between the dots.



**alternatives to inkjet printers**
Although inkjet printers are by far the most commonly used output devices, they are not the only technology available. Small 'postcard' printers using dye-sublimation or thermo-autochrome, offer high-gloss, high-quality 'fade-proof' prints, albeit at a higher cost. You can now also take a disk or memory card full of images to a high-street photo developers to have them printed onto conventional photographic paper.

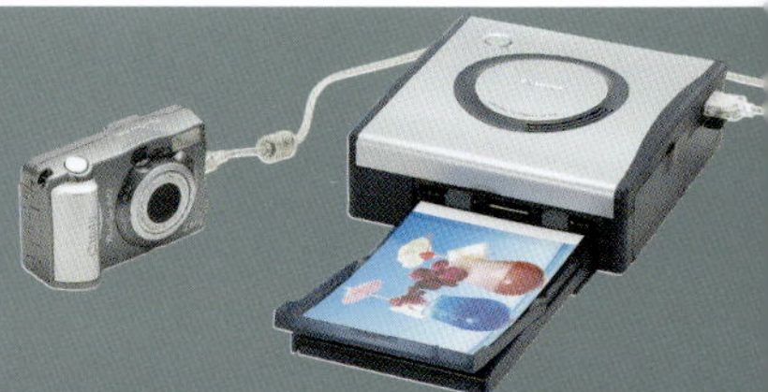

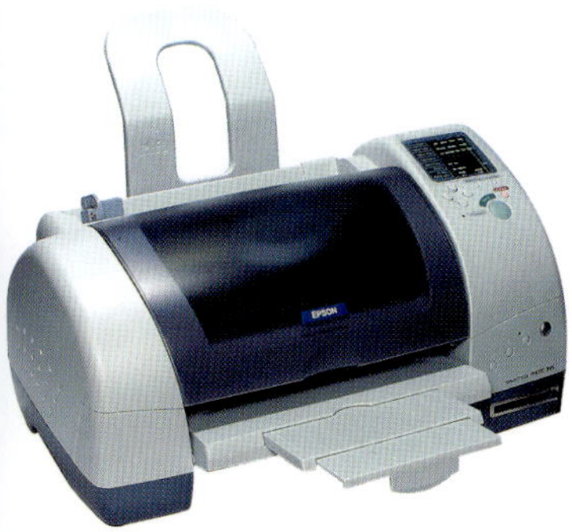

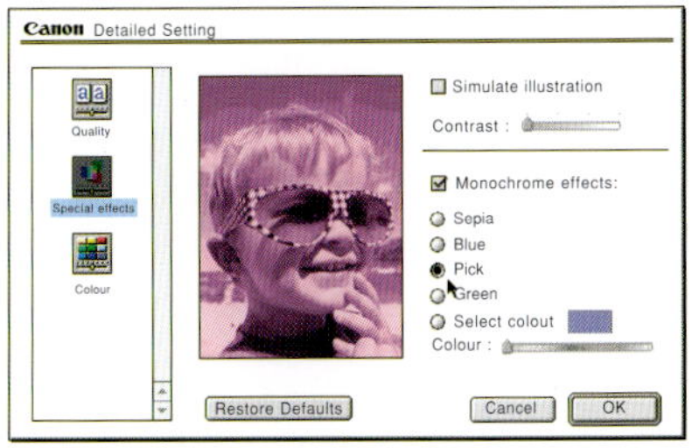


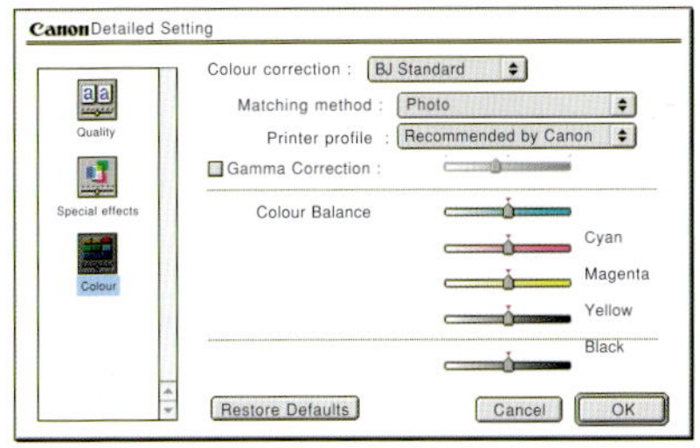


Virtually all home printing is done using a color inkjet device. These have developed rapidly over the last few years and can offer quality that rivals conventional photographic prints. Best for photographers is a 'photo-quality' printer that combines high resolution with six-color printing and advanced driver software.

Other printer technologies, including dye-sublimation, are used in small postcard printers and offer excellent quality as well as direct print capabilities with some digital cameras.

The driver software provided with a printer is as important to the quality of the print as the hardware itself.

Using the best possible paper is essential to getting good results from an inkjet printer. There are plenty to choose from so it is worth experimenting until you find one or two you really like.

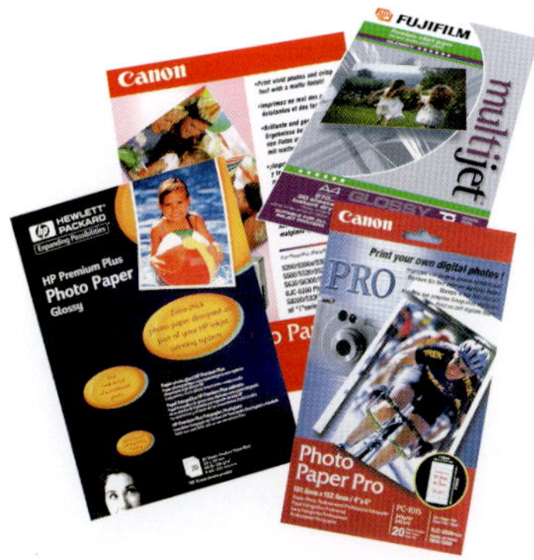

**Some of the hundreds of different inkjet photo papers on the market. As well as the usual gloss and matt, there are a variety of special surfaces available, including cloth, watercolor paper and stipple.**

## Printing tips

- Print your images at between 200 and 300 pixels per inch (ppi) for the best possible quality on an inkjet printer. In Photoshop, use the Image Size command to change the resolution (making sure the Resample Image option is off) as shown on the right.
- Don't confuse the resolution of your printer, measured in dots per inch (dpi), with image resolution (ppi).
- Most inkjet prints fade in direct sunlight, so keep copies of your digital images safely, that way you can reprint at a later date.
- Always use high-quality inkjet photo paper – anything else will reduce the quality of your output.

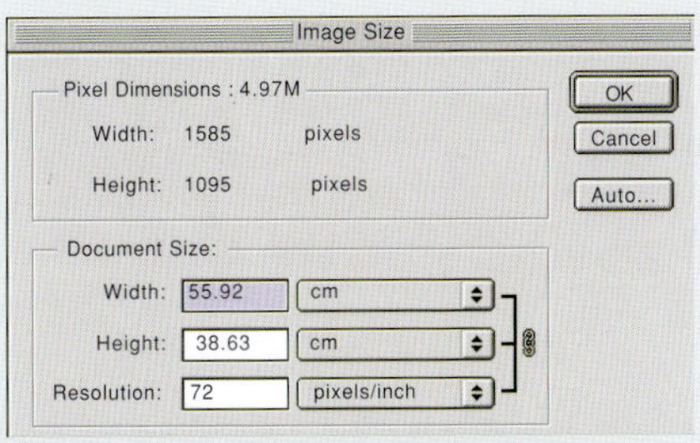


**▲ The resolution of an image refers to the number of pixels, but print resolution is measured as pixels per inch. This file is 1585x1095 pixels, but the output resolution is set to 72 pixels per inch, making an enormous print (55.92x38.63cm).**

**▼ By altering the physical output size, but not the number of pixels in the file, you increase the print resolution to 200 pixels per inch – perfect for photographic-quality output.**

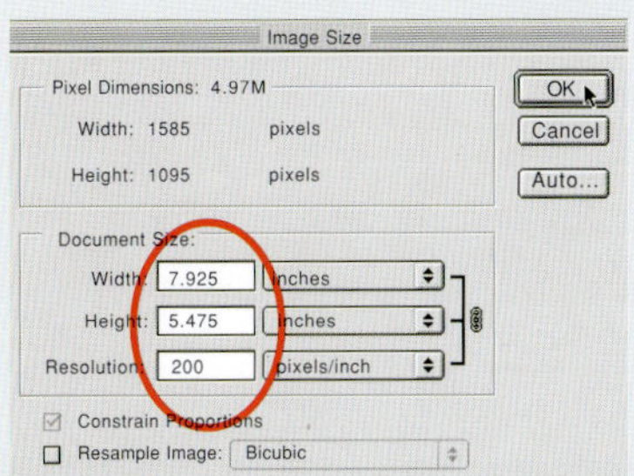

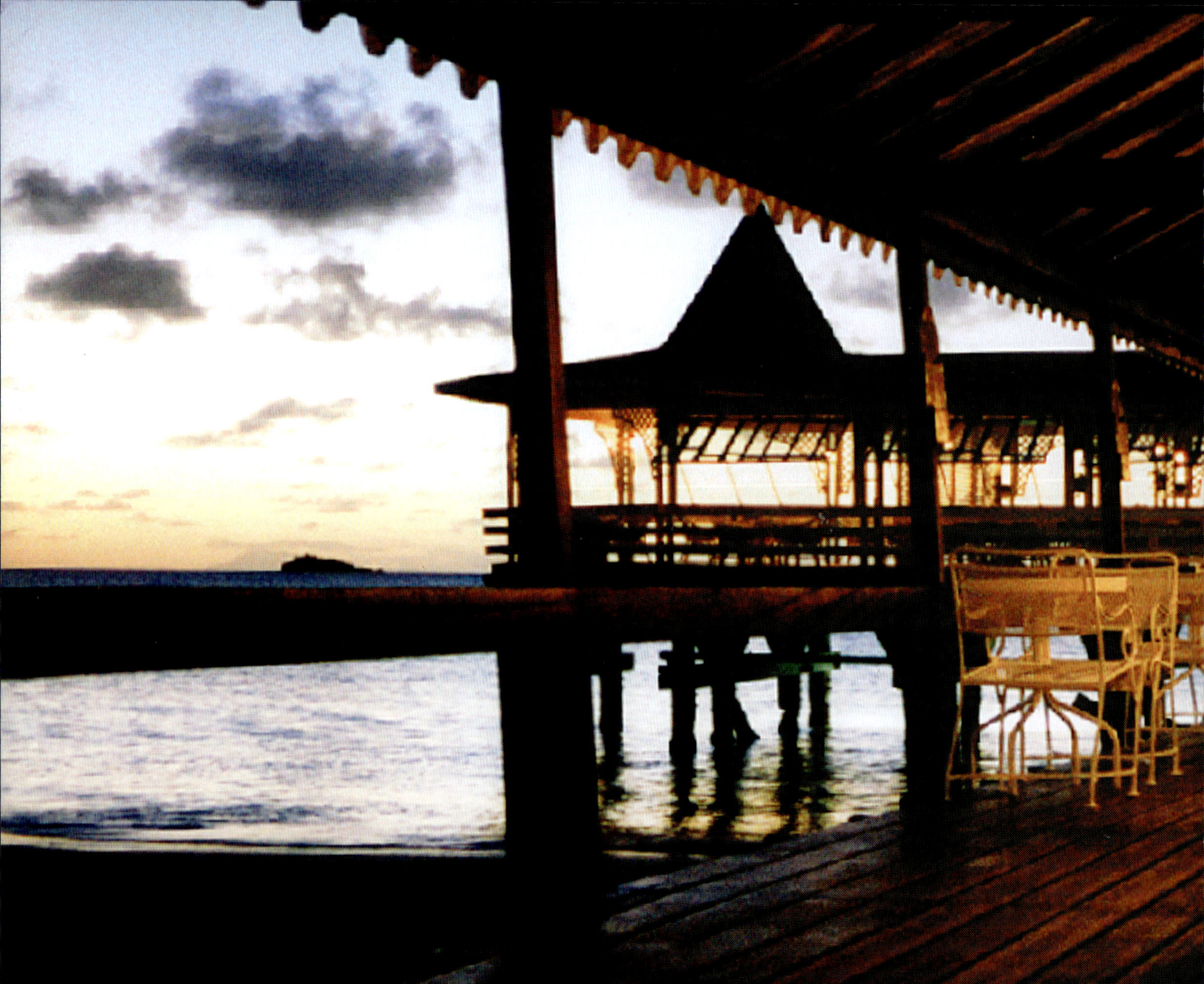

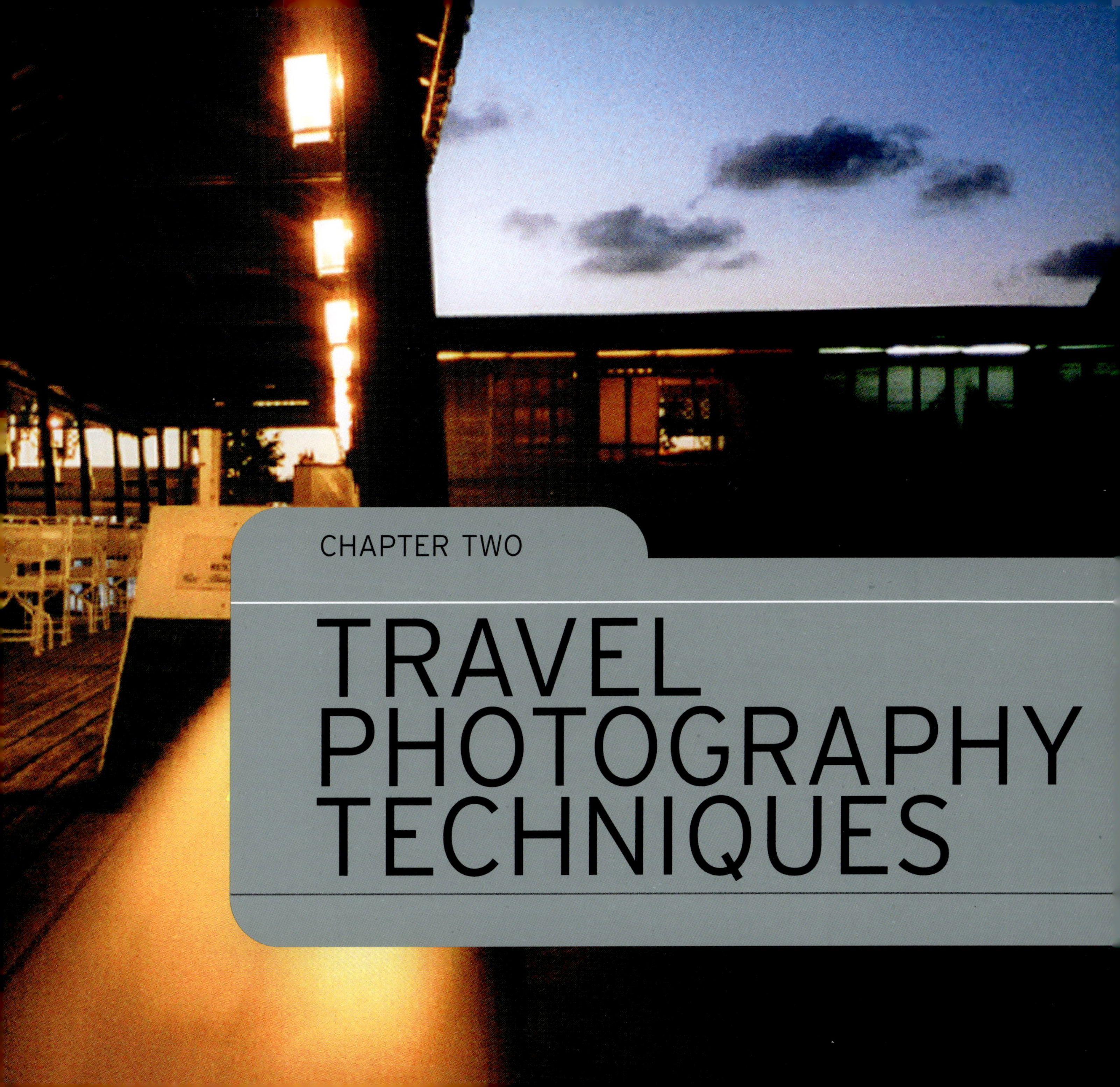

CHAPTER TWO

# TRAVEL PHOTOGRAPHY TECHNIQUES

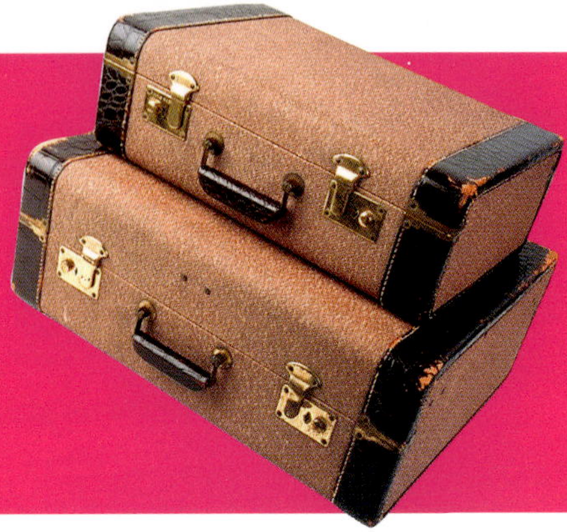

# Before you go

Whether you're embarking on the trip of a lifetime or a week by the beach, the key to coming back with a worthwhile selection of photographs lies in a little careful planning.

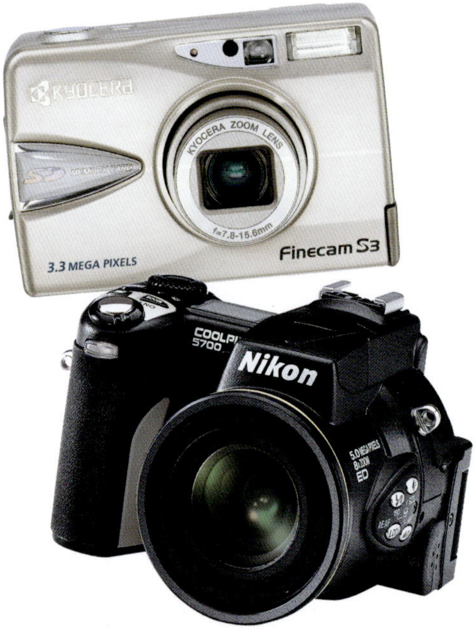


**Although a simple compact camera (top) will produce perfectly nice photographs, a more sophisticated model will offer more control and shooting versatility.**

**Equipment**

Professional travel photographers always take more equipment than they need and try to double up on everything in case of technical breakdowns or theft. On the other hand the last thing that you want on a holiday is to be loaded down with lots of unnecessary equipment.

What you decide over equipment depends on your priorities and whether a heavy camera bag would be more annoying for you than potentially being without a camera for part of your trip.

If photography is your priority then the least that you should have is a spare camera and, if you are using interchangeable lenses, then you should make sure that you carry a couple of spares of similar focal lengths with you.

You should make sure that you are familiar with any equipment that you take overseas, and that everything has been tested before you go. Allow time when buying equipment to get used to using it and allow time to return it under warranty if it is faulty. The last thing that you want when trying to take a picture is to be fumbling with kit that you don't know how to use.

Many cameras take special batteries, which you may not be able to find overseas. You should always make sure that you have at least one complete set with you. If you are planning on photographing at night or taking close-up shots then you will need a tripod. Make sure that it is large enough to be stable, but small enough not to weigh too much.

All of this kit needs to be stored somewhere safe, and you should invest in a good-quality camera bag. This should protect your equipment from damage, rain and dust, but still allow easy access.

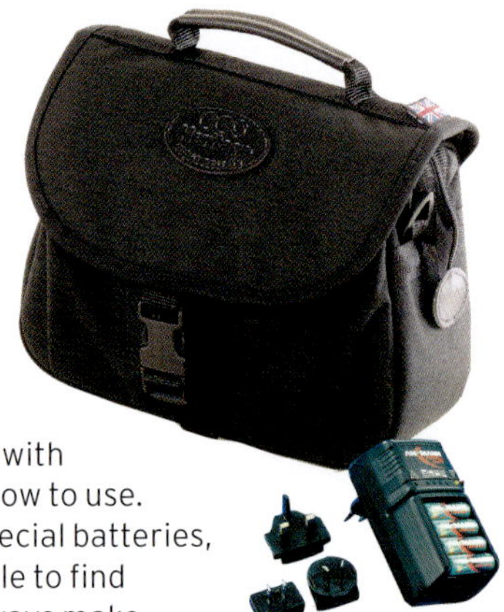

**A good weatherproof bag and spare batteries - with international charger - are essential.**

**keep in mind**

Never take a camera - digital or otherwise - on a 'trip of a lifetime' having just bought it. Most serious faults develop within the first few days of use and, equally importantly, you really need to get to know your camera before you put it to any serious use.

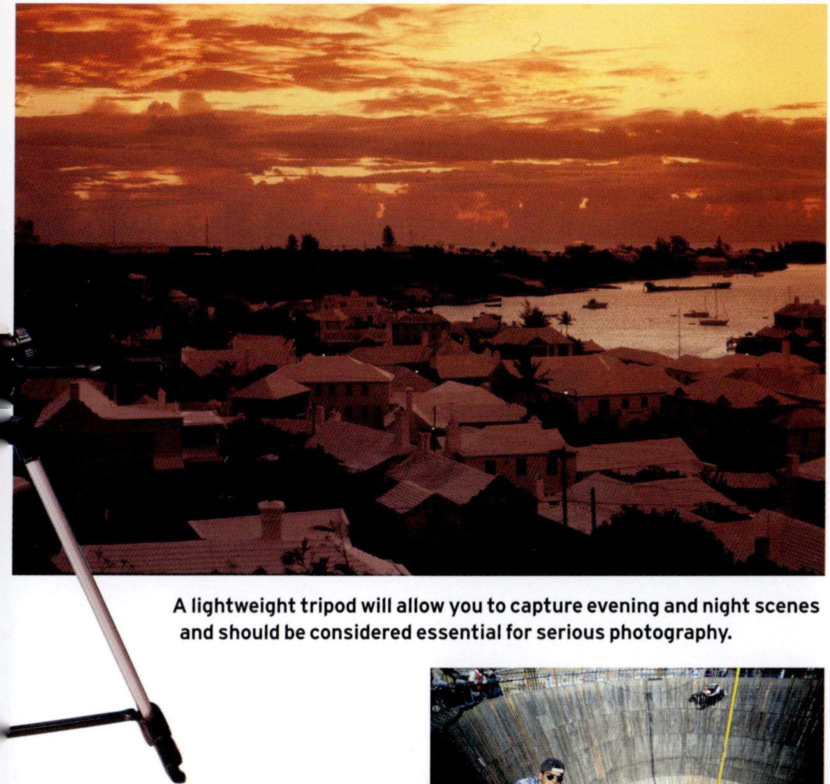

**A lightweight tripod will allow you to capture evening and night scenes and should be considered essential for serious photography.**

## Insurance

Insurance is vital when you are travelling. You should consider separate cover for your camera as often, normal travel insurance doesn't adequately cover expensive pieces of equipment. Ensure that any photography that you do is covered, for example dangerous sports. You should also be careful if you occasionally try to sell your pictures. Your insurance company may deem you a professional. Also, consider 'new for old' cover. It costs more but means that you will be able to replace equipment without having to hunt round for second-hand items.

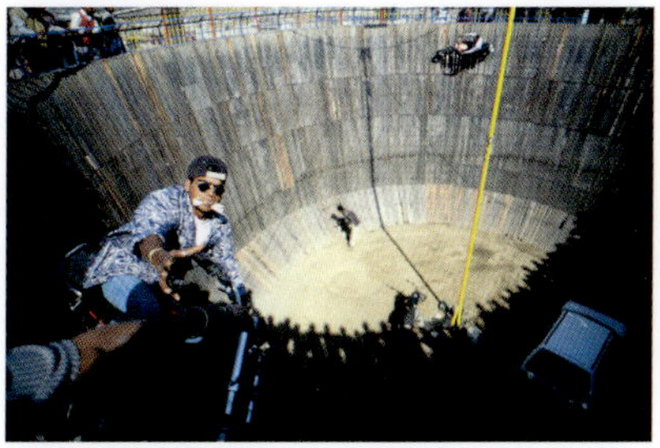

**Check your insurance cover for anything that constitutes a dangerous pursuit.**

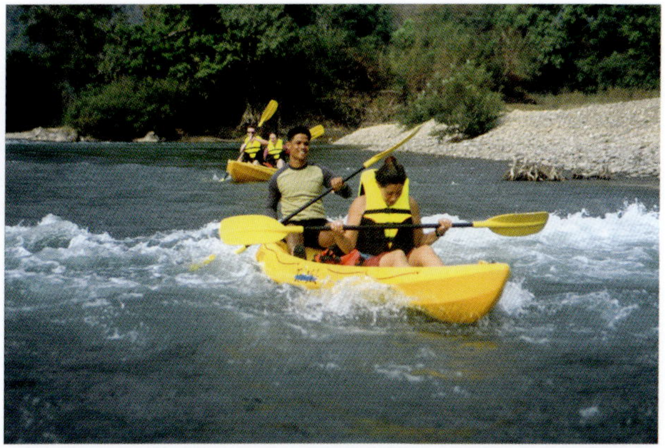

**navigator**
Shooting tips: night p42
The digital camera p16

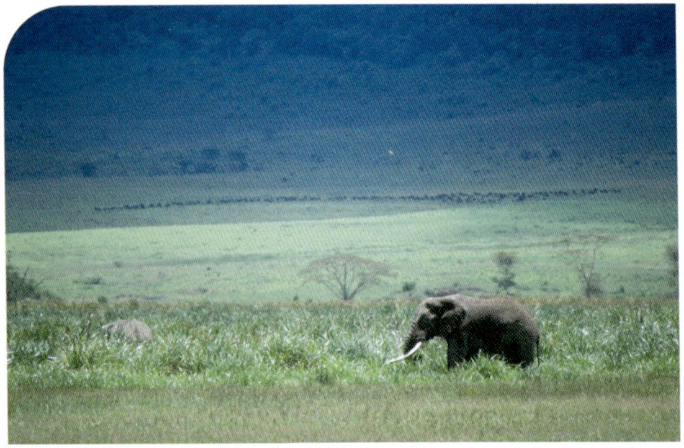

A long lens, or lens extender, is essential on safari.

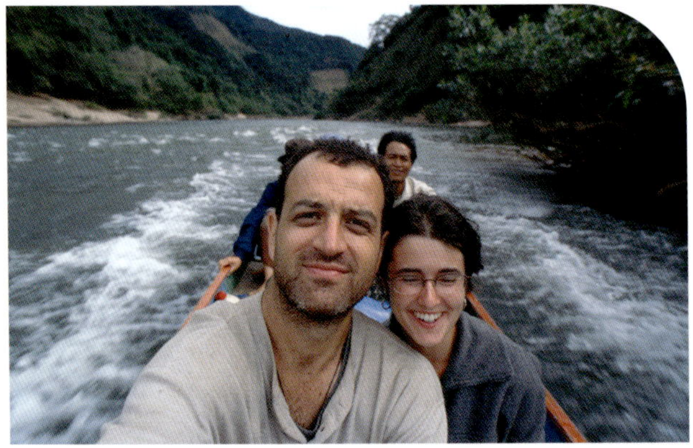

Cameras don't like water, so take care!

**Additional equipment**

There are a few additional pieces of photographic equipment that you should consider taking with you on your travels. If you have any intention of using a compact camera in wet, sandy or very humid situations it may be worth considering a weatherproof or waterproof housing. Although pricey, they are a lot cheaper than a new camera. Remember, electronic devices do not like sand or water, especially salt water.

As most digital cameras have a relatively high sensitivity, you should pack at least one neutral density filter if you want to have blur in your pictures, or use a narrow depth of field. Polarizing and graduated filters can also be useful. A flash is essential for a range of photographic techniques and a reflector is useful for taking portraits. See pages 42-43 for photographic techniques that use this equipment.

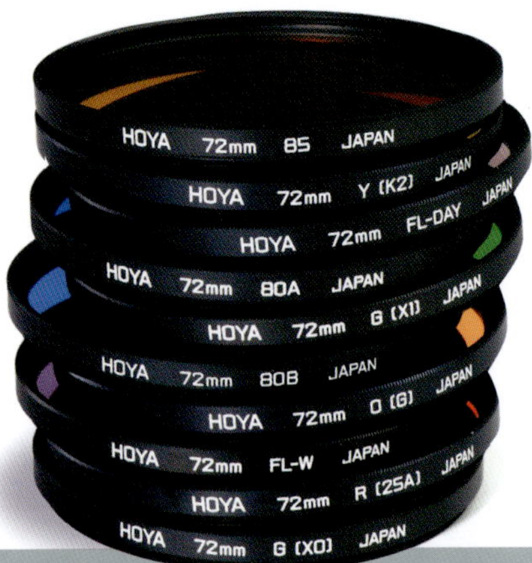


Screw-in glass filters.

**Storing your pictures**

The biggest problem with digital travel photography is storing your ever-growing collection of images. There are a number of ways of doing this. Spare memory cards can boost the capacity of your camera, but you might find it cost-effective to buy a back-up hard drive or even take a laptop computer with you so that you can safely download and back-up images.

There are other options though. In many countries round the world it is possible to download images in internet cafés. These can then be emailed back

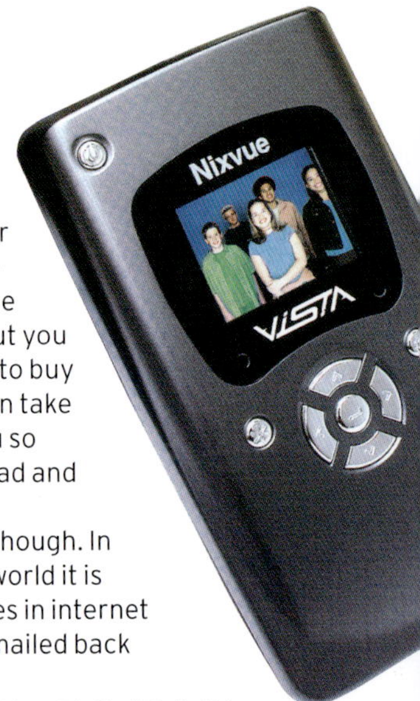


A hard drive 'Digital Wallet' for downloading images in the field.

**keep in mind**

Choosing the right quality setting on your digital camera is a compromise between quality and quantity; the lower quality setting you use, the more pictures you take.

Avoid the temptation to use too low a setting as you are unlikely to be able to return and retake the picture once you get home. Instead, invest in plenty of extra cards or some form of back-up system.

I'd recommend using the best JPEG setting on your camera; save the uncompressed (TIFF and RAW) modes for 'shots of a lifetime'.

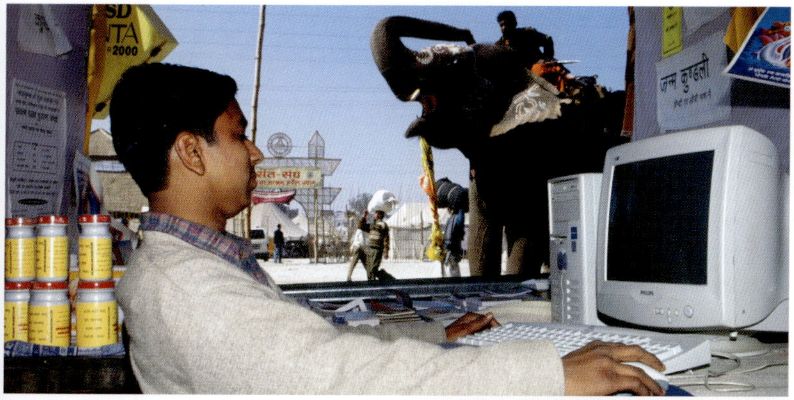

**Internet café in Cambodia.**

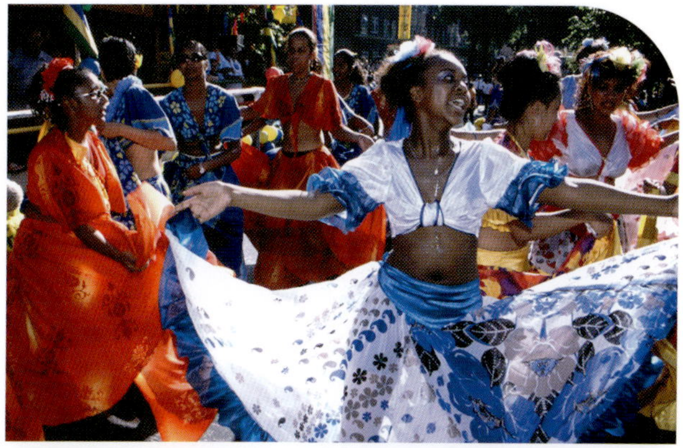

to your home account, making sure that you have the capacity in your mailbox to receive them all, and that it will be checked periodically so emails won't be bounced back. More and more internet cafés are offering CD-authoring for digital photographers where your images can be archived at very reasonable rates. It is not just in developed countries that you will see this service. I have seen it offered in the depths of Cambodia.

Whatever method you choose for storing images, you should always take a spare memory card with you in case one gets corrupted.

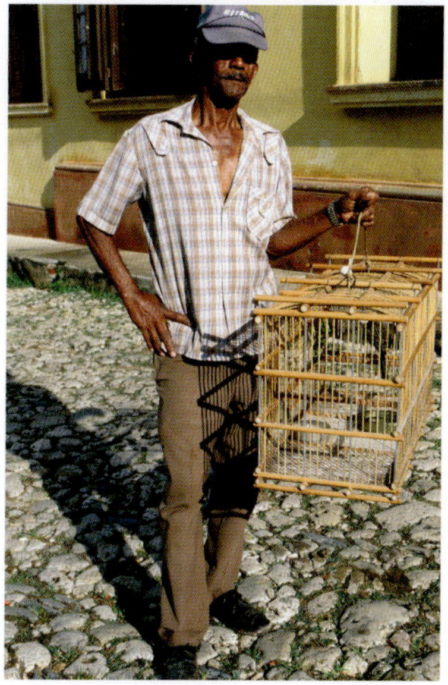

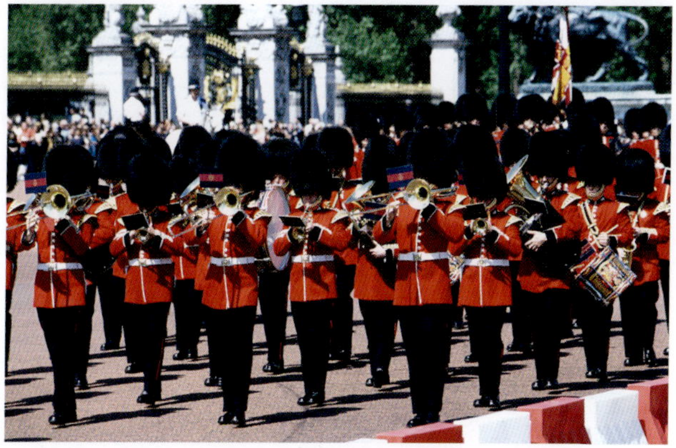

**If you are serious about your photography, then you should carry out some research before you go. This will give you an idea of what to look out for, as for example, Cuban men taking their caged birds for an evening stroll (left).**

# Travelling with your camera

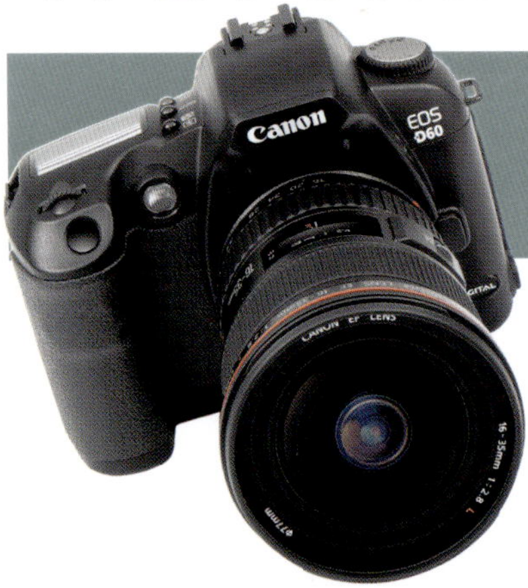


**Travelling with a digital camera requires more than a little planning. Here's some essential information to ensure your photography is a pleasure, not a chore.**

### Security

One of the biggest problems is keeping equipment secure, especially in poorer countries where even a relatively modest camera can seem like a fortune. Conventional wisdom says that you should be careful about showing cameras in these situations but it is difficult to take pictures when you are hiding your camera. The best advice is just to read each situation as best you can and be careful.

It is always worth only taking out the equipment that you think you will actually use and leaving the rest safely locked away in your hotel. Leave all valuables with reception or in a room-safe. This way, if you get robbed, you will not lose all of your equipment.

### Flying with your camera

When flying you should always hand-carry your equipment and any media cards, and certainly any film. The X-ray machines used for hand luggage are much less powerful than those that are used for hold bags. There is also less chance of equipment being lost, stolen or damaged if it is with you. You should also be aware of the customs restrictions of countries you are travelling to; it is also worth carrying a list of equipment, copies of purchase receipts and serial numbers in case you come across an officious customs officer.

### Protection from the elements

In many countries dust or moisture can be a problem. Resealable plastic bags keep equipment safe when you are not using it and minimize the amount of time it is exposed to harsh conditions. Lenses are especially susceptible to moisture. A couple of silica gel bags can help, as can an umbrella; especially in the tropics when rain can be very heavy, and the sun can be very hot.

Be careful of overzealous cleaning. A small amount of dust on the lens will not affect the picture quality as much as a scratched lens. You should also keep a skylight filter over the lens to protect it. Be careful about carrying too much equipment with you – it is supposed to be a holiday after all – but also avoid the

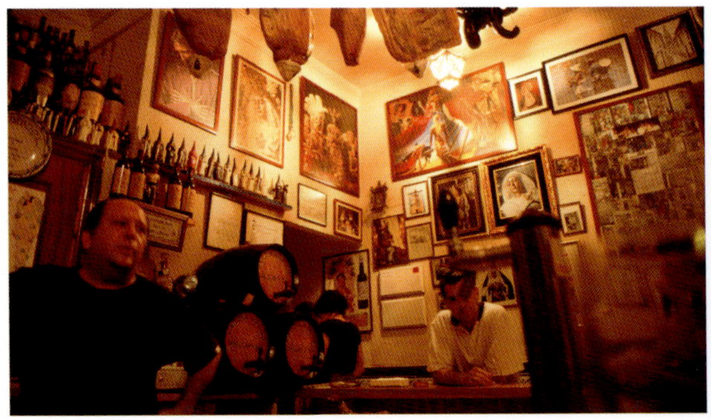

**As this shot in a tapas bar in Seville, Spain shows, it is worth carrying a small camera with you wherever you go.**

**keep in mind**

If you are photographing an event like a local festival, you cannot choose the lighting or the time of day. You might have to use all of your skills as a photographer to make the most of the pictures, but you should keep shooting whatever the conditions.

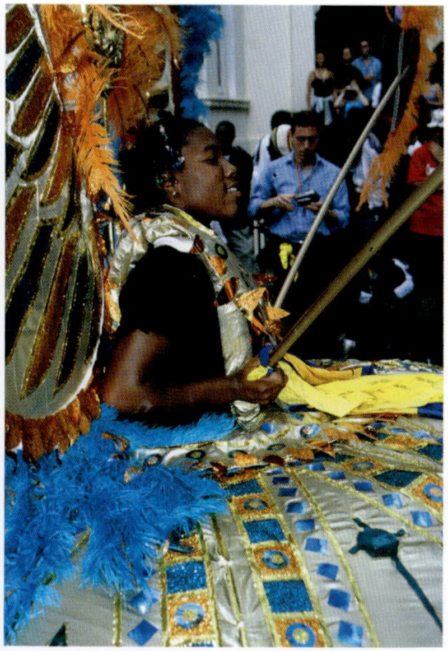

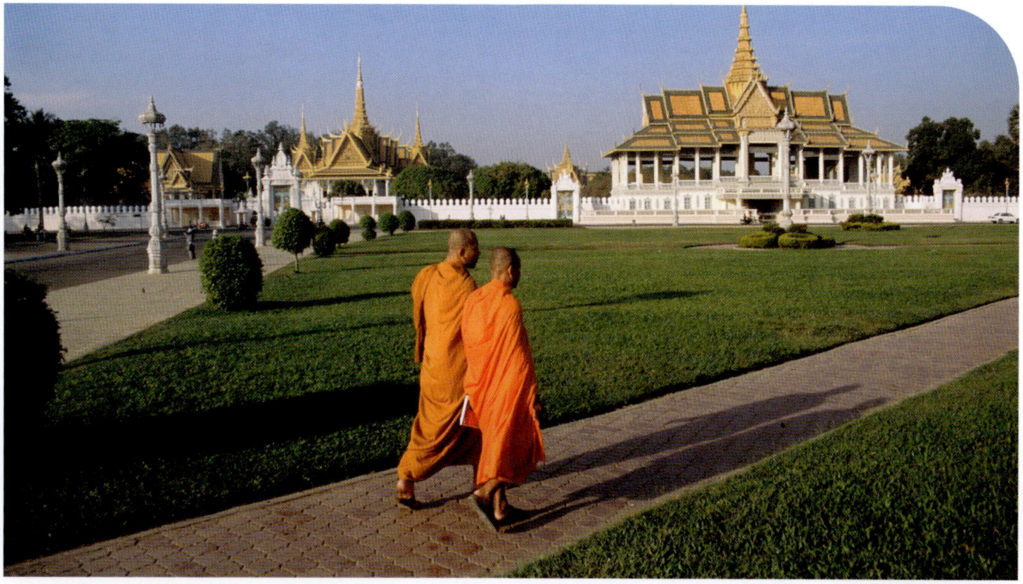

frustration of not having certain key bits with you. For instance, a flash is pretty much always vital - and not just at night (see page 46). The frustration of seeing a picture when you don't have a camera with you is greater than the hassle of carrying it everywhere.

**When to shoot?**

The photographer's maxim of only shooting in the early morning or late afternoon is valid, but only up to a point. The light is certainly much better during these times and, consequently, so will your pictures. However there are times when this just isn't possible. If you are on a family holiday, then keeping photographer's hours might not be possible. Moreover, certain events - such as the Changing of the Guard at Buckingham Palace in London - happen closer to noon. The light is often harsh but in situations such as these, you don't have a choice! The pictures are still worth taking. You can dramatically improve shots later on the computer by lightening shadows and reducing the contrast.

There are instances where harsh sunlight won't be an issue at all. Interiors are obviously possible at any time of day and, by using a simple technique called fill-in flash (see page 46), you can take portraits whenever you see someone to photograph, at any time of day.

**Shooting at the end of the day results in much longer shadows and more interesting lighting.**

**navigator**

Shooting tips: night p42
The right lens p36
Other color tools p68

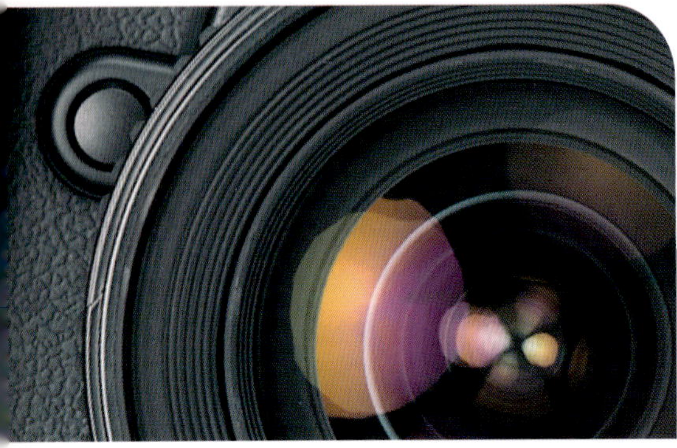

# The right lens

**Whether you have a simple camera with a zoom lens, or an SLR type with interchangeable lenses, you need to learn a bit about lenses and depth of field.**

The power of a lens depends on its focal length. They can be broken down into three basic types: wide-angle, standard and telephoto. A simple camera with a zoom lens will cover all three, but if you have a camera that takes interchangeable lenses you can use ones with a more pronounced effect.

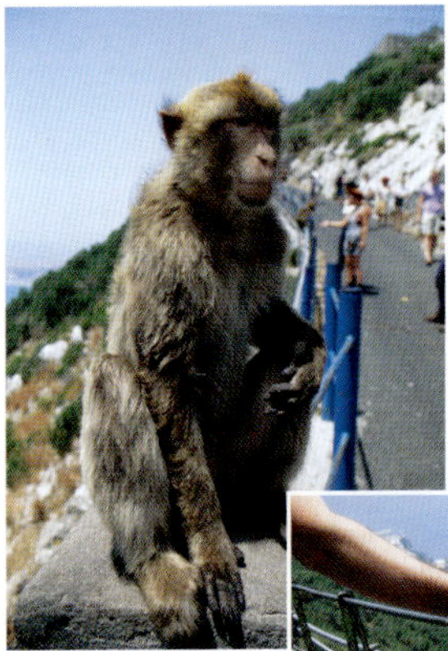

**A short telephoto lens isolates the subject and creates narrow depth of field.**

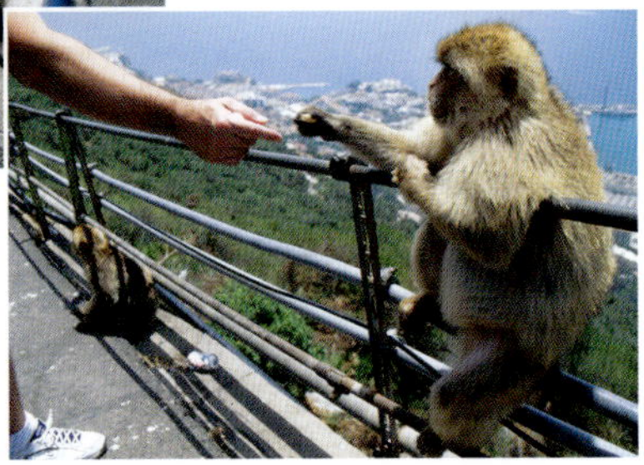

**Shooting with a wide lens gives context and a completely different perspective.**

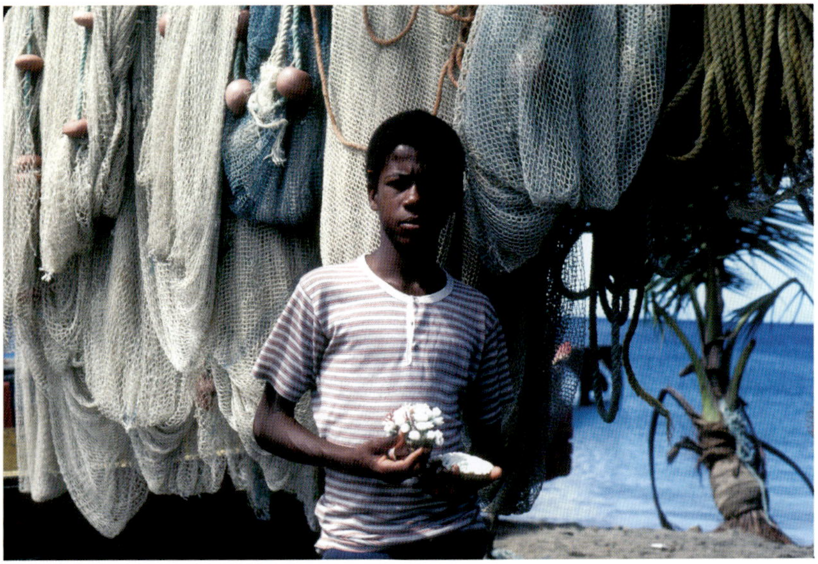

**Standard lenses**

Standard lenses have a perspective that is fairly similar to the human eye. They are a good all-round lenses and can produce a pleasing perspective. However there will be times when you want to get closer to, or further away from a subject.

**keep in mind**

Many compact cameras with short zoom lenses can be extended with clip-on or screw-on lenses. Although they cause a slight reduction in overall sharpness, these additional lenses bring real wide-angle and long telephoto capabilities to point-and-shoot cameras, and are well worth considering.

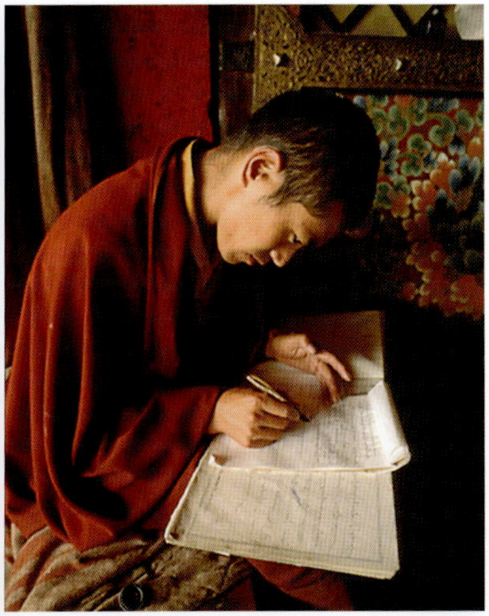

### Telephoto lenses

A mild telephoto lens is perfect for portraits and produces a flattering perspective.

A very powerful telephoto lens can be used to make far away objects seem much closer. It also compresses the perspective, making distances between objects seem less than they are. The flattening effect can be used as a creative technique.

If you have a digital SLR type camera that takes interchangeable 35mm lenses, then the effect of the chip size being smaller than the 35mm frame will increase the focal length by about 50%. This means that an average telephoto turns into a powerful super-telephoto.

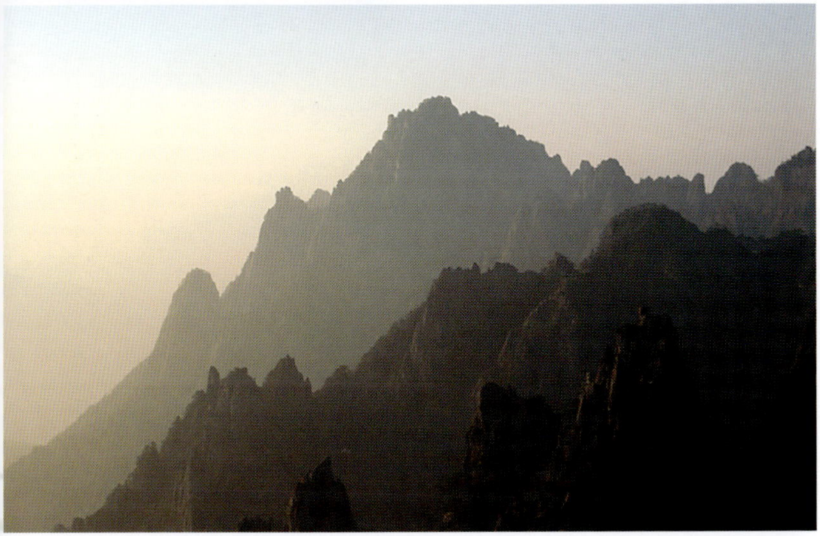

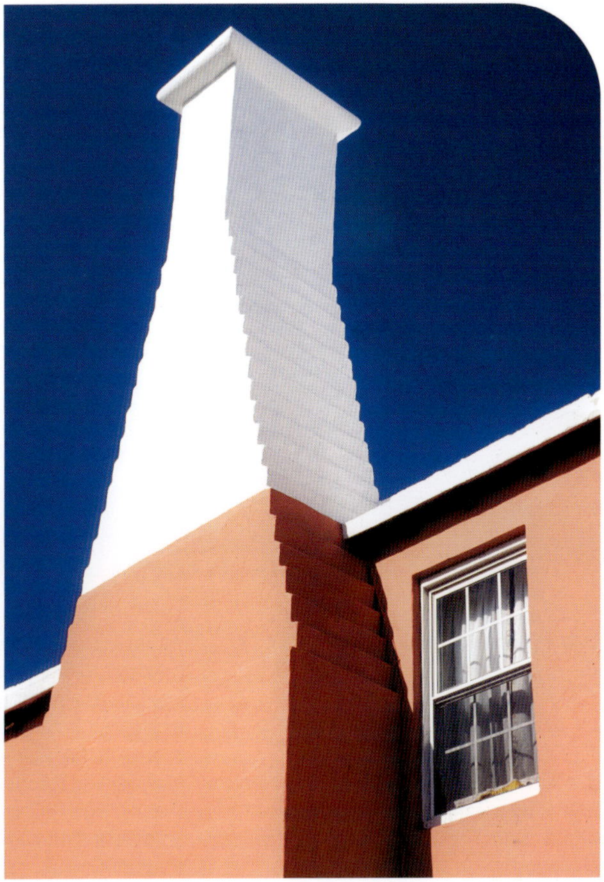

**navigator**
The digital camera p18
Converging verticals p86

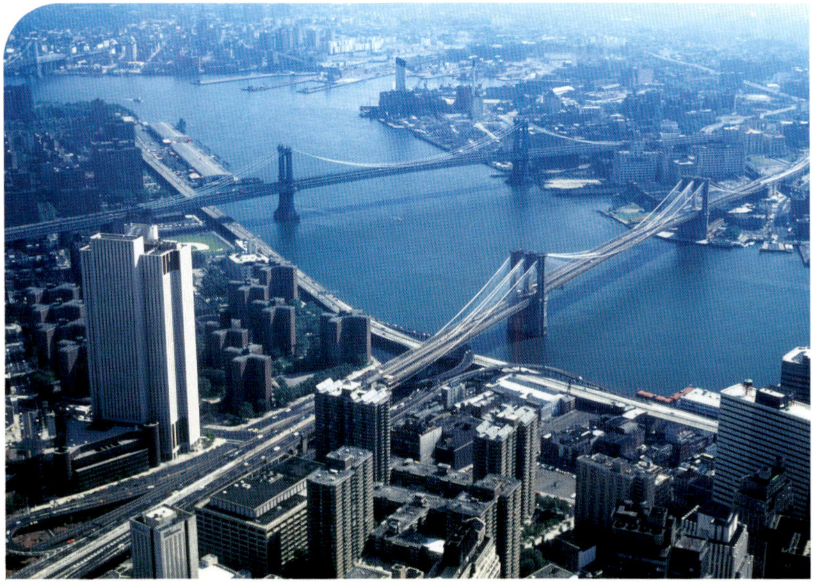

If this all sounds to good to be true, there is a downside. At the other end of the scale, your wide-angle lens will suffer a similar fate, making really wide views difficult with most digital SLRs. To combat this lens manufacturers produce even wider wide-angle lenses and zooms, while a new generation of digital SLRs with full frame sensors has removed the problem entirely.

Any wide-angle lens will give some sort of distortion – especially at the edges of the frame. However, professional photographers – especially news and reportage photographers – use this as a creative effect. A wide-angle lens is very useful for getting more into the frame, especially for juxtaposing things at the edge of the picture with things in the middle. If you are using a very wide-angle lens then people at the edge of the frame might not even know that they are being photographed!

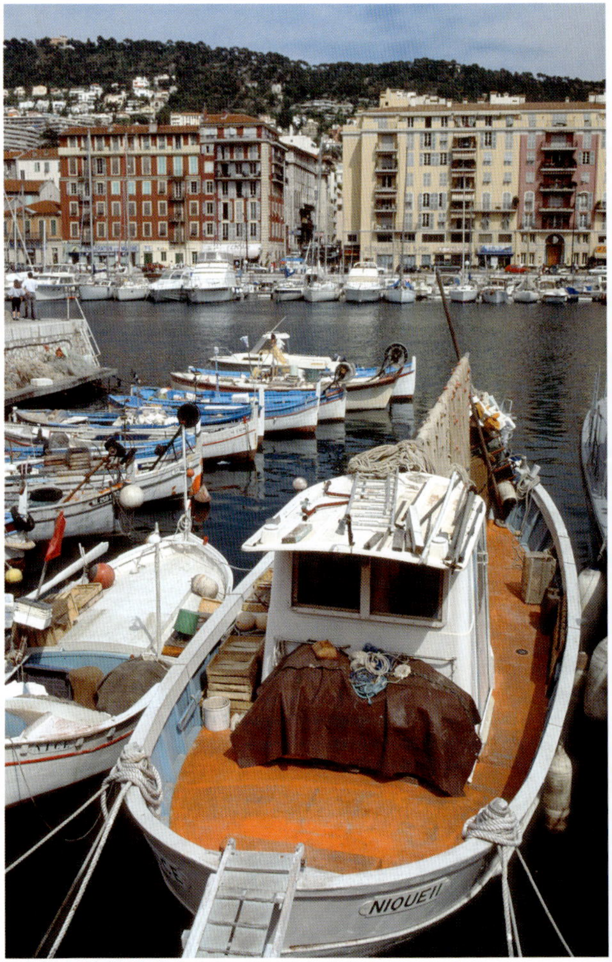

**A wide-angle lens gives exaggerated prominence to foreground objects.**

**keep in mind**
The digital zoom function offered by many point-and-shoot cameras is to be avoided at all costs. All the camera does is to enlarge the central portion of the image, without adding any detail. You can do this yourself later with much finer control.

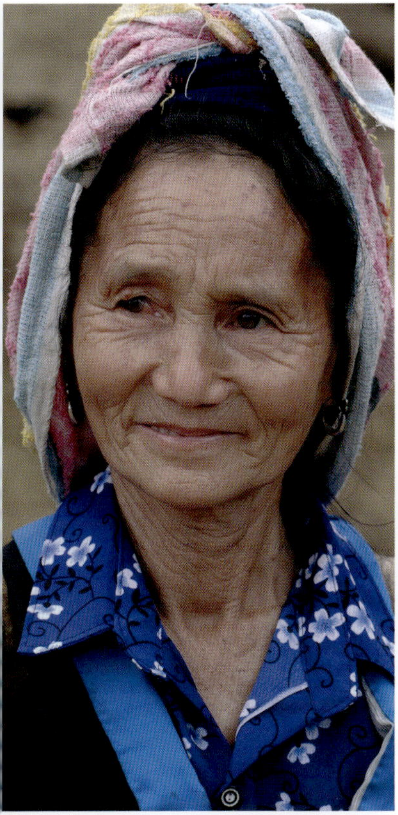

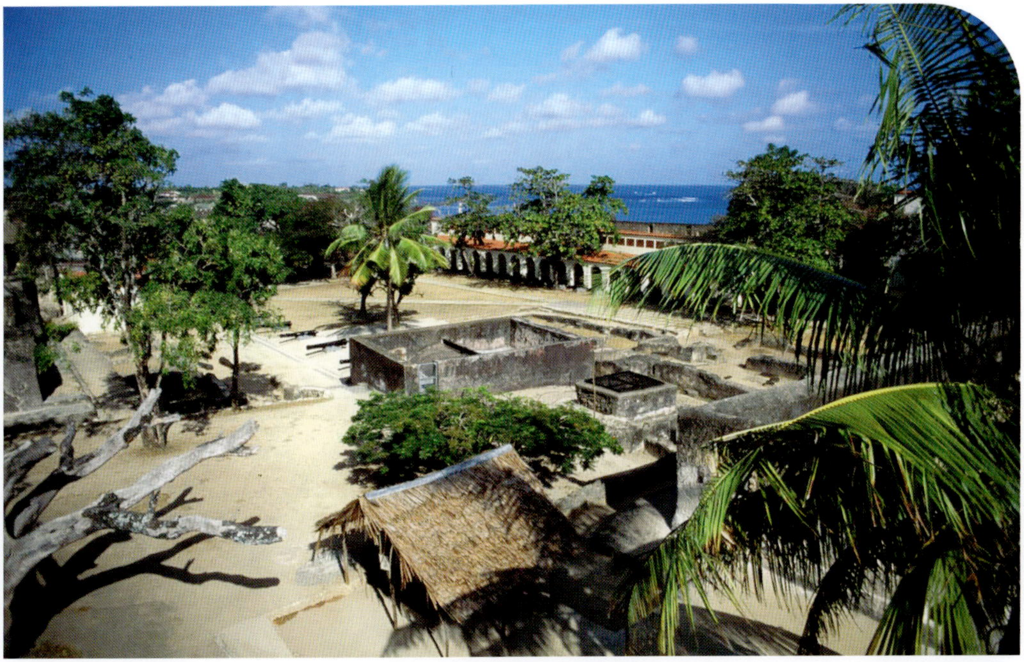

**Depth of field is considerably less when using a telephoto lens (above) than a wide-angle (above right). This allows you to throw the background out of focus for flattering portraits or keep everything from foreground to background sharp in scenic shots.**

Your lens choice - along with the aperture of the lens - will also have an effect on the depth of field. This is the amount of your picture - in front of and behind the thing that you are focused on - that will also be sharp. A wide-angle lens will have much greater depth of field than a telephoto lens used at the same aperture setting.

You can use the small depth of field of a telephoto lens to throw the background of an image out of focus so that it doesn't interfere with your subject, whereas a wide-angle lens can be used to keep both the foreground and background objects completely sharp.

**navigator**
Cropping & rotating p62
The digital camera p18
Converging verticals p86

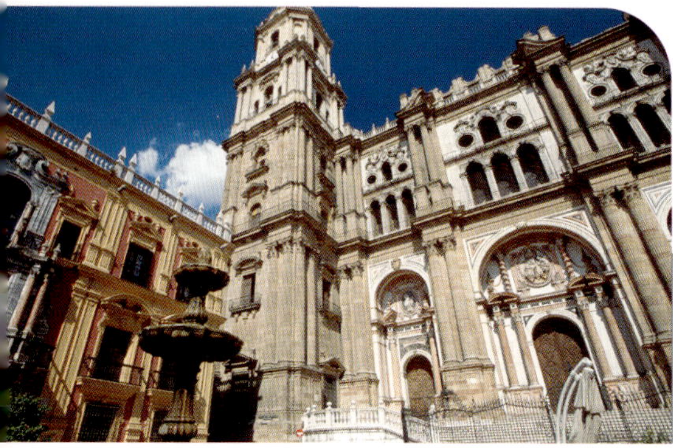

# Shooting tips: places

If you want to bring back more than a couple of standard tourist shots it makes sense to prepare well and take some time to really capture the spirit of a place.

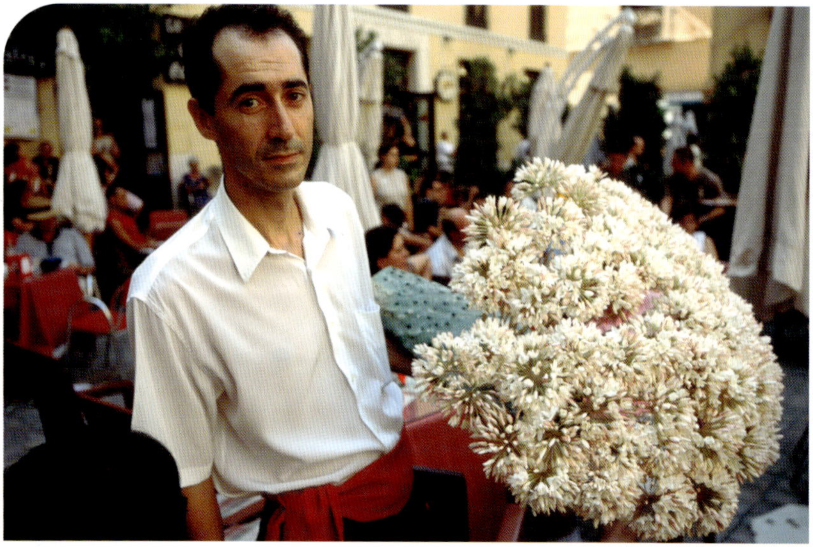

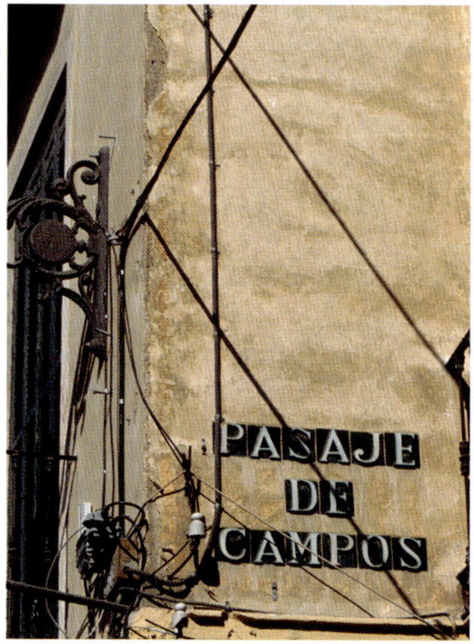


Shooting a place – whether it be a single building such as the Taj Mahal or a whole city – allows you to build up a series of images which will work together to show much more about your subject than you could achieve with a single photograph. It will also allow you to use a range of photographic techniques and styles. The pictures on this page are from Malaga in Southern Spain. This is the gateway city to millions of beach holidays a year, but most people never bother to look round – just heading straight out to the concrete strip of the Costa del Sol. As you can see, even the most familiar of holiday destinations can be fertile ground for the imaginative photographer.

**technical details**
Fujifilm FinePix S1 Pro
Digital SLR
Nikon 28-70mm lens

**keep in mind**
Don't overlook the effect that tourists themselves have on a city. The contrast between mass tourism and a traditional destination can provide fascinating photographs.

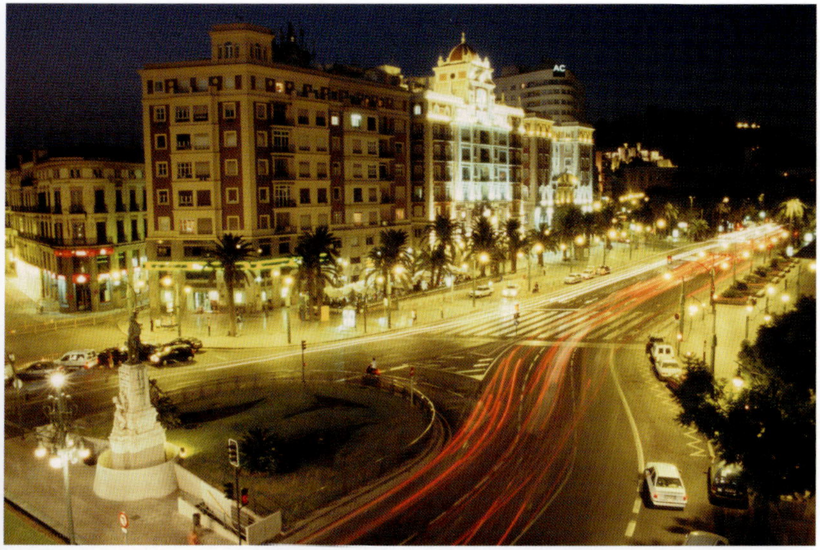

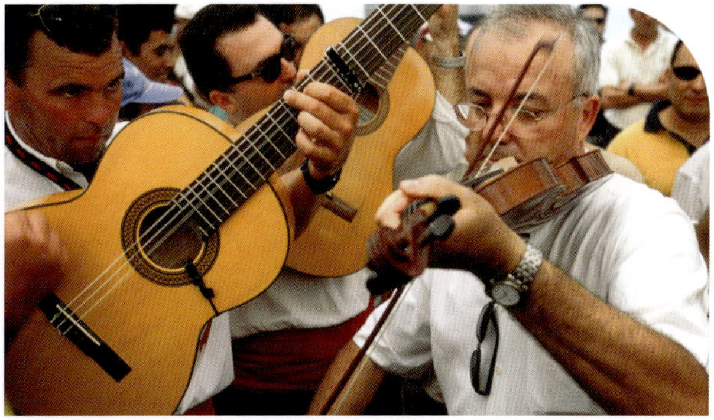

## Get the most from your destination

Make sure that you have enough time to take pictures. Vacations are ideal, giving you time over a period to visit - and re-visit - your subject. You should also try to learn something about where you are shooting. Read at least one guide book to find out if there are any special things that you should look out for. Once you reach your destination you can carry on your research by speaking to the tourist office and also looking at various postcards that are being sold.

Don't limit yourself to one style of photography. Try out everything in this book - even if you don't always get it right. Your pictures, if successful, should work on two levels; the subject matter itself, and the photographic execution.

Try to revisit places at different times of the day. Photographing familiar scenes at night gives them a whole new atmosphere - and often a much more effective shot. You should also look out for small details, such as architectural flourishes, and try to photograph typical shops or bars. Even the food that you eat can be a subject for a photograph - especially if it is a particular local delicacy.

## Do your research

It is well worth trying to coincide your visit with any special events if at all possible. Although this might mean that accommodation costs are higher, you will often be able to get a much truer impression of a city. Venice, for example comes alive at the annual carnival, and the people of Malaga hold an exuberant Feria every August where they decorate the town and drink and dance in the streets, often wearing traditional Andalucian costume.

Whenever you visit, your pictures will benefit from a degree of research. For instance, Malaga is the birthplace of Pablo Picasso and in a park on the outskirts of town there is a lively statue of him. Capturing details such as this will help to convey something about the place that you are photographing - things that the casual photographer will often miss.


**navigator**
Shooting tips: people p48
Shooting tips: night p42
Removing elements p74

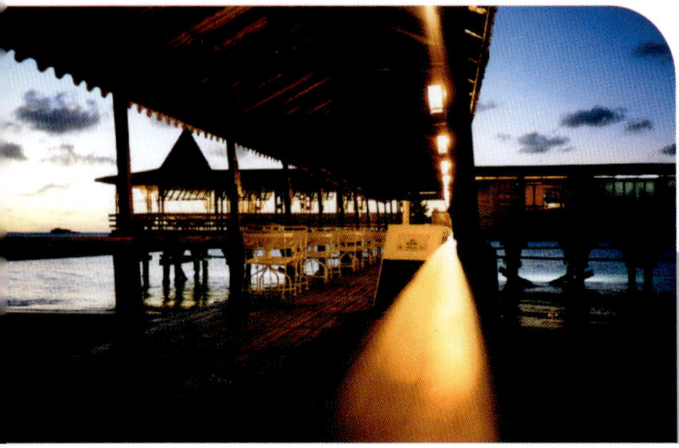

# Shooting tips: night

**There is no need to stop taking pictures as the soon as the sun goes down – in fact shooting at night can produce the most dramatic photographs of all.**

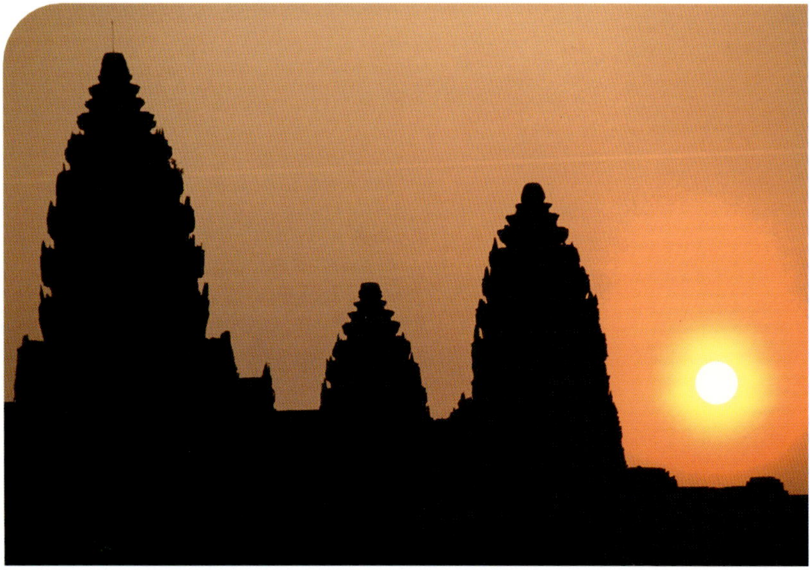

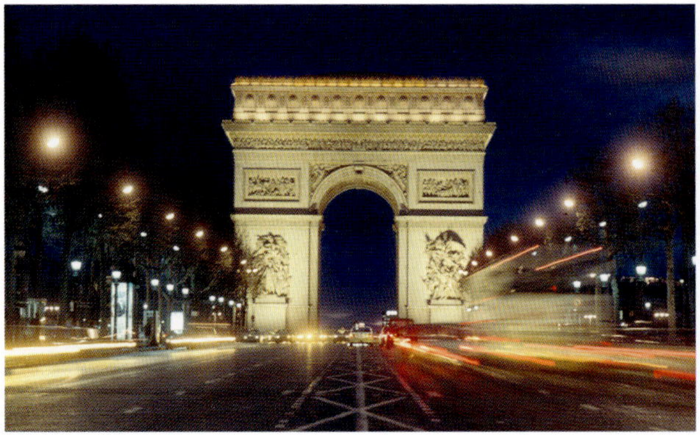

Night time provides a rich source of atmospheric images and often conditions and exposures will be more forgiving than in daylight. If you have been unlucky with the weather on your trip then it might be the only option open to you. Poor weather can often enhance photography at the end of the day. Stormy skies will show up the colours of the setting sun and wet pavements and roads will reflect lights to double their effect.

**Shooting sunsets**

Generally speaking, you will find the best sunsets just before and just after the sun slips below the horizon. This will give the warmest possible light and if the sun is still in the frame, it will be less bright, ensuring that it won't bleach out.

Sunsets always look better if there is something in the foreground. This gives your picture a sense of place and also a perspective. Choose something with an identifiable shape as it will be reduced to a silhouette by the backlighting.

**technical details (top)**
Nikon Coolpix 990
digital camera
Self-timer, flash off



**keep in mind**

Long exposures will produce camera shake. Although this can be used to effect, you will probably want to avoid it. If your shutter speed is under about 1/60th of a second you'll need to use something to stop the camera moving during the exposure. A tripod is the best solution, but you can improvise. The image at the top of this page was shot by resting the camera on the wooden railing and using the self-timer to take the picture.

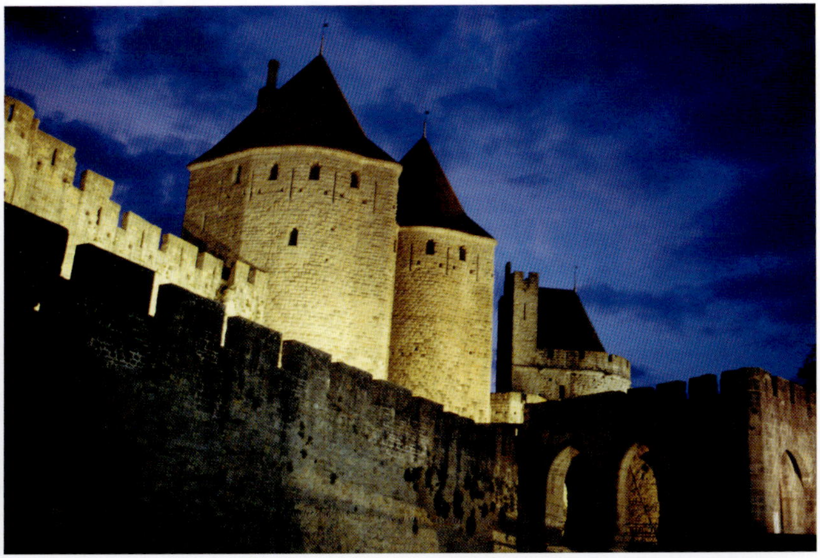

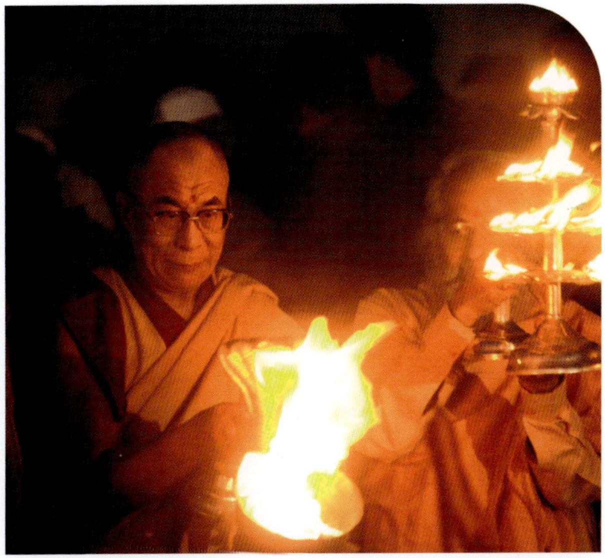

Sunsets are very dynamic, so keep taking photographs as the subject develops. The time difference between the perfect shot and no shot at all can be only a few seconds.

**Shooting at night**

The best time to take night shots - even of floodlit buildings - is at dusk, when there is still some light in the sky. Typically the perfect conditions last for a short time after the sun goes down.

If you do take photographs after this time then you should avoid wider shots; use a telephoto lens to fill your frame with a floodlit building. This will give it more prominence and avoid it being swamped by inky black skies.

**Night exposure**

Exposure is often thought of as being a real problem with night photography, but in reality you will find both sunset and night photography much more forgiving than daylight photography. Many photographers use a technique called bracketing to take a number of shots at different exposures so that they can later choose the one that is correct. In this area of photography it is difficult to work out what right exposure is, and quite different settings will yield good, yet strikingly different images.

Anything can make a good subject for night photography, but some of the favourites are views over cities, floodlit buildings and busy roads.

A tripod will allow you to use longer exposures. This will produce a number of interesting effects in your picture. People will become blurred - with longer exposures they blur so much as to disappear - and the lights from cars will form long sweeping lines of color. Experiment with various exposure times until you get the effect that you are after. Some of the shots on this page had exposures exceeding ten seconds.

**keep in mind**

Automatic cameras will always try and use flash at night. Remember that unless your subject is less than a few feet away the small built-in flash simply won't provide enough illumination. It is much better to disable the flash altogether if you want an atmospheric shot.

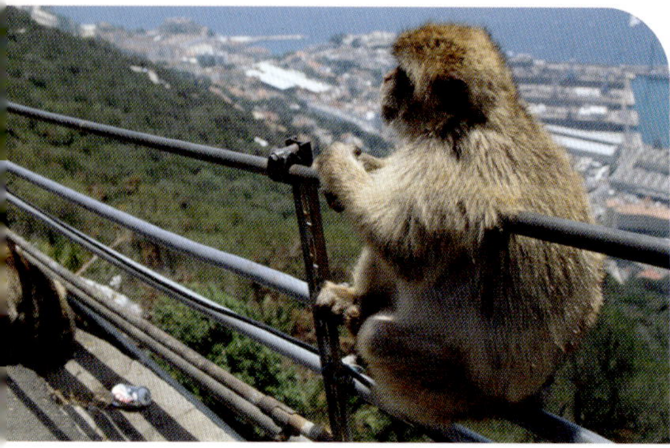

# Shooting tips: wildlife

Animals are one of photography's perennials. And you can find wildlife just about anywhere you travel - even if you're not off on an African safari.

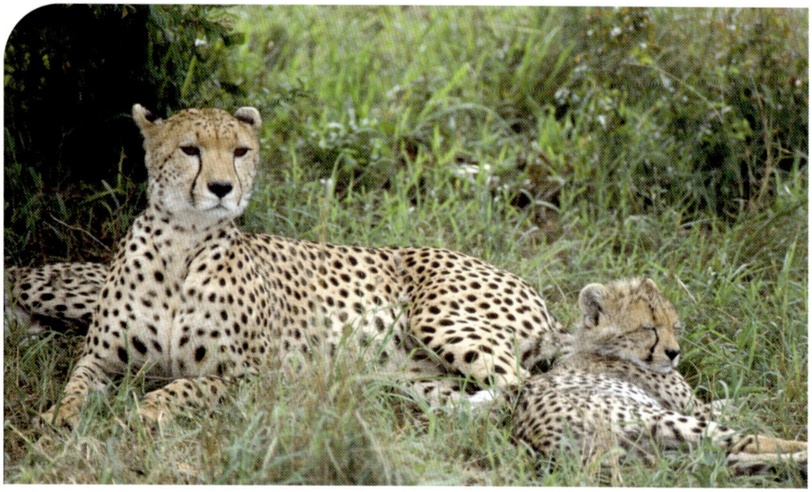

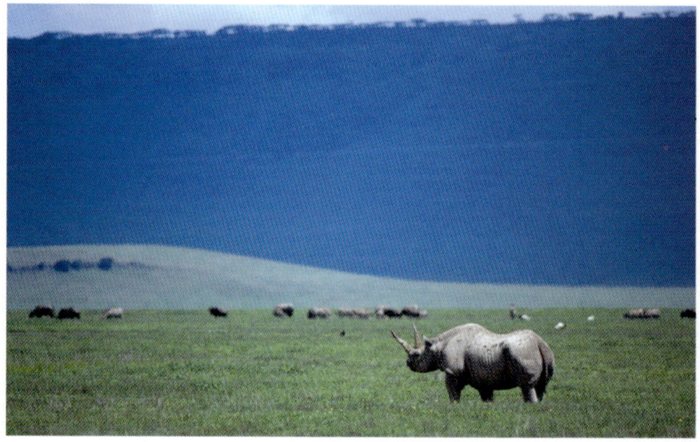

Mention wildlife photography and most people will think of the big stuff, such as African wildlife safaris. These are compelling subjects, granted, but you can find interesting wildlife in virtually any travel destination if you go looking for it. There are always animals - especially birds - wherever you go. In some places you will find animals that are used to people and even beg for food from them. These animals, such as the Barbary apes in Gibraltar, are very easy to get close to and you can photograph them with even the simplest equipment.

**Shooting on safari**

If you are lucky enough to get to one of the big wildlife destinations such as Africa, then there are a few rules that will help you get some incredible photos.

For most wildlife photography you will need some sort of telephoto lens. A zoom lens on a good digital camera should be powerful enough for some of the bigger wildlife that you will see on a safari and you can always crop the image on a computer to make the subject fill the frame. If your camera does not have

**keep in mind**

You don't need to go on safari to see interesting and photogenic wildlife. Most major cities have zoos, many of which offer loads of photographic opportunities. You'll also find interesting local wildlife wherever you travel - from pelicans and crocodiles in Florida to exotic birds and lizards in the islands of the Caribbean.

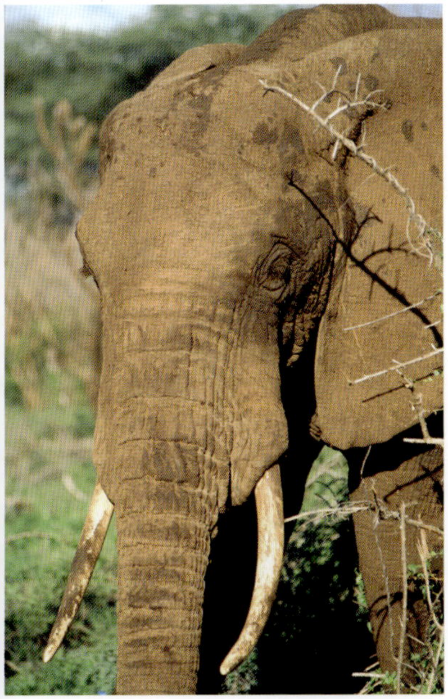

a powerful enough telephoto lens to get in close to the subject, then compose your picture in such a way that you place the subject within the environment. Basically, you are shooting a landscape with an animal in it.

Even if you do have a telephoto lens, remember the rules of composition. Don't always point the camera directly at a subject and shoot it dead in the middle of the frame. Remember, though, if you do place the subject off-centre make sure your autofocus system doesn't focus on the distant background. Moreover, when something happens, it will do so very quickly – anticipation is the key to successful wildlife shots.

If you are on an organized trip you will have a guide to find the wildlife for you, but if you are on your own research the animals that you wish to photograph. This will give you a better chance of finding them and getting your pictures.

In hotter countries, the best time to take pictures is during the first and last few hours of the day. The animals will be more active and the light will be much better.

**Getting the best shot**

There are lots of people taking wildlife pictures and, if you want yours to stand out, you should try to do something different. For the shot of flamingos taking off I had to use a slow shutter speed because there wasn't much light. I combined this with panning to compensate, but also to shoot a more interesting picture.

If you witness some action from your wildlife, and your camera has the facility, you should try shooting sequences. This should ensure that you catch the action. Professional photographers always get through a huge amount of film taking wildlife shots but, working digitally, you will be able to delete the images that don't work, freeing up memory space.

When you are taking pictures of wild animals remember that your subjects can be dangerous. You might think that a camera will stop an elephant charge. The elephant won't!

Sometimes you will come across animals that you can't 'hunt' by driving round in a vehicle. This is a much more difficult form of wildlife photography requiring a large amount of concealment and patience.

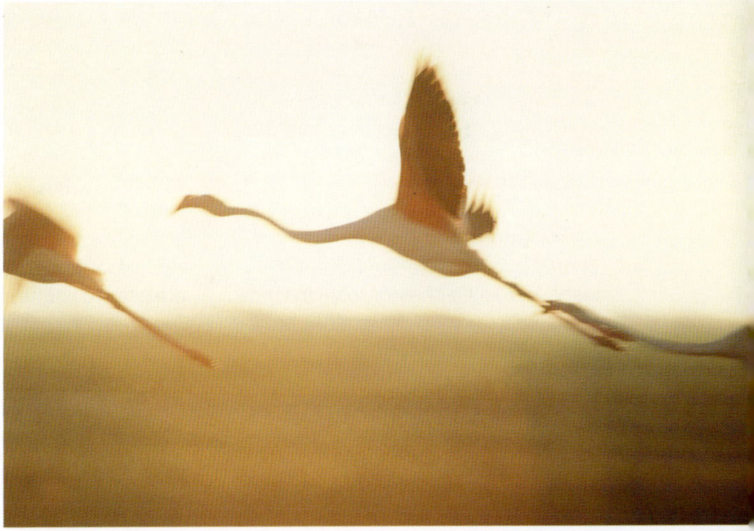

# Professional techniques

**There are a number of photographic techniques that are regularly used by professional photographers – to correct things that aren't quite right, and to produce some creative effects. Bring them into your own photography, and reap the rewards.**

### Fill-in flash

There are always going to be times when the light just isn't quite right. Our eyes are good at adjusting between shadows and highlights, but the camera isn't. The problem is trying to balance two different light levels, which is when professionals use a technique called 'fill-in flash'.

Most people only use a flash once the light falls below the point that a hand-held exposure is possible. However, if you use flash when your subject is backlit, or standing in shadow, then you will get a much more evenly lit subject. Even the simplest camera should allow you to manually switch on the flash.

A more sophisticated camera-flash combination will give you much more control over the levels of fill-in, even allowing the use of a long cord to hold the flash away from the camera, but the basic technique is the same.

If the background is relatively dark, then select the slow-synch flash setting if your camera has one. This gives a longer exposure for the background and will make sure that the flash does not overpower it.

### Filters

Professional photographers use a wide range of filters in their photography. Often these are simply to correct color casts produced by a mismatch between the light source and the film. This is an area where digital photography excels; even the simplest cameras will automatically 'white-balance' to ensure that your images have a neutral color. However, there are a number of other filters that you might consider adding to your camera bag.

Not every digital camera can take separate filters, but if yours does then a polarizing filter is always useful. Used carefully it can cut haze from skies – especially near mountains. It can also reduce reflections on water or glass. A more pronounced effect of a polarizing filter is to darken and enhance blue skies. Another filter that has an effect on skies is a graduated filter. As the name suggests, these start dark (either with a color or a neutral mask which will darken an image without changing the colour) and blend through to clear. They can be used to

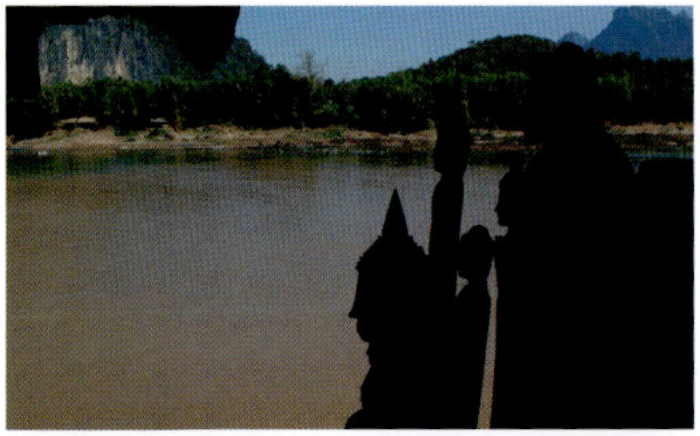

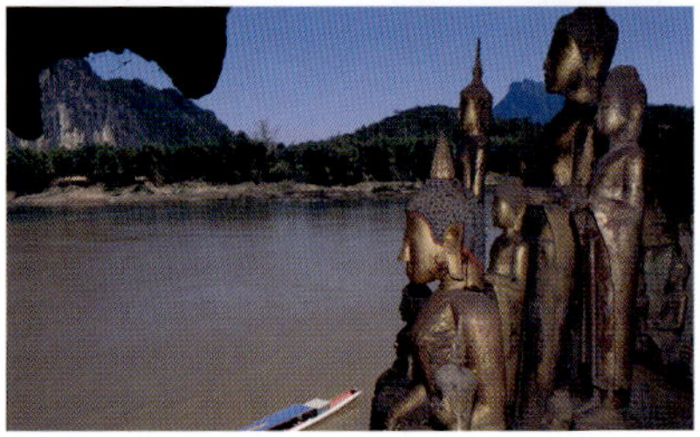

**(Top) A straight shot without flash, which produces a silhouette. You could meter for the statues, but the result would be to overexpose the entire background.**

**(Above) The result of adding some 'fill-in' flash: a balanced exposure that would be otherwise impossible.**

**keep in mind**

Digital cameras can often be too sensitive to allow blurring in bright light, as they have fairly fast relative film speeds. Counter this by using one or more neutral density filters. These block off two or even three stops of light without affecting the colour balance. Choose the smallest aperture possible (or choose 'landscape' mode) and the camera will use the slowest speed that the conditions allow.

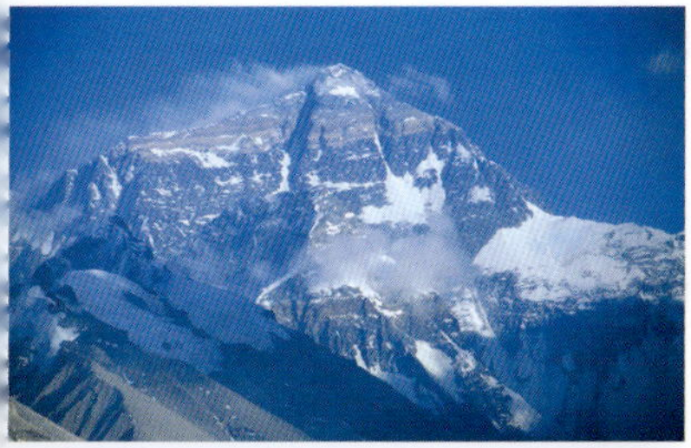

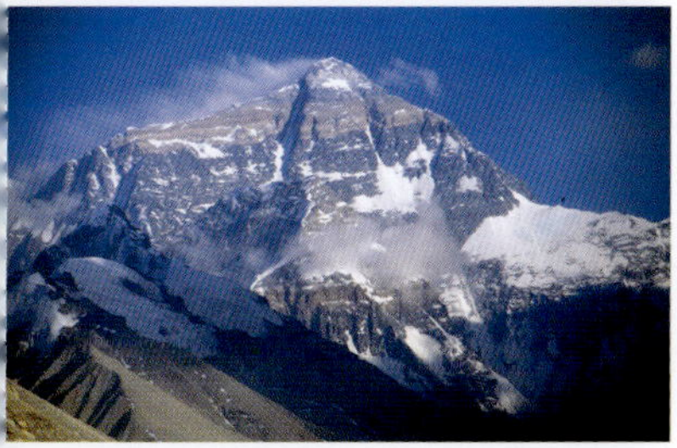

**A polarising filter is essential when shooting in bright weather for saturated blue skies. Compare the shot with (above) and without (top).**

add colour or just selectively darken a sky. Of course both of these effects can be done on the computer later - see page 78 for a description of the techniques involved.

### Blurring

You can often add atmosphere to a photograph by introducing blur. By selecting a slow shutter speed, you can allow the subject to move during the exposure. Simple blur - where the camera is kept still and the subject moves - can easily be recreated later on a computer, but many professionals use a technique called panning.

### Panning

Panning is where the camera is moved along with the subject and produces a much more dynamic image - which would be very difficult too recreate on a computer. The background will be blurred but part of the subject will be sharp, as it won't have moved precisely in line with the camera. If you combine panning with using a wide-angle lens, the effect is completely different as distortion is introduced to the image as well.

To pan an image, select the slowest speed that you can, typically around a second or longer. As your subject passes you move the camera at the same speed and squeeze off the shutter. Keep the movement going before and after the exposure and the effect will be smoother. This is not a precise skill so be prepared to take a number of shots and experiment until you get an effect you are happy with.

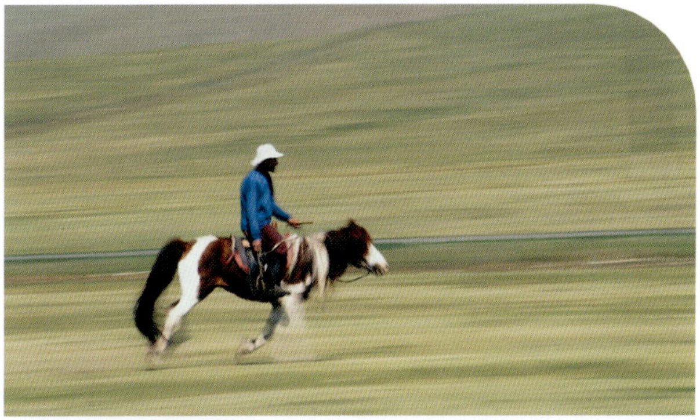

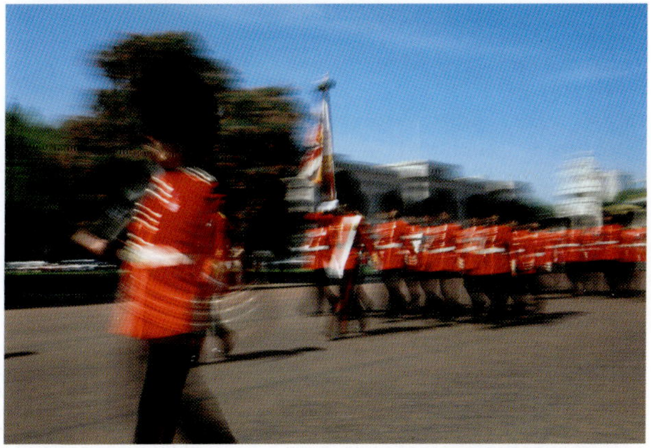

**(Top) Panning gives a real sense of action.**

**(Above) Blurring: using a slow shutter speed.**


**navigator**

Zoom blur p90
Graduated filter p78
Using levels p64

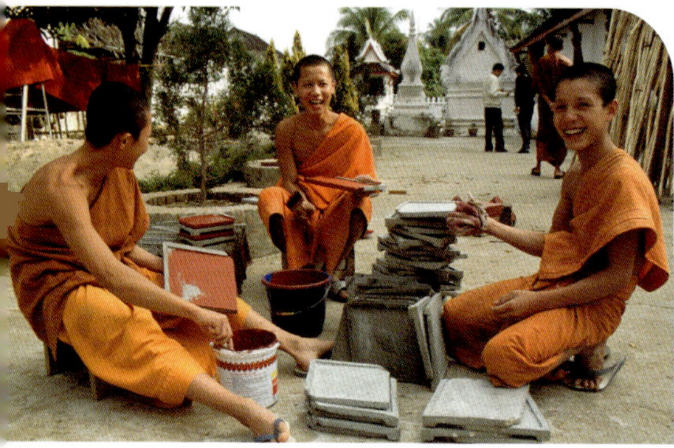

# Shooting tips: people

**People give a place its identity, they are its heritage and its future and they are the most fascinating of photographic subjects. From candid snaps to posed portraits, here are a few tips.**

In the early days of photography, Western explorers used photography to record the indigenous people and cultures that they saw on their expeditions. Often the people in the pictures look uncomfortable and unhappy with being photographed. As more of us travel to remote, and often less affluent, parts of the world, the issue of how to ensure that we return with good-quality photographs without, in the process, offending people from far-away places, is a sensitive one.

Semi-organized events are often a good way to see local culture without being too intrusive. Local entrepreneurs often make arrangements with local villages to allow visitors and even put on a show.

Some people are against paying locals for pictures as they say it corrupts, but small amounts of money, responsibly given, in return for a service (modelling) are a boost to the local economy, which is often cut out from the benefits of a boom in tourism. It is also an incentive to preserve and

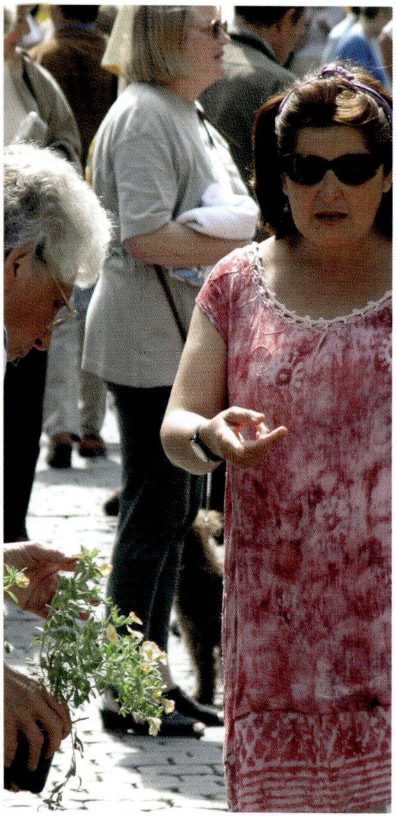

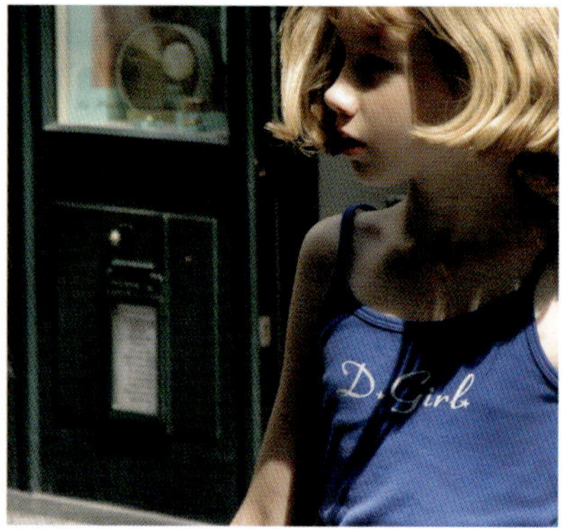


**Candid photographs need a long lens, a good eye and fast reactions. A digital camera with a tilting or swivelling LCD monitor allows you to face in a different direction to your lens, ensuring you stay incognito.**

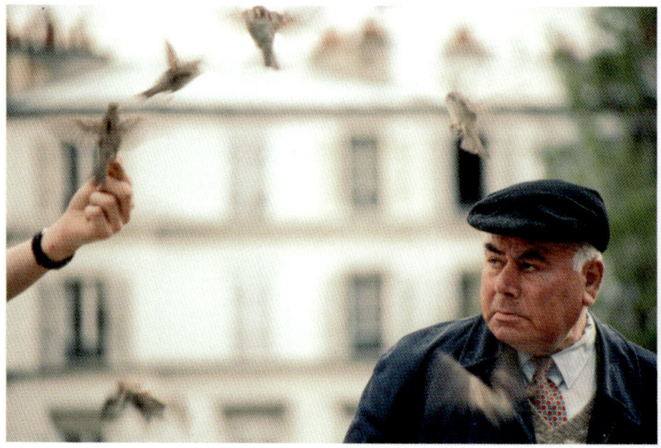

**keep in mind**
The beauty of candid photography is that you can shoot people who are acting totally naturally, in their own environment. Don't forget though, not everyone likes their picture being taken, so discretion is essential.

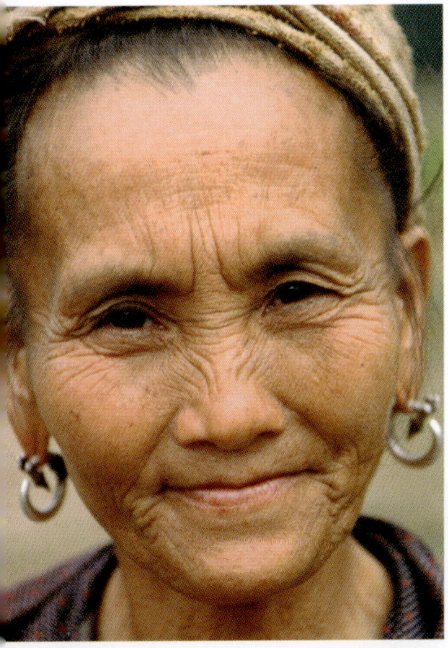

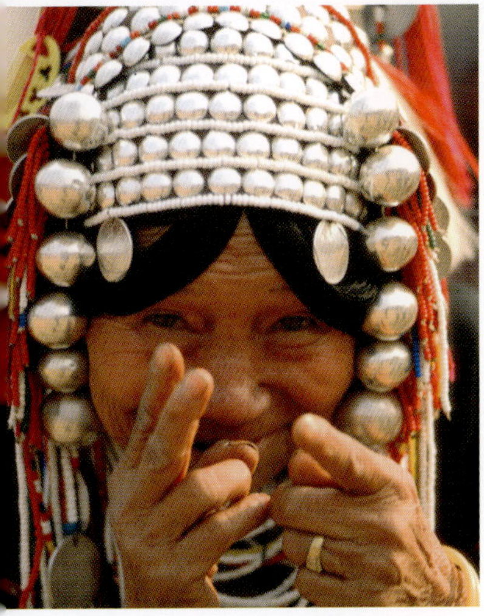

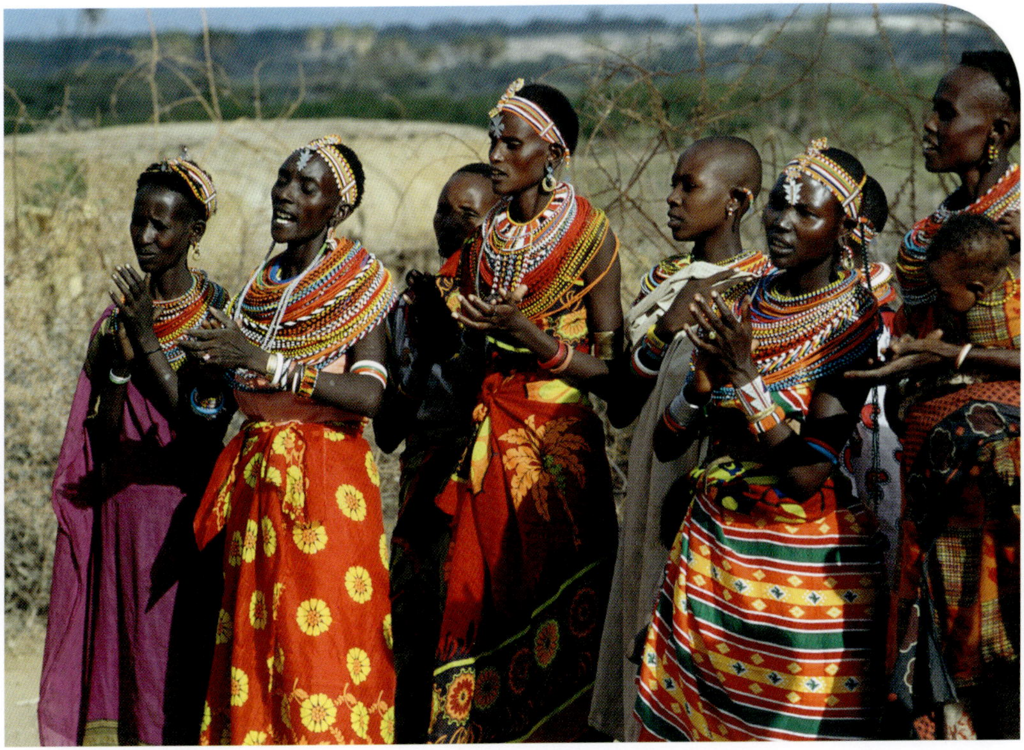

value local traditions that are under threat from the onslaught of Western culture. If we are prepared to pay for it, it must have value. At this Samburu village in Kenya, villagers were using donations from visitors to restock their herd of cattle, which was decimated by drought. The other advantage of taking pictures in these circumstances is that the people are actually choosing to be photographed, and are generally more familiar and happy with the process. Although the Akha woman in Northern Thailand (bottom left) is playfully counting the number of shots that I have taken to work out a 'bill', it makes for an engaging picture and shows her spirit, humour and power.

**navigator**
The right lens p36
The digital camera p18
Travelling with your camera p34

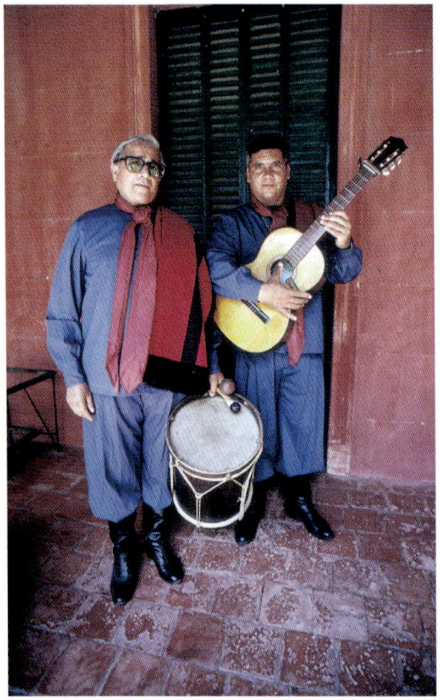

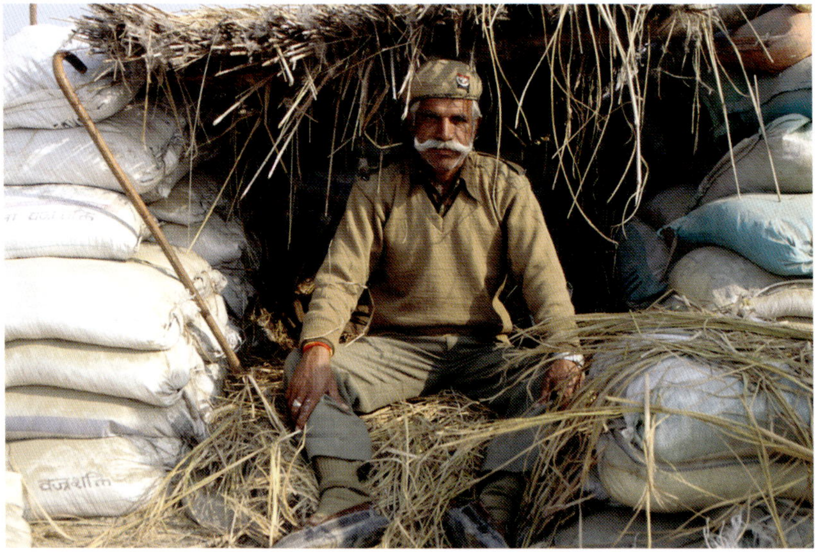

**Etiquette**

Outside of such organized encounters, if you see someone you want to photograph, whether it be a holy man in India or a newspaper seller in London, the basic courtesy is the same: ask their permission! This doesn't have to be an obviously posed question, it can be a non-verbal exchange. If you are holding a camera, catch someone's eye and smile at them; you can generally tell if they are happy for you to go ahead and take their picture or not.

If someone indicates that they don't want to be photographed, even if they only look uncomfortable or turn away – then you should respect this and move away immediately. You should also be sensitive to private events such as funerals or religious services. Just because people are 'poor' or 'culturally interesting' does not mean that they don't have the right to privacy.

**Getting natural portraits**

One of the problems of photographing people from non-Western countries is that they tend to pose very formally for portraits – standing up straight in the Victorian tradition.

To get round this you should try to spend a bit of time with people until they relax or try to photograph them when they are engaged in some familiar activity that draws attention away from them directly.

If someone just won't relax then crop in tight so that you just show their face, which will often look much more relaxed and expressive when isolated from a stiff, tense figure. Using a telephoto lens will allow you to get in close in the picture without having to intrude into their personal space.

Keep taking pictures. People's expressions change, even people who are posing formally will often visibly relax after the first picture has been taken and they think that you have finished. Work fast though, so that you aren't pointing the camera at your

**keep in mind**

The more pictures you take, the more likely you are to get a winning shot. You can always delete those you don't like later. Remember; you are not using film!

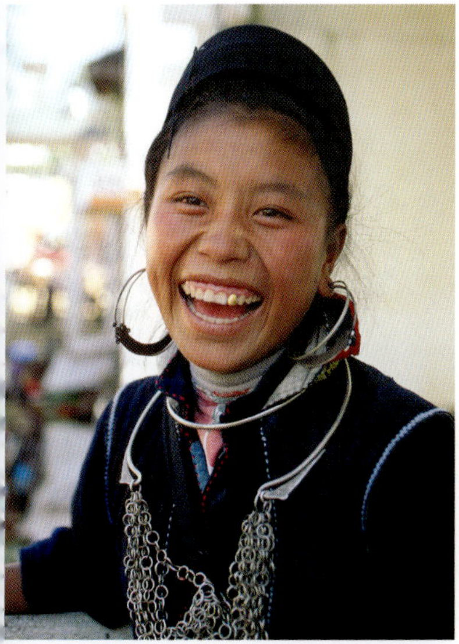

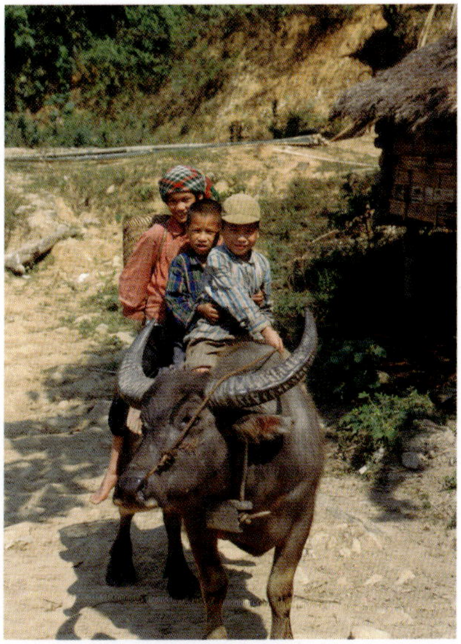

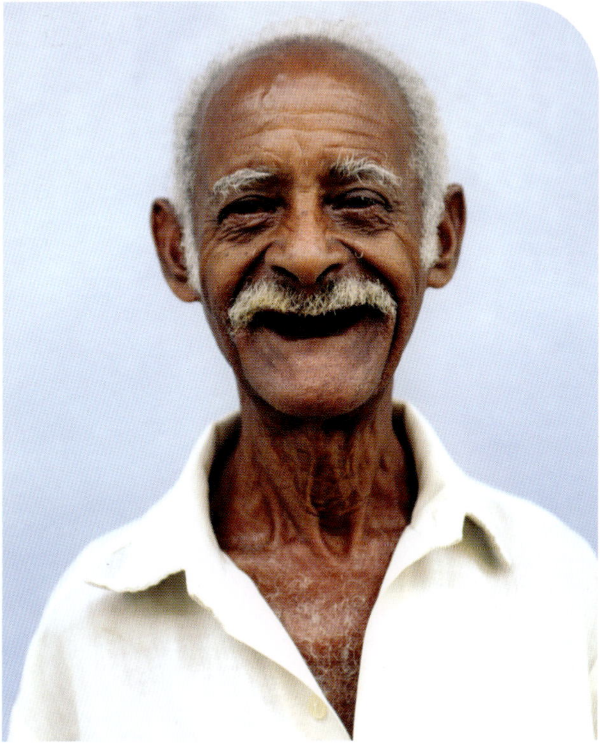

subject for a long time. Digital cameras with LCD screens can be ideal for this type of photography; not only will you be able to compose the picture without having the camera as a barrier between you and your subject, but you will be able to show them the picture afterwards - a great ice-breaker.

Children are always another good way of getting people to relax. Get the child to relate to you and the parent to react to the child and you will instantly have a natural-looking picture.

Often people will ask you for copies of pictures. You should never promise to do this unless you are actually going to go ahead and do it. Bearing in mind the cost of postage from overseas, if you are really serious about photographing people then a small portable printer connected to your digital camera will win you a whole lot of friends, although you might be expected to take more pictures than you bargained for.

**Avoiding offence**

There are cultures round the world that have taboos about being photographed, and others that have reservations about their children being photographed. You should do some research first. A good guidebook should point out such cultural issues. Don't necessarily rely on local guides for this information. Some of them can be exceptionally insensitive to other cultures in their own country. If you use your own judgment, not only will you come back with a number of pictures that you are proud of, you will also have some amazing encounters with local people.

**navigator**

| | |
|---|---|
| The right lens | p36 |
| The digital camera | p18 |
| Travelling with your camera | p34 |

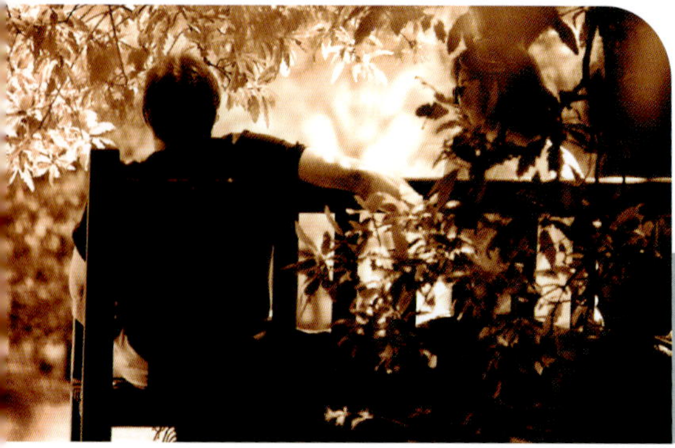

# Working digitally

Shooting digitally is subtly different to using film. The most important point is that you can take less than perfect shots safe in the knowledge that you can put things right later on the computer.

There are many times when there is something wrong with the view that you want to photograph. There might be a crane in the picture, or a parked car; an ugly poster or some litter. In the days before digital, photographers often would just give up and not take the scene as they knew that the only way to improve it was with very expensive ink-and-brush retouching that was beyond the reach of all but the most committed professional on a high-budget shoot.

These days, everyone has access to retouching software and you can plan shots with a view to correcting them later. Before the advent of digital manipulation I wouldn't have bothered photographing this London pub because there was a crane in the background but, removing it and a few other minor enhancements, such as concealing the white van, only took a few minutes.

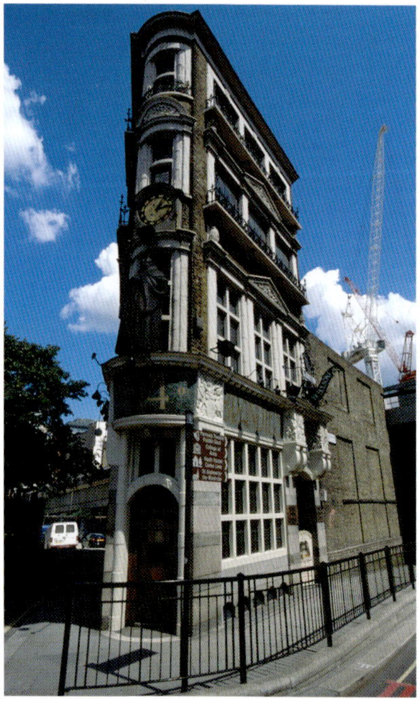

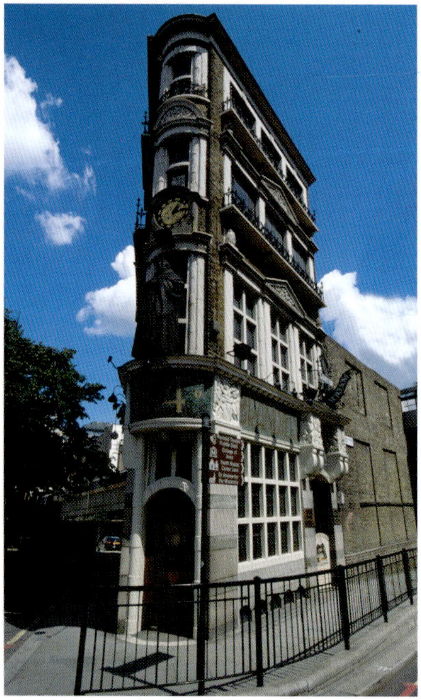

**This image of a pub in London shows clearly the advantage of shooting digitally. The original shot (left) has been subtly enhanced (right) to remove ugly distractions, such as the crane on the skyline and the white van centre-left.**

**keep in mind**
No matter how powerful your computer or how developed your image-manipulation skills, there is no substitute for good photography. The important point here is that it is always worth taking a shot, just in case it can be improved upon once you get home.

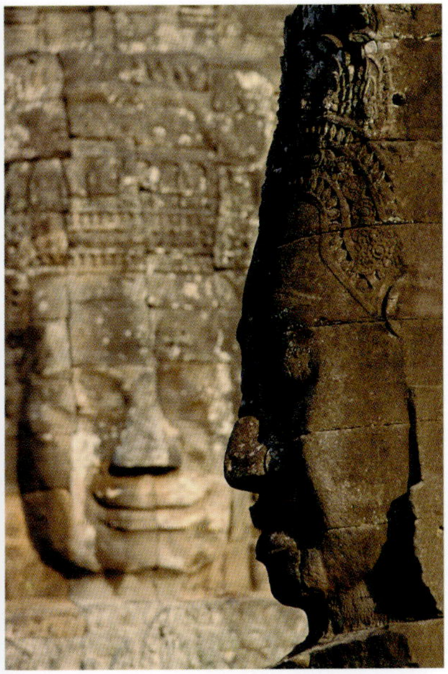

**This shot, taken in the harsh light of the midday sun, has been rescued with a little lightening of the shadow areas.**

### Other enhancements

You shouldn't just restrain your creative skills to removing unwanted clutter. There are myriad other enhancements that can be made to images. Some come in useful if you are on a vacation and cannot devote as much time to your photography as you would like. Most partners are not happy being woken up at five in the morning on their week in the sun so that you can 'catch the light', and few appreciate hanging around for hours waiting for the beach to clear.

When the sun is too high in the sky the light can be very harsh, with deep dark shadows obscuring much of the detail in a subject. If you have to take pictures during this time, you can at least do some corrective work on the computer later. The shadows can be lightened dramatically without losing the detail in the highlights. This gives the impression that the shot was taken at a much better time of day.

This same technique can be used if the contrast level is too high in your photograph, for instance if there is a bright white wall in the frame. Expose for the highlights and then use the computer to balance to shadows.

If the contrast range is too great, such as a building against a washed out sky, then you can take two shots of the same scene using different exposures. These can be combined on the computer later, so that both have enough detail. This technique works particularly well if you put the camera on a tripod and keep the frames identical, making the post-processing relatively painless.

A more extreme version of this technique is when you use a sky from a completely different photograph to boost a shot. This technique has to be used with care; if the foreground is flat and lifeless and you drop in a sunny sky, it will look wrong.

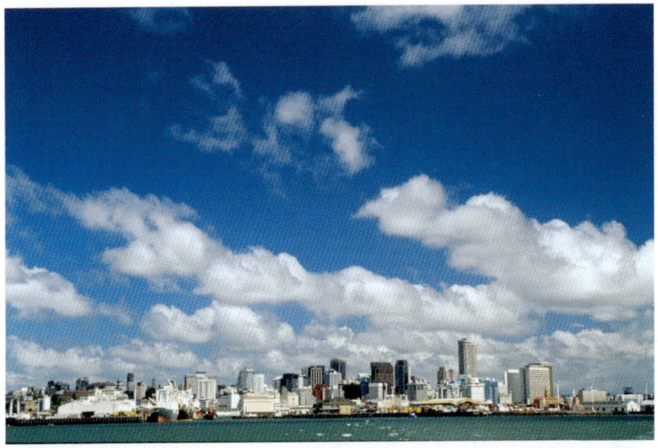

**Adding a new sky can transform an otherwise dull shot. You need to decide whether to go for a realistic effect, which is much more difficult, or a more stylized feel.**

If you do a lot of montages in this way, you should use your camera like an artist's notebook, photographing elements that you can use later. In this way you will soon construct a library of images for future computer manipulations.

**navigator**
Basic corrections p58
Removing elements p74
A new sky p80

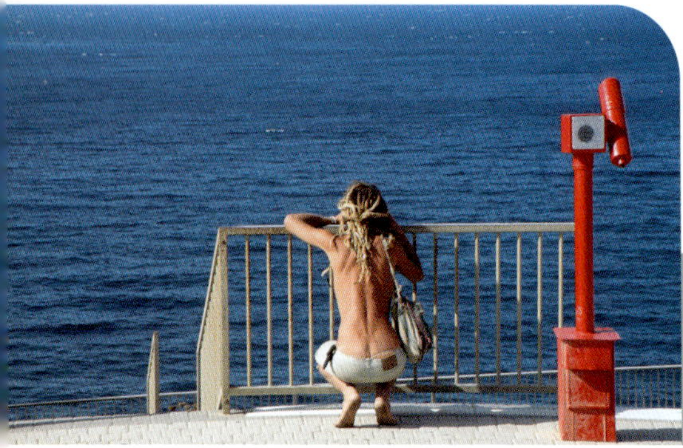

# Vacation photos

**Not all travel photography is about great expeditions. More often than not your picture-taking will be secondary to a relaxing vacation, but you could still bring home some stunning shots.**

The key difference between travel and vacation photography is summed up by the word 'vacation'. There is no point in coming back with some of the best pictures on earth if your partner is divorcing you, your kids have put themselves up for adoption, and you are twice as tired as when you left.

If you are supposed to be on holiday, then make the photography fit it, not the other way round. There is a lot you can do in an hour or so in the morning or afternoon, taking the rest of the day off.

### Off the beaten track

Even at some of the most developed holiday resorts there are small, tucked-away areas that have some degree of local culture – a historic 'old town', for instance. In most resorts you will find places where local people live, and you can often find images there that sum up people's lives. The shot of an old American car (above right) was taken in what must be the most developed holiday resort in Cuba, but still sums up the country perfectly.

There is also the day trip. Most package tour companies will try to sell you a day trip to a local beauty or cultural spot. This can be a good opportunity to sample a bit of local culture and also get some good photographs. The small town of Ronda is only a few miles from the busy Costa del Sol in southern Spain, but is about as traditional a town as you will ever find in Spain. It is easy to get a tour bus there and, as well as giving you the opportunity to take some pictures, it will you a real taste of the country.

Don't forget that the vacation itself can make an excellent photographic subject. Things like children's toys in the sand, beach parasols and shells can not only capture the atmosphere of your trip, but also produce iconic images. If you are lucky enough to go to somewhere beautiful, the beach itself can be a rich source of photographic inspiration. In many parts of the developing world, such as India and the Caribbean, people still fish from tourist beaches, although you will generally

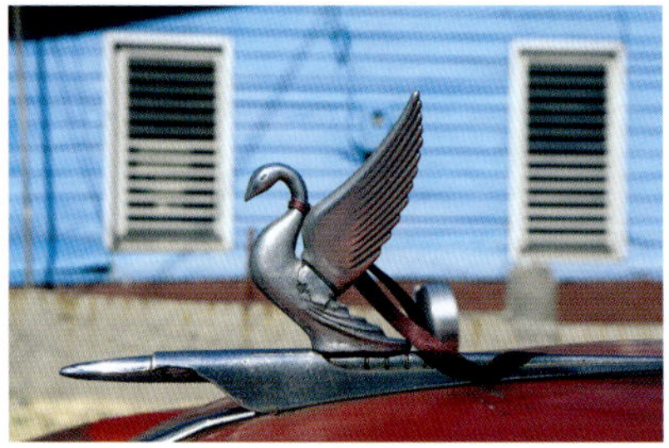

have to get up early to watch them landing their catches or sorting the fish.

Many holiday resorts will have organized displays, cabarets or dancing. These can sometimes be very tacky, but with a little care and a telephoto lens, they can give a true sense of the culture or heritage of a place.

**keep in mind**
Even the most unpromising vacation destinations will offer a wealth of photographic opportunities. Look for local life, unusual flora and fauna and, most importantly, arise at least once before the crowds arrive for a unique view of tourist areas.

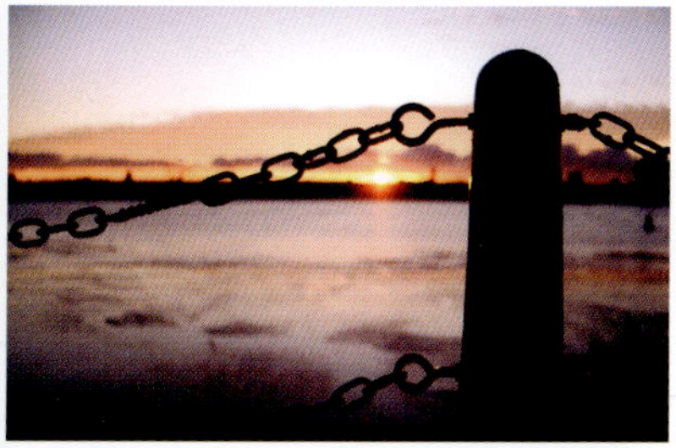

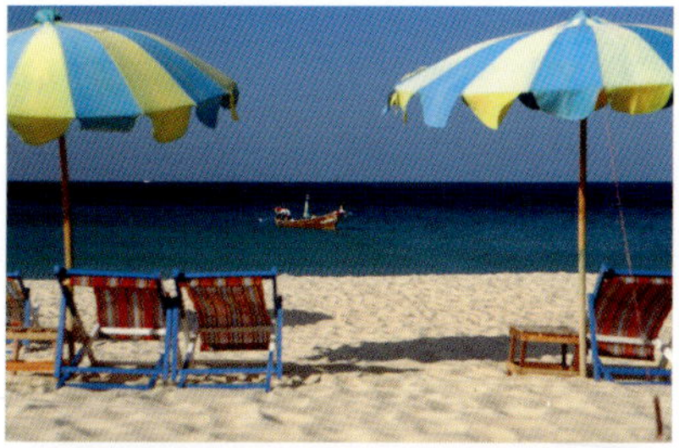

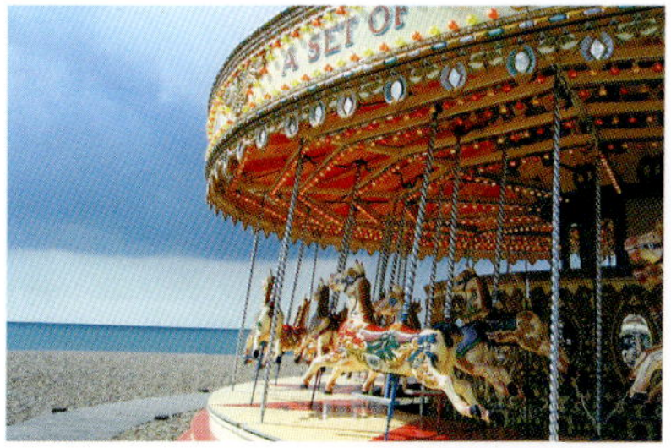

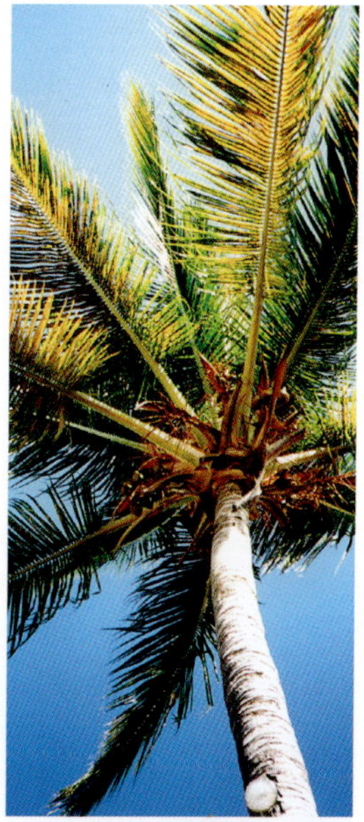

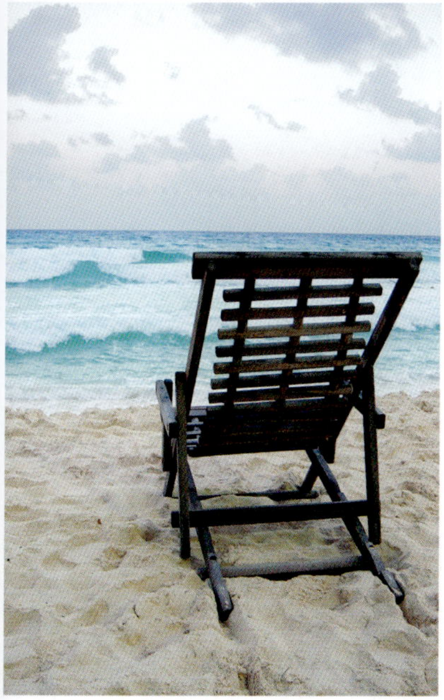

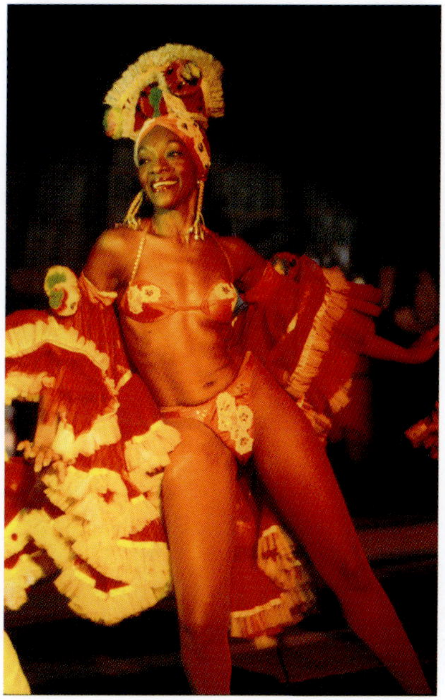

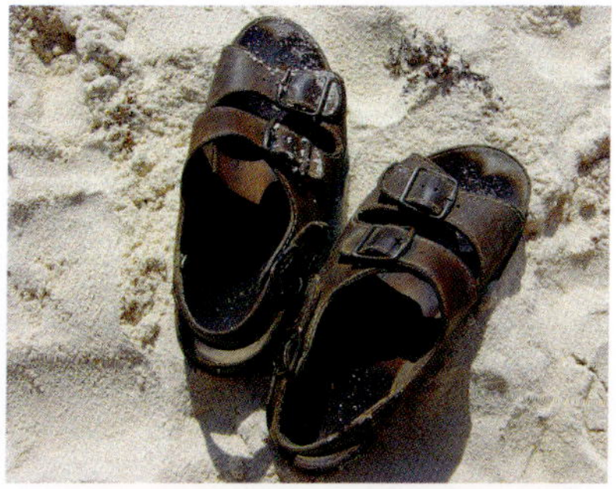

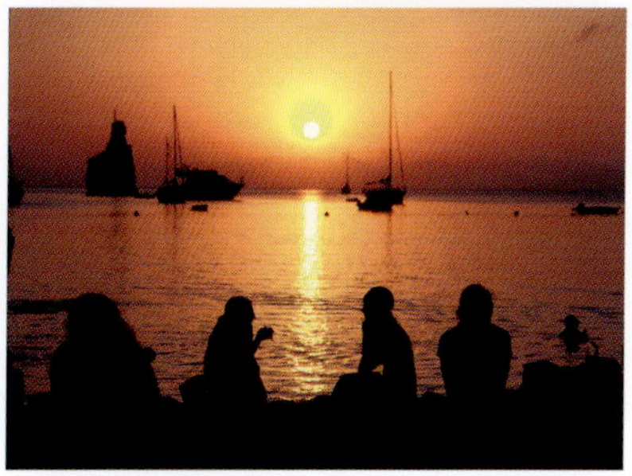

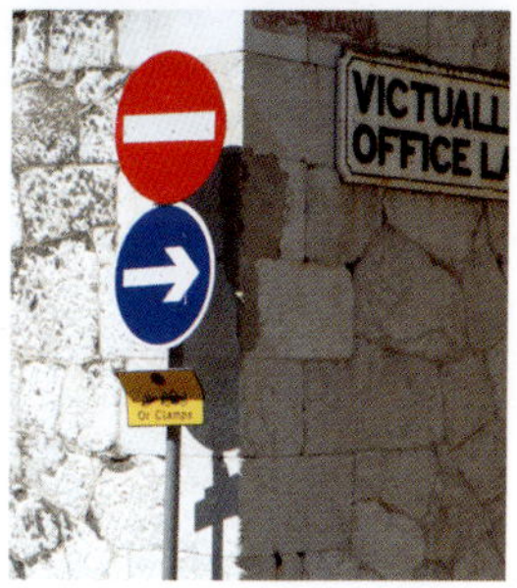

**Follow a few simple rules and your vacation photos can easily be a lot more than sunburnt family members enjoying a piña colada. Local festivals, sunsets and sunrises, even an empty beach chair, can all offer rich photographic opportunities. Beaches photograph best at dawn or dusk (when they are also usually empty), so make at least one early morning visit with your camera.**

**navigator**
Playing with color p92
Removing elements p74
Cropping & rotating p62

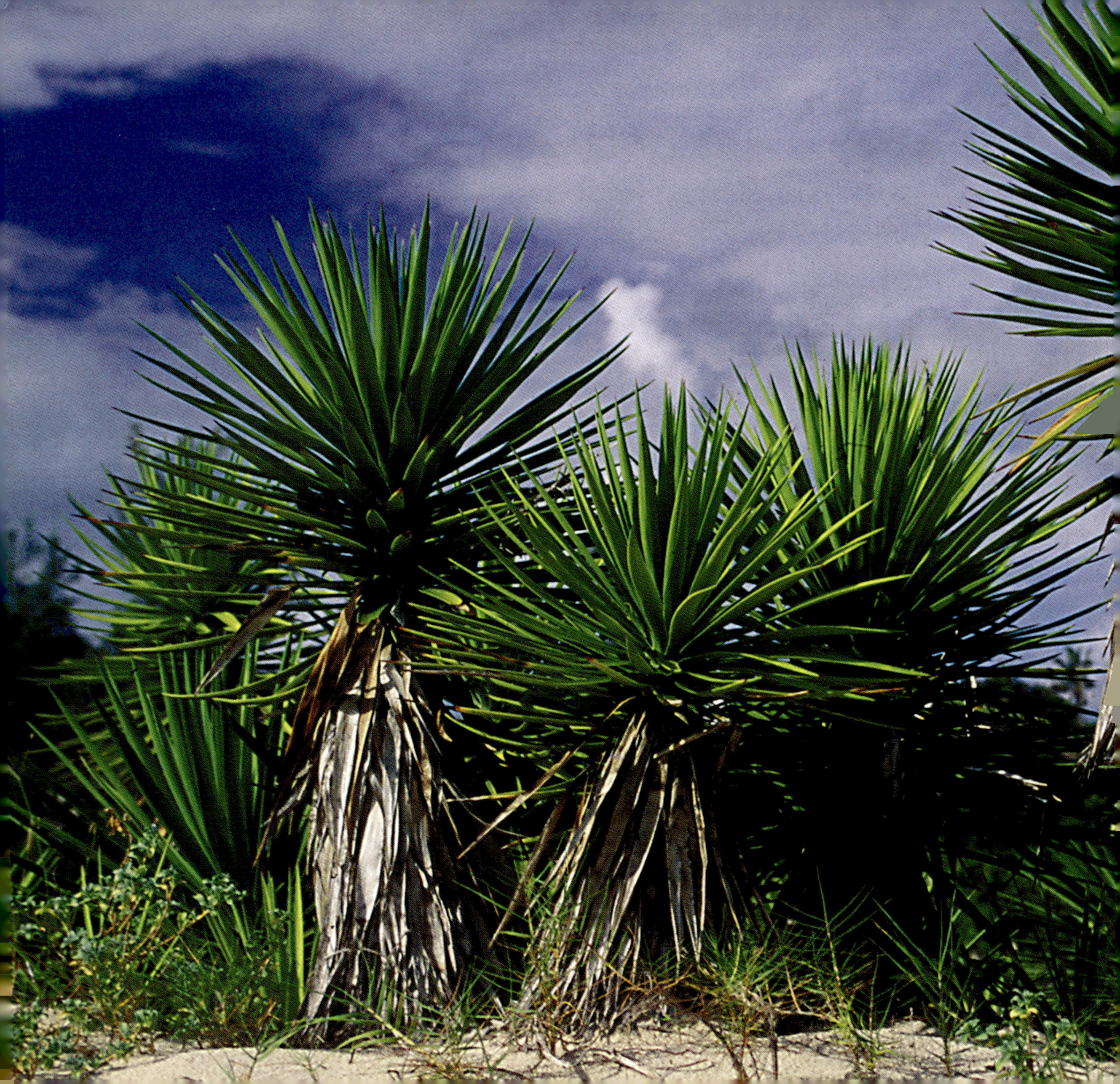

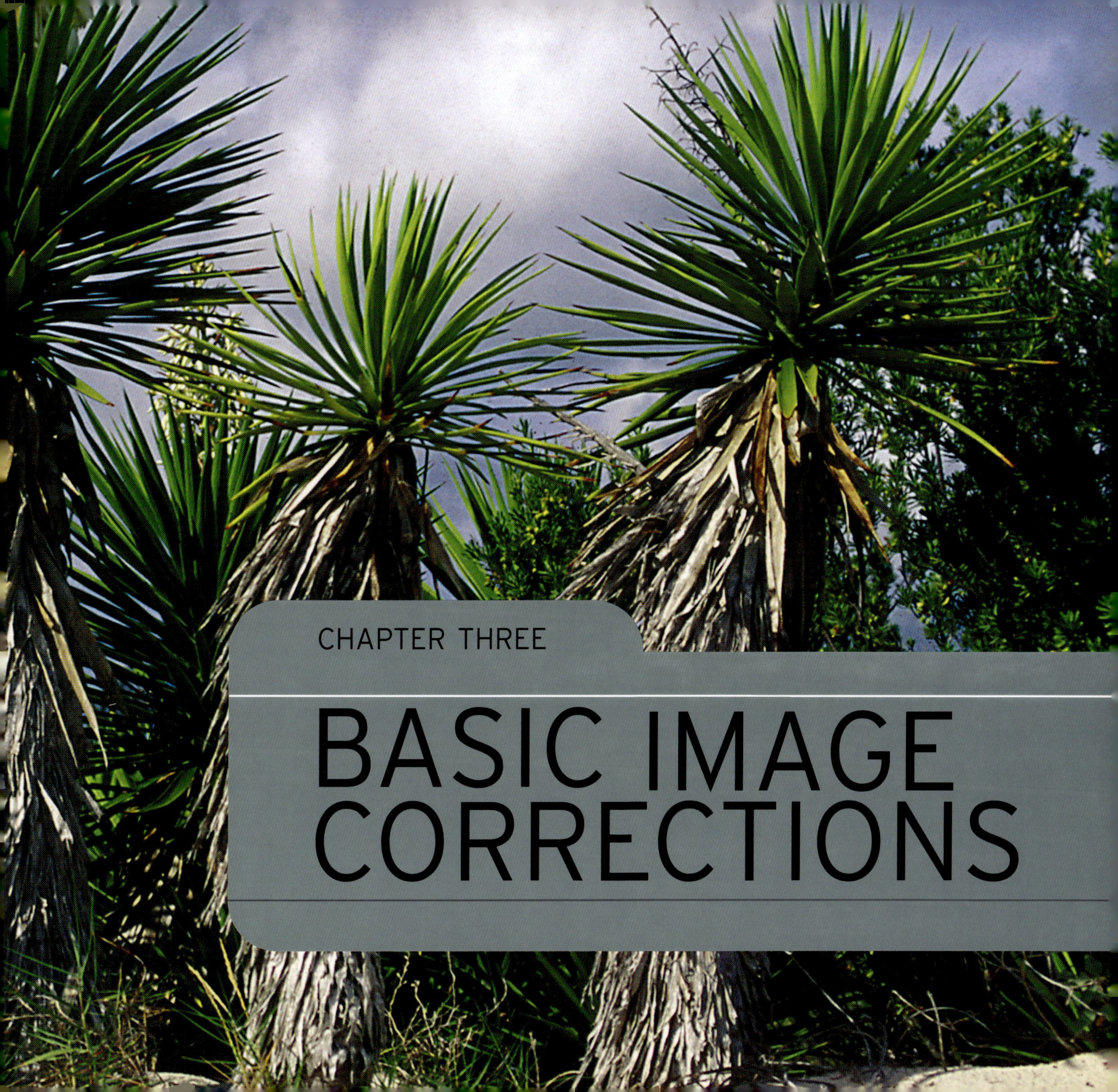

CHAPTER THREE

# BASIC IMAGE CORRECTIONS

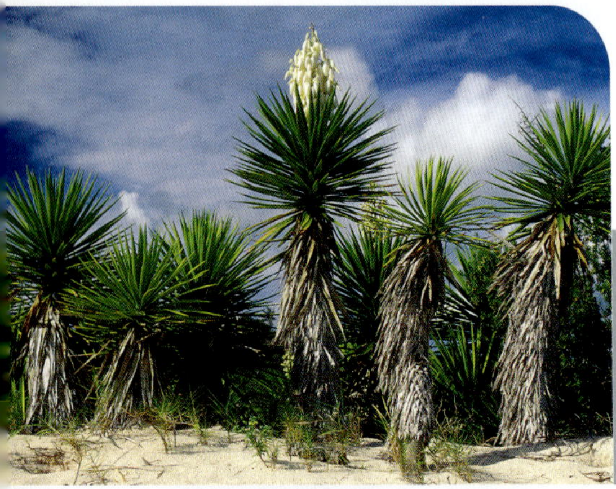

# Basic corrections

Most digital images need some basic corrections, from simple adjustments to brightness and contrast , color balance, sharpening, and the removal of dirt and scratches on scans. The next few pages show you how these are executed.

input

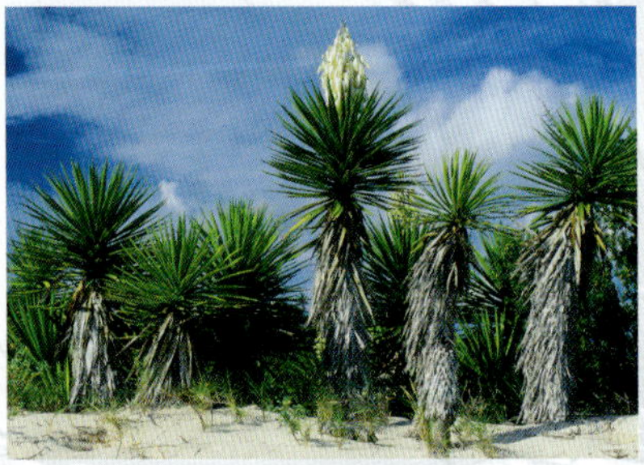

**01** The basic principles apply equally to scans and digital camera shots, with the exception of the dust- and scratch-removal, which is only necessary when scanning your prints or slides. We'll start with a raw scan straight out of a typical flatbed film scanner with a transparency adaptor.

process

**02** After cropping (if necessary), the first job is to correct the exposure and contrast. If the color looks right but the exposure or brightness look wrong, choose Image > Adjust> Auto Contrast. If there is also a color cast, try Image>Adjust>Auto levels.

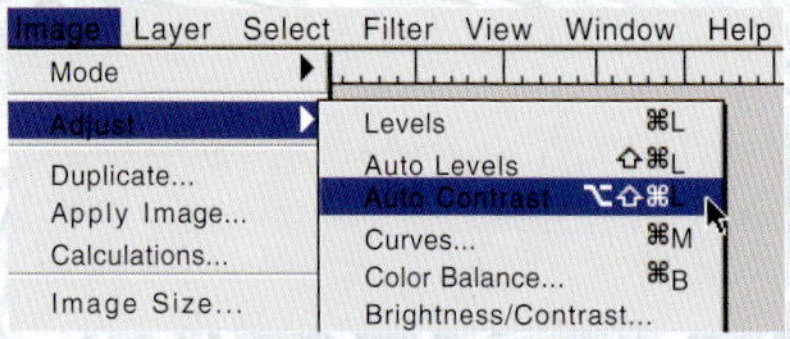


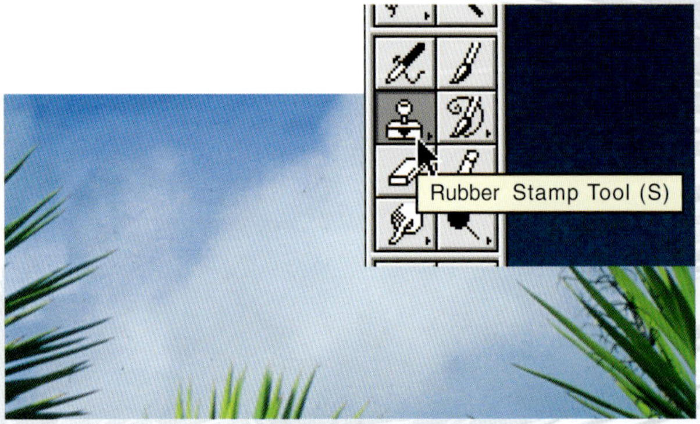


**03** Dirt is a common problem with film scanners, but can easily occur with flatbeds too. Take a look at this enlarged section from our original scan. The whole frame is covered in dust spots and scratches. Many applications offer automatic dust and scratch removal, but this will also remove fine details from the image. The tool we're going to use to 'rub out' the spots and scratches is the Rubber Stamp (a.k.a. the Clone tool).

**technical details**
Canon A1
28-70mm Canon llens
Kodachrome 64
Adobe Potoahop 6.0

**tools**
Scanning
Cloning

**keep in mind**
You can save yourself hours of retouching work by simply ensuring your originals are kept absolutely dust- and scratch-free, and by cleaning your flatbed scanner's glass plate with computer screen cleaner.

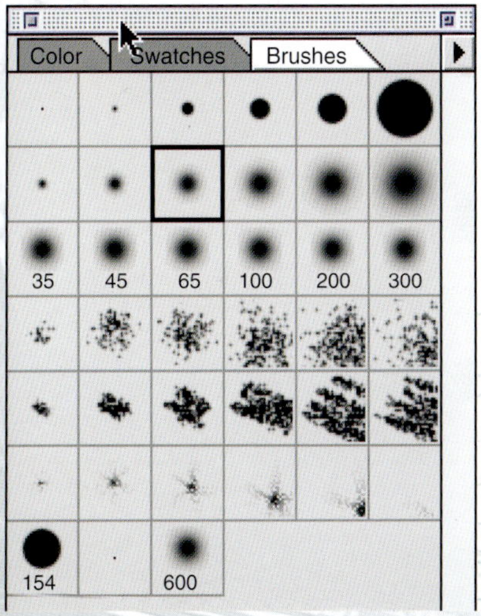


**04** The Rubber Stamp acts in the same way as the Paintbrush. You can change the shape and size of the brush itself by selecting any one of the presets in the Brushes palette. You can also change the opacity of the brush from 1–100% (via the Tool Options palette, double click on the Rubber Stamp icon in the toolbar). For this purpose, leave it set to 100%.

To define the source point (that's the pixels you are cloning from), alt-click. To paint with the source pixels, simply click and move the mouse like any other paint tool (without holding down the alt key).

### Cloning tips

- Use a soft-edged brush for a more seamless clone.
- Do not place your source and target points too close – you will end up with a 'zebra-stripe' effect by repeatedly cloning the same small group of pixels.
- Make sure the area you clone from has a tone and texture that matches the target area.

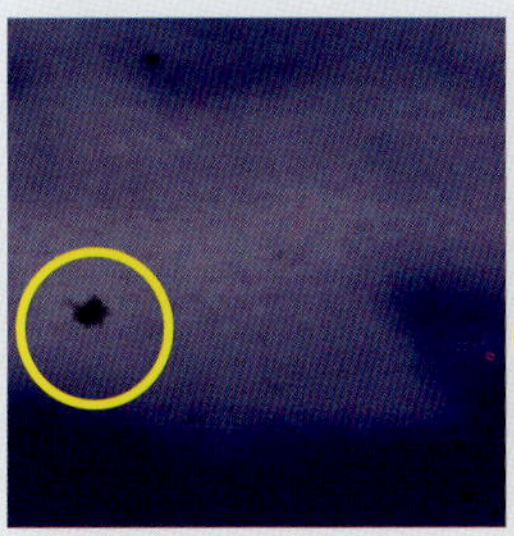

**In the above example, we need to remove the circled dust spot.**

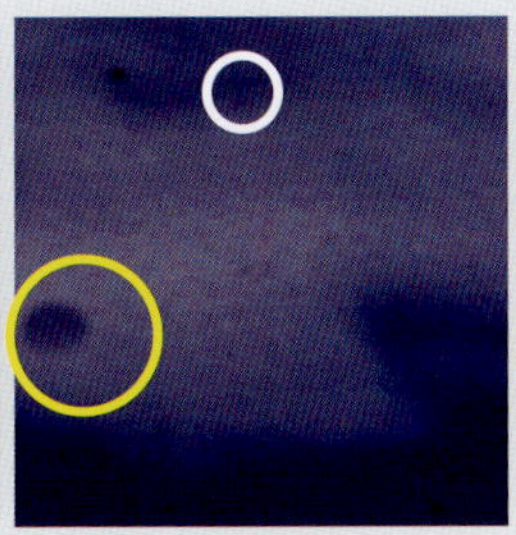

**Using a darker sample point results, unsurprisingly, in a dark blob.**

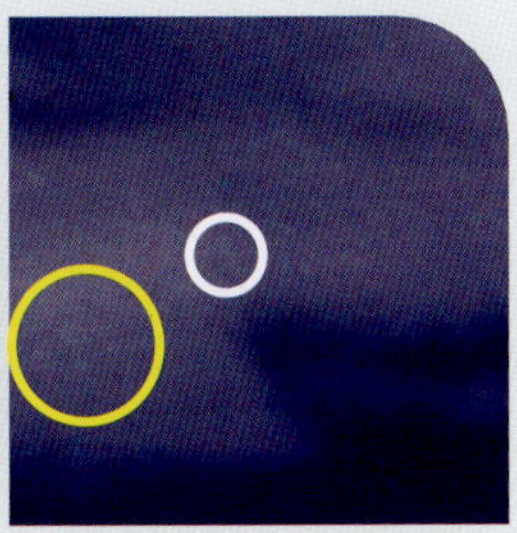

**Choose a point to clone from that is in an area of similar tone for a seamless result.**

### Dust and scratches filter

Photoshop offers an 'automatic' dust-removal filter (Filter>Noise>Dust and Scratches). The trouble is that when it is used at a high-enough setting it also obliterates all the fine detail in the picture too. As ever, there is a way around this problem, and it provides a fast way to remove large amounts of dirt in your scans.

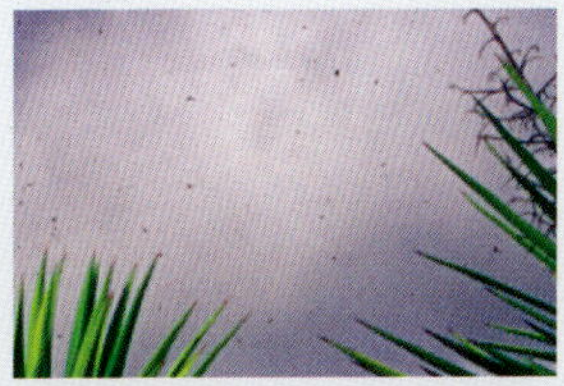

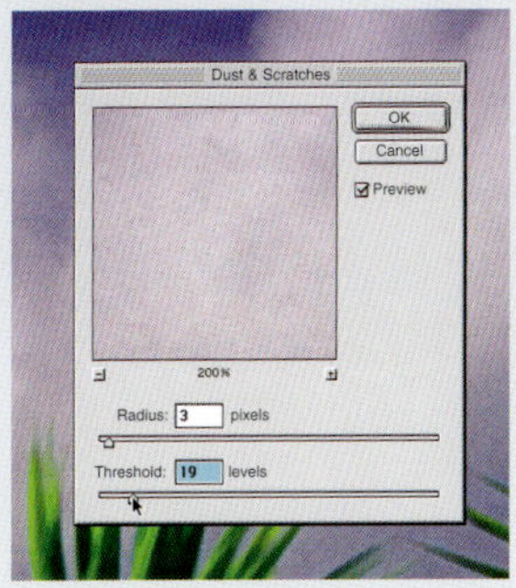


First make a duplicate of your image in a new layer. Select the lower (original) layer and run the Dust and Scratches filter. Move the Radius slider to the right until all but the largest dust spots have disappeared from the preview. Now move the Threshold slider to the right until they just reappear again. Finally, reduce the threshold until the spots just disappear.

Working on the upper (duplicate layer) use the eraser (and a soft-edged brush) to remove the spots one at a time. As you erase parts of the upper (dirty) layer, the lower (filtered) layer shows through. This way, the Dust and Scratches filter won't remove any vital image detail.

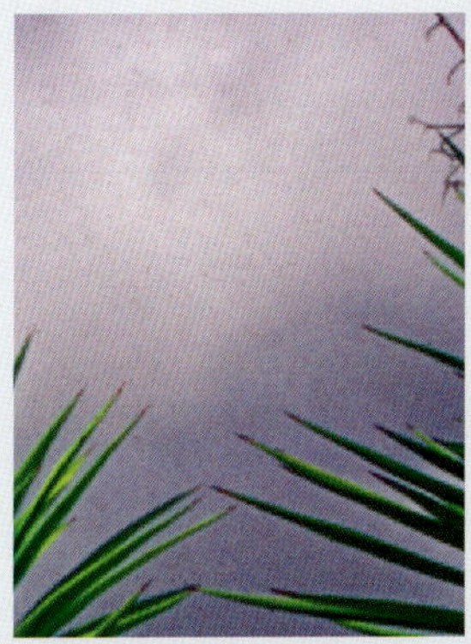

**05** The final step in the clean-up process is to sharpen the image. Most scanners and virtually all digital cameras produce images that benefit from a little software sharpening. Although most applications offer a simple 'Sharpen' command, it pays to get into the habit of using 'Unsharp Masking'. Unsharp Masking (USM) allows you a high degree of control over how the image is sharpened with visual feedback in the form of a preview screen.

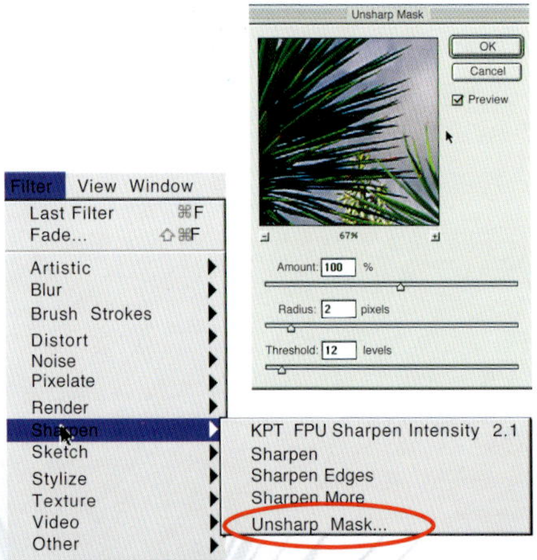


### What is unsharp masking?

Despite the rather confusing name, USM is a process that makes pictures look sharper. It does this by locating pixels that differ from surrounding pixels by a user-defined amount (the 'Threshold') and increasing their contrast by the 'Amount' you specify. The 'Radius' figure specifies how many surrounding pixels each pixel is compared with. This increases the contrast of edges, enhancing the appearance of sharpness.

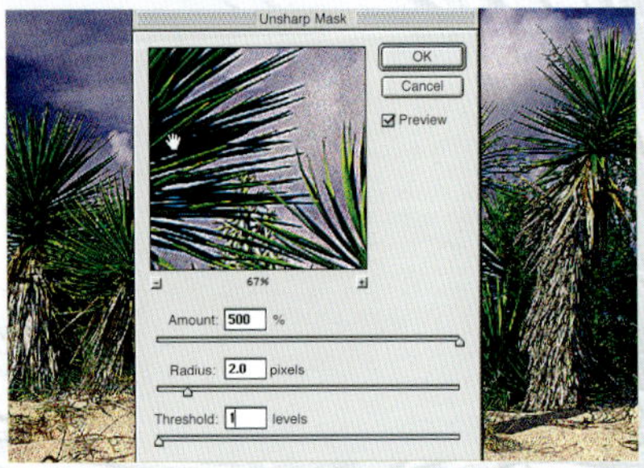


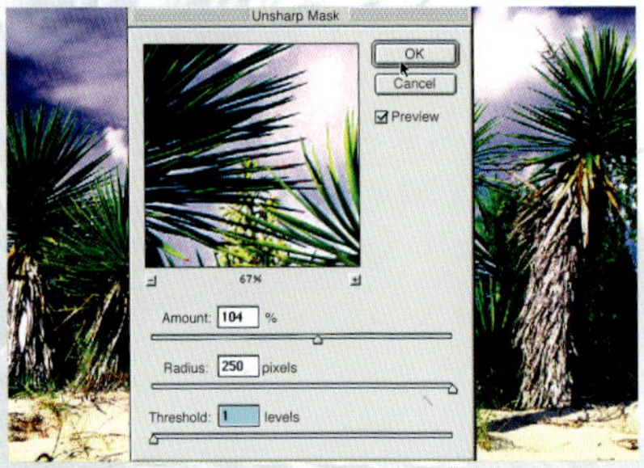


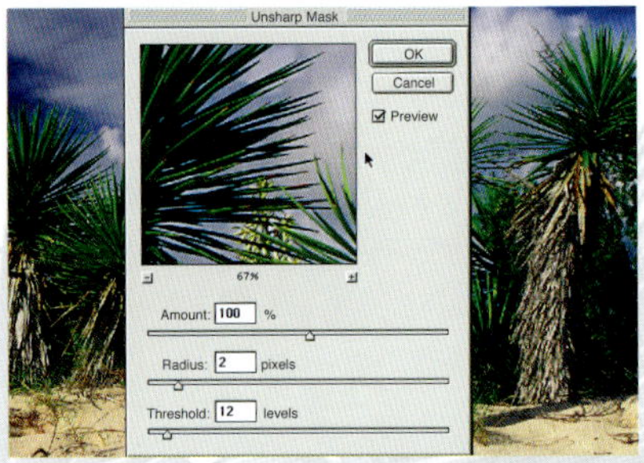


**06** The figures you enter into the USM dialog will depend on the resolution of the image, the quality of the picture and what you intend to use it for. Experiment with the settings to get a feel for what effect they have on the image. The Amount figure simply changes the strength of the sharpening. You will rarely want to go above 120%.

**07** The Threshold figure defines how different two areas need to be before being considered by the filter to constitute an 'edge'. The effect is to protect areas of continuous color from the sharpening. 'Radius' defines how far from each pixel the filter looks for an edge. Increasing the figure beyond about 50 results in 'contrasty' images, and it is usually left under ten.

**08** Scanners or digital cameras almost always needs the same degree of sharpening, and this is at least a starting point. The figures shown in the box above - Amount 100%, Radius 2 pixels and Threshold 12 - are the settings I use for my 35mm scanner. My digital SLR (with its own sharpening off) needs the Amount increasing to 200%.

**Photoshop keyboard shortcuts**

| | |
|---|---|
| Zoom | spacebar and control/⌘ |
| Rubber stamp | S |
| Change brush size | [(smaller)] (larger) |
| Color balance | Control-B/⌘-B |

**keep in mind**

Software sharpening always produces results that look much more marked on screen than they will when printed. Remember too that over-sharpened images look worse than soft ones.

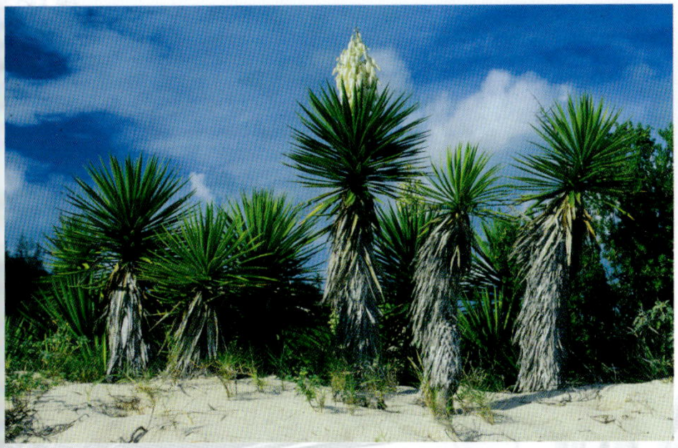

These basic steps – scan (or shoot digitally), crop, correct exposure, remove imperfections (from scans), sharpen and save – represent the 'bare essentials' of the digital process. It is a rare photograph that would not benefit from at least two of the stages. The difference even a few minutes work can make to the final print is remarkable.

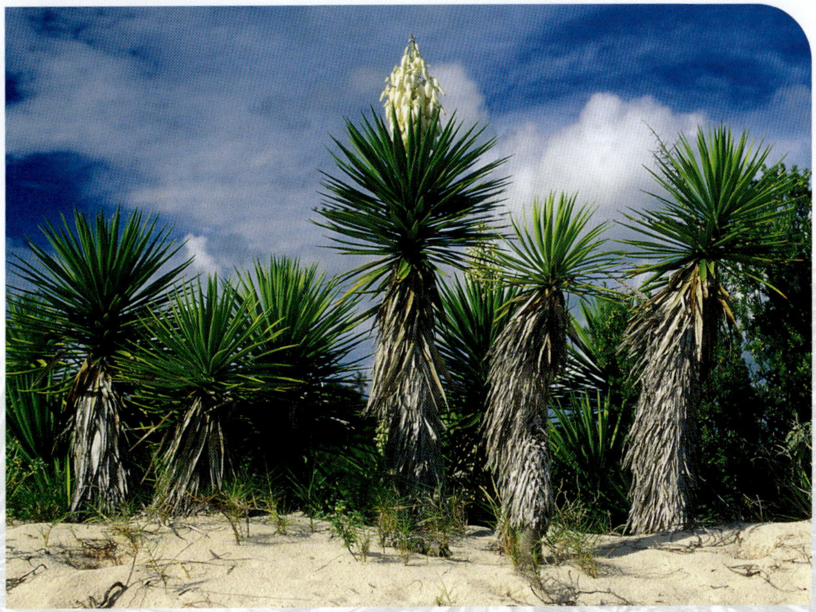

**Correcting digital camera images**

- Digital camera images are often flat and dull-looking, but lurking inside the most unpromising shot is often a much more colourful, vivid photograph.
- Use Levels or Auto Levels to correct the brightness and contrast and you'll see a massive improvement.
- Take care when using Unsharp Masking on JPEG images; too much and you'll exaggerate the artefacts and fringes created in the compression process. This is the strongest argument for using the best-quality setting on your digicam, or even opting for the uncompressed option, if available.
- Photoshop allows you to create and save a series of corrections that can be run on a single image or a whole batch of files. These 'Actions' are useful if your camera consistently produces results that need the same corrections.
- Digital camera files are inevitably created at 72dpi (screen resolution). Remember to resize to a higher resolution before printing (see page 27).

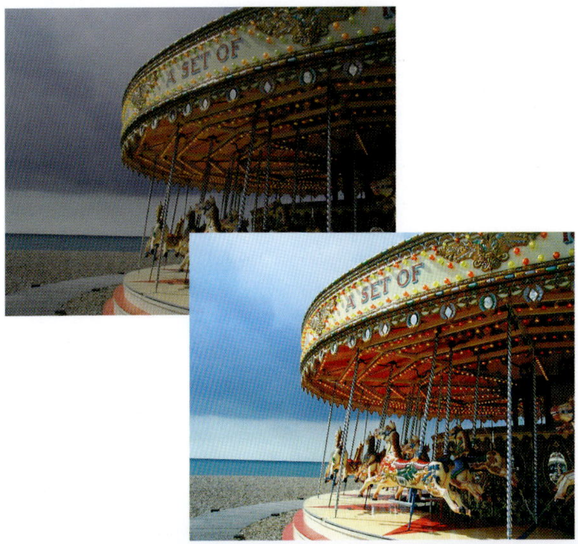

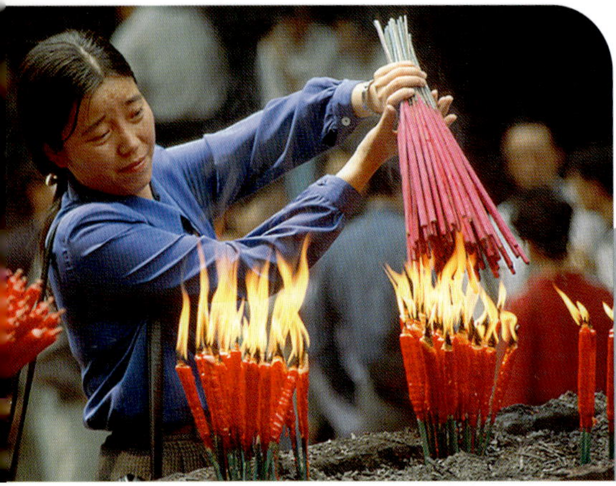

# Cropping and rotating

It may be one of the simplest edits you can perform on an image, but a little judicious reframing can add a new dynamic to a landscape or concentrate attention on the main subject. It can also fix those drunken horizons.

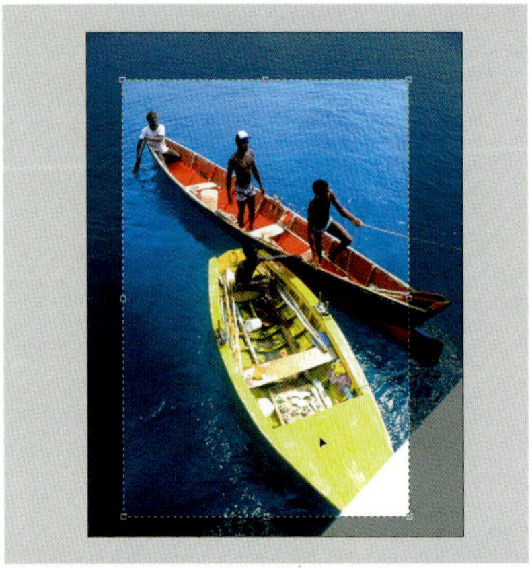

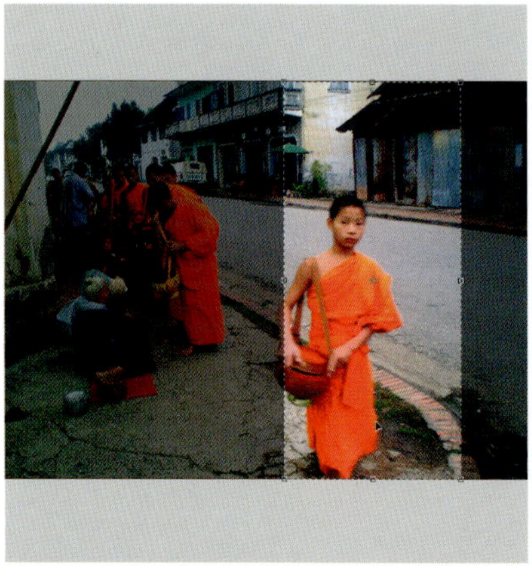

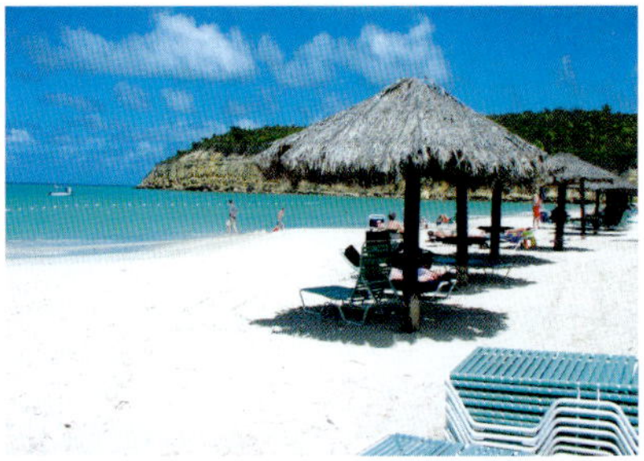

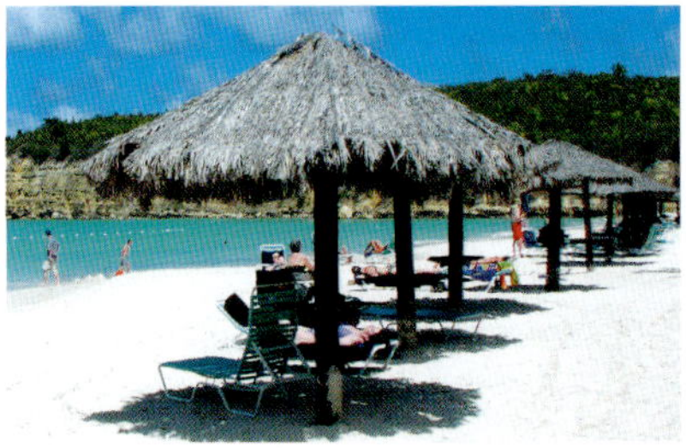

**01** There really is nothing more to cropping an image than clicking with the crop tool and dragging out a rectangle to define the new frame. Applications such as Adobe Photoshop 7.0, make the process even easier by greying out areas outside the new crop.

**02** Although most cropping is to create a more panoramic frame or simply to 'tighten' the composition (whilst preserving original proportions), feel free to experiment. Remember that a vertical panoramic frame can look as dramatic as a horizontal one.

**03** Cropping is effective with even the most unpromising image!

**Photoshop keyboard shortcuts**

| | |
|---|---|
| Crop tool | C |
| Perform crop (after selecting frame) | Double-click or Enter |
| Marquee | M |
| Free transform | Control- T/⌘-T |

**keep in mind**

Unless you are using a telephoto lens for a particular reason (for example to compress perspective), it makes sense to include a little more in a scene when shooting than a little less. This gives you greater compositional freedom at the processing stage.

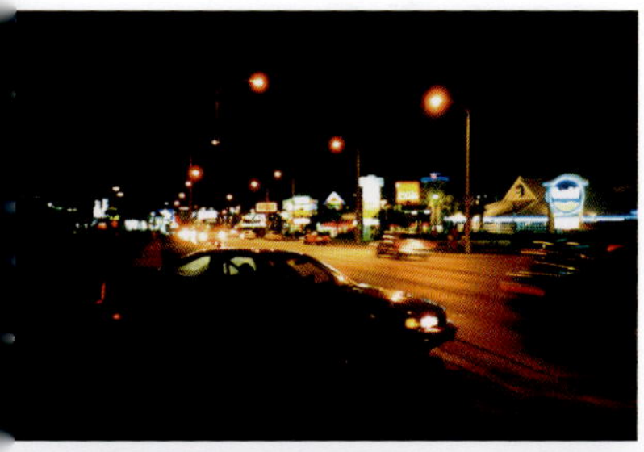

04 One of the most effective uses of cropping is to create a panoramic frame. The beauty of digital photography is that you can plan for this kind of editing when you shoot, creating stunning panoramas without carrying any special equipment. Other times the cropping to panoramic format only occurs after the picture has been taken and scanned.

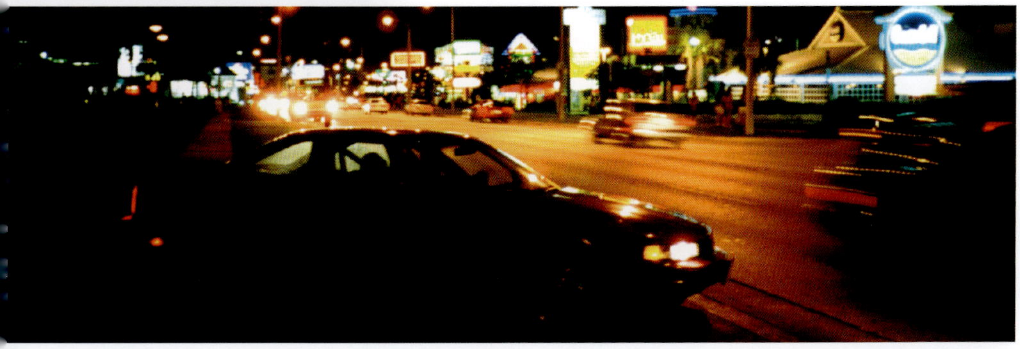

### Straighten up

Whether due to a wonky scan or poor composition, a slightly skewed horizon is a real distraction from what could otherwise be a winning shot. Here's how to correct it.

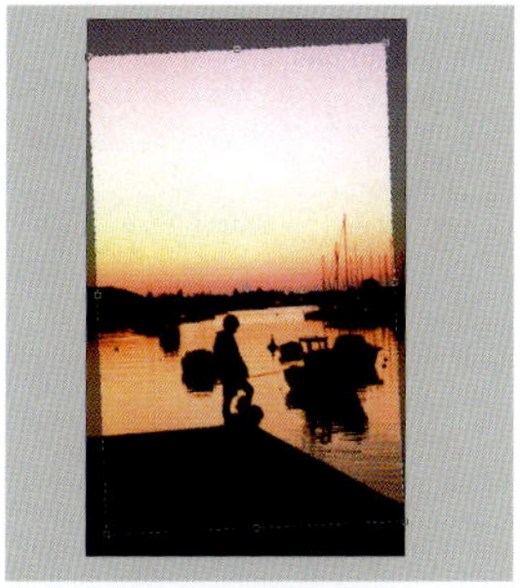

**The cropping tool usually allows you to rotate the frame at the same time.**

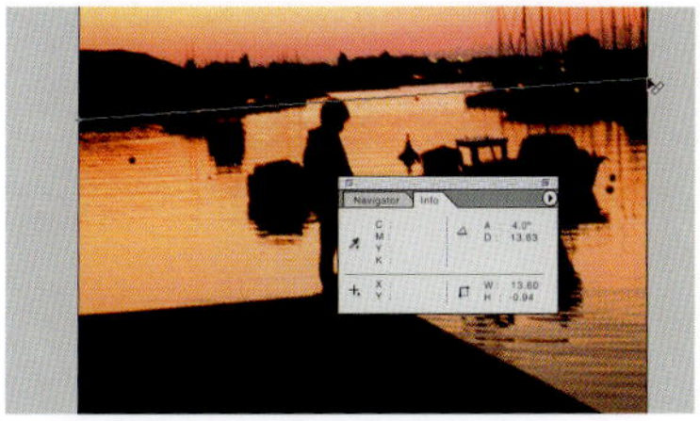

**If you don't trust your eye, use Photoshop's measure tool to draw along the horizon. The info window will now show the angle. You can now use the Image>Rotate Canvas>Abritrary to rotate by the exact amount required.**

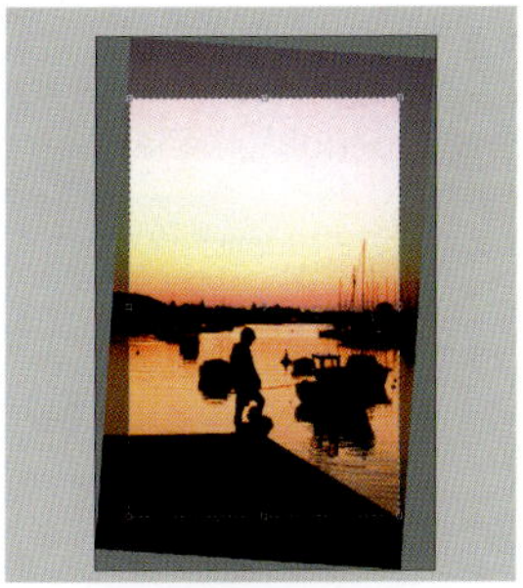

**The final step is to re-crop the image to remove the white corners.**

### Cropping tips

- Square crops can be very effective for landscapes, as the popularity of 6x6cm cameras for this type of photography illustrates.
- Photographs taken in landscape orientation can easily be converted to portrait (and vice versa) using the cropping tools.
- Remember that cropping removes pixels, and if you remove too much you may be left with an image with too low a resolution for satisfactory printing. If you are scanning your pictures and intend to crop, make sure you increase the scanning resolution enough to make up for the loss of pixels.
- If your digital camera only has a wide-angle lens but offers a digital zoom, don't use it (the zoom that is!). Shoot instead at the best quality setting and use cropping to create the same effect with less loss of quality.
- Check out the section on border and edge effects for tips on adding special effects to the edges of your crops (page 102).
- As with all digital imaging, experimentation is key to getting good results when cropping for creative effects.

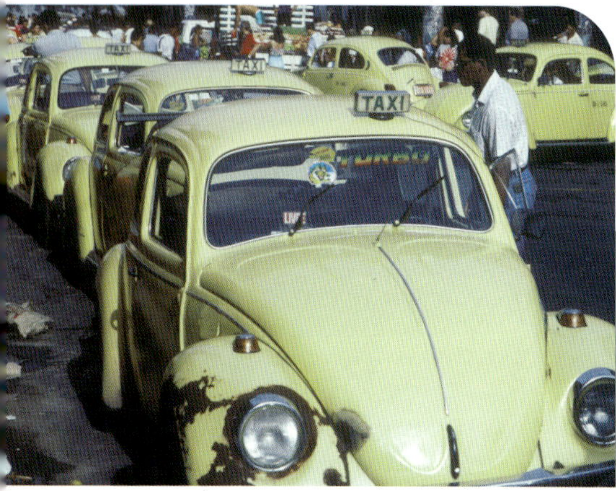


# Using levels

**Auto-correction functions and basic brightness and contrast settings are a good starting point, but an understanding of image histograms and Levels controls is essential for fine-tuning your photographs.**

input

**01** We'll start with an image lacking in contrast and underexposed. Using the Levels controls (Image >Adjust >Levels), we see from the histogram that there are no pixels with brightness values at the high or low ends of the scale.

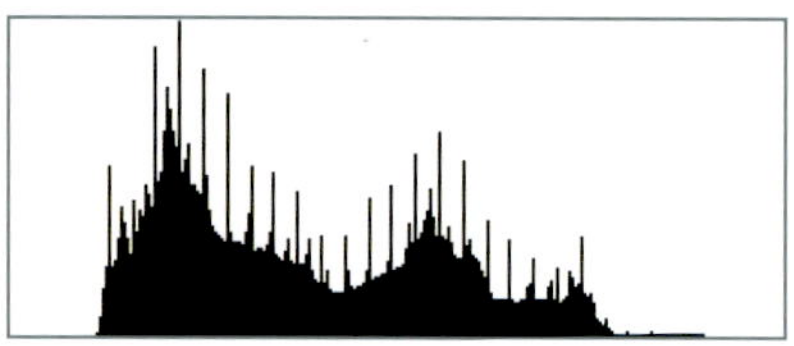

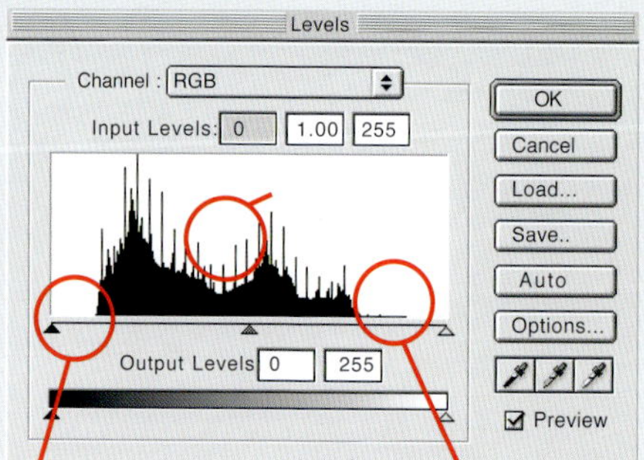


This end of the scale shows the darker (shadow) tones.

This end of the scale shows the lighter (highlight) tones.

### Interpreting histograms

This is the Levels dialog for the image as opened in Photoshop. The graph area is known as a histogram and shows the number of pixels at different brightness levels in the image.

The grey gradient at the bottom of the dialog shows the entire range of tones possible, from black (0) to white (255). We want to use as many of these tones as we can. Here, the distribution of tones falls short at both shadow and highlight end, explaining the rather flat look of the image. We can use the Levels dialog to remap each pixel's brightness, so that the darkest point corresponds to black (0) and the lightest to white (255).

### Auto corrections

Photoshop and high-end applications, offer 'automatic' brightness/contrast functions. The first of these, Auto Contrast, attempts to perform the process described in steps 02-04 opposite. Auto Contrast does not affect the color balance of an image. The second option, Auto Levels, also attempts to 'neutralize' the color of the image - often successfully. Both functions need to be used with care, as they can clip highlights and shadows.

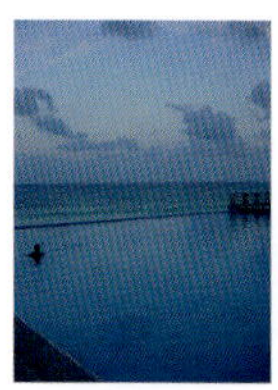

*Original image*

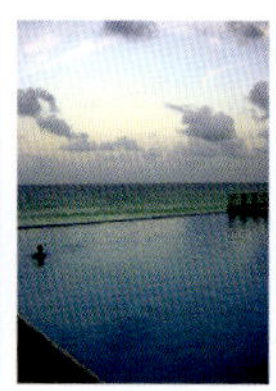

*Auto Contrast*

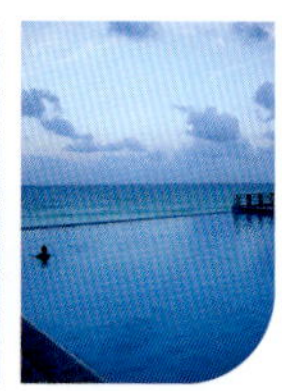

*Auto Levels*

**technical details**
Nikon F3
35-70mm f2.8 Nikkor
Fujichrome Velvia
Adobe Photoshop 5.5

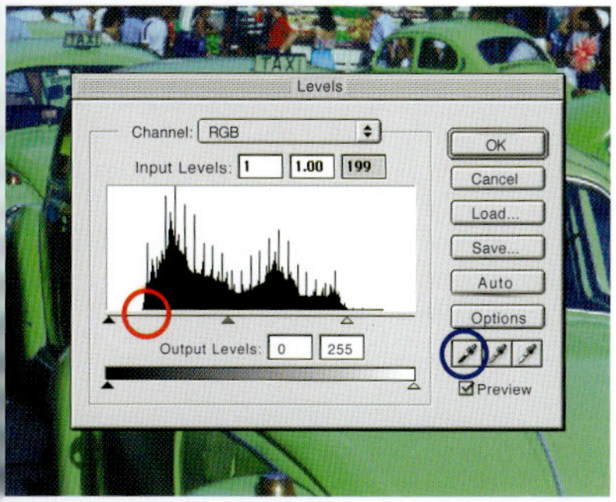


**02** First we'll fix the shadows. Drag the black slider to the right until it is under the point where the graph first shows values (circled in red), or use the black point eyedropper (circled in blue) to select the darkest point in the image - however, this can be hit and miss, and may also introduce a color change.

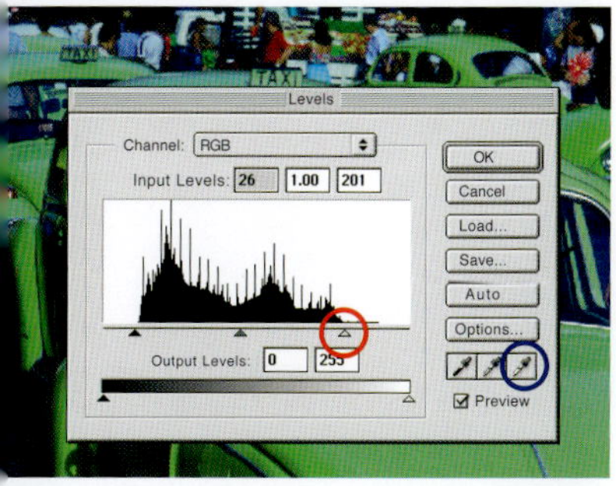


**03** Now for the highlights. Move the white slider to the right until it is under the point where the graph first starts to rise. Watch the preview image , as you will probably need to go a little further to the right (some of the brightest levels will be specular highlights, and therefore, spurious). You can select your own white point using the eyedropper.

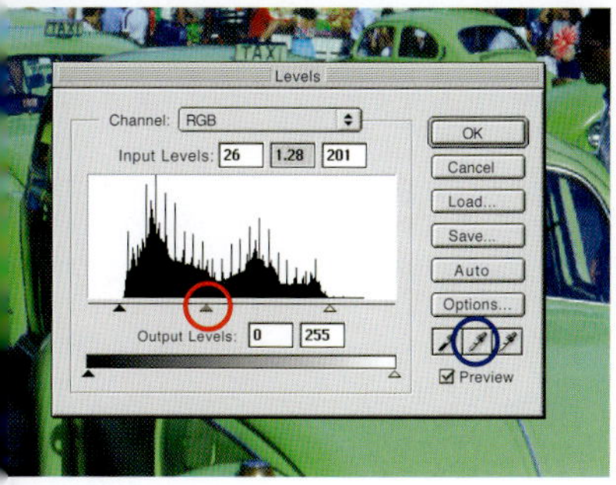


**04** Finally the midtones. By moving the middle (grey) slider right or left, you can darken or lighten the midtones without affecting the highlight or shadows (white and black points). Don't use the grey eyedropper (circled here again in blue) to set the grey point unless you want to change the overall color balance.

**Levels tips**

- When using Levels, turn off the preview (using the checkbox) and hold down the alt key whilst moving the white or black sliders to work in 'threshold mode', allowing you to see where the brightest or darkest points in the image are.
- Make a selection first to apply brightness changes to a specific area of an image.



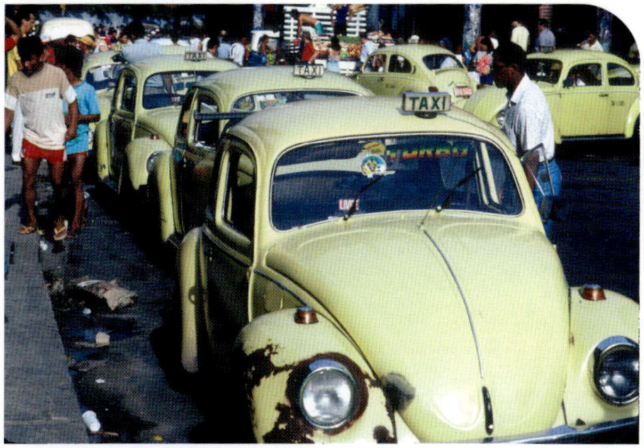


**05** Our final result. You will need to experiment with the Levels controls to discover exactly how to get the best results from your photo printer.

**Using Levels for color correction**

The grey eyedropper in Photoshop's Levels window can be used to apply an overall colour change. Using it is simple; just select the eyedropper (circled here in red) and click anywhere in the image that should be a neutral grey (shown below circled in yellow). The entire image will then be re-mapped to make that point grey. You may need to try a few times to find the right point to click on, checking the preview image each time.

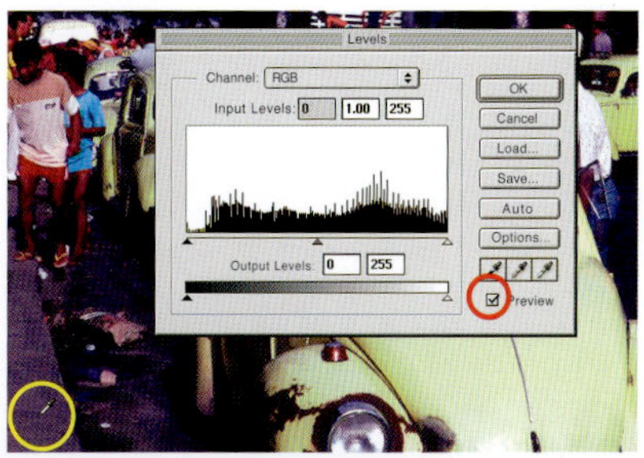

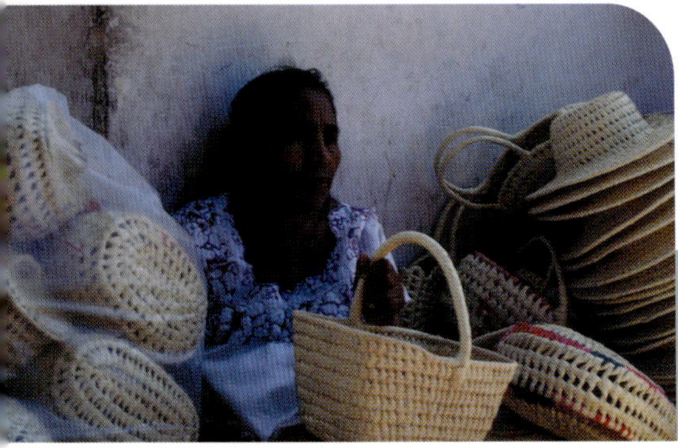

# Using curves

**Often ignored by digital photographers because of the rather daunting interface, the Curves controls are even more powerful than Levels for adding subtle or dramatic tonal changes to an image.**

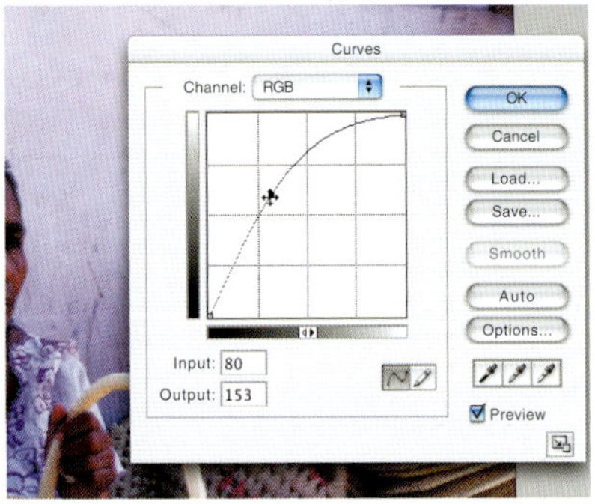


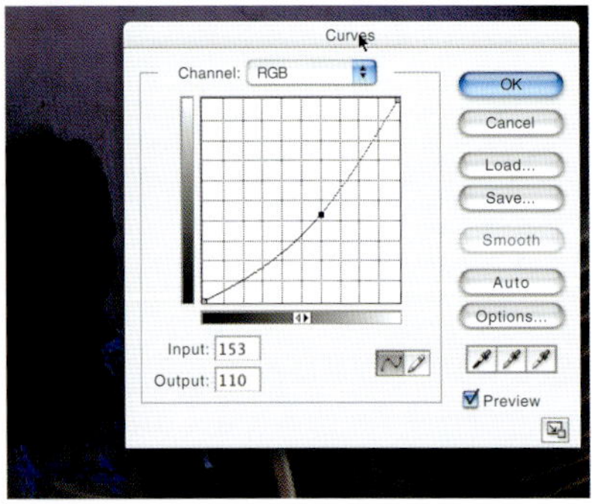


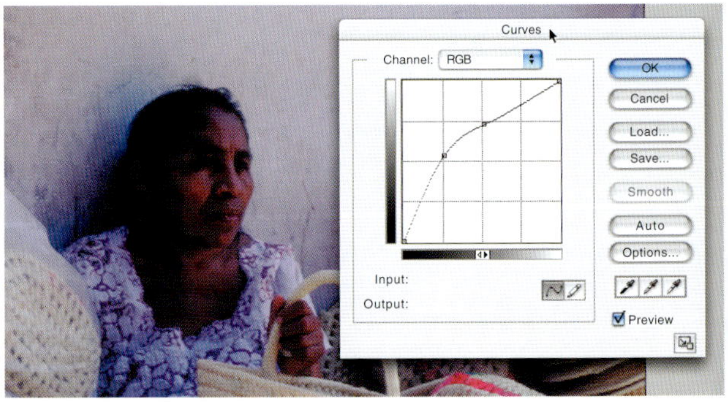


**01** The curve is simply a graph that shows input (original brightness values, on the horizontal axis) versus output (the new brightness values, on the vertical axis). When you open the Curves window(Image>Adjust>Curves in Photoshop), the graph is a straight line at 45°. By clicking on the line and dragging it, you add 'anchor points' used to change the straight line to a curve. Pulling the middle of the line up (as above) lightens the midtones in the image.

**02** Conversely, dragging the curve the other way (down) darkens the midtones. Note that the highlight (white point) and shadow (black point) values are not changing in either case, as the line still starts and ends in the same place. Although the 'Auto' button is good at fixing exposure problems, using the Curves controls to fix exposure is not as easy as using Levels (see pages 36-39), so I start in Levels for a rough fix before moving to Curves for fine-tuning.

**03** By adding a second point to the curve we can start making more complex shapes, such as one shown here. The lightening is being restricted to the mid- and mid-dark tones, with the highlights relatively unaffected. You can add points at will and still 'protect' certain parts of the image from any change by leaving that part of the line as a 45° straight section. With practice, you can fine-tune the curve to get the best range of tones out of the most difficult original.



**technical details**
Canon A1
28-70mm Canon lens
Kodachrome 64
Adobe Photoshop 6.0

**tools**
Curves

**keep in mind**
Curves, like many image adjustments in Photoshop, can be applied via an Adjustment Layer, allowing you to mask areas of the image you want to protect from changes.

output

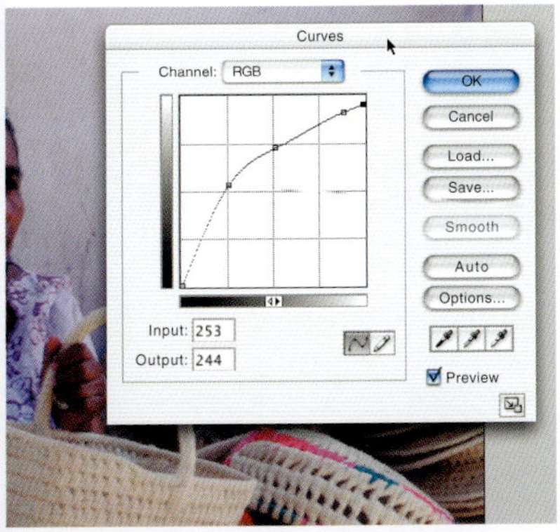


**04** Here I've fine-tuned the curve for this image even further, using four anchor points to lift the mid-dark tones and darken the highlights slightly. It is vital to have a correctly set up and calibrated monitor when performing manual corrections such as these, since you rely totally on the accuracy of the on-screen preview.

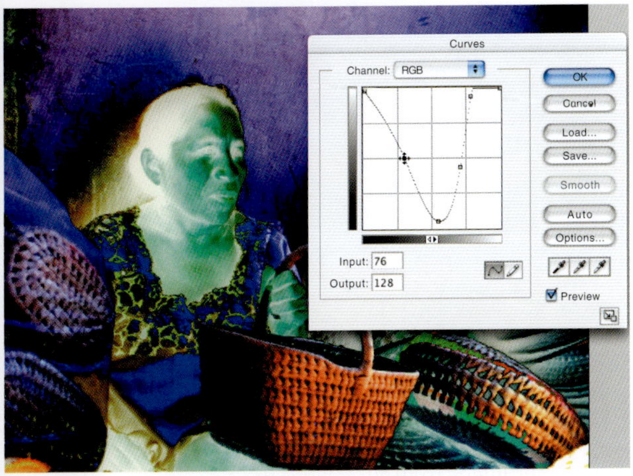


**05** The key to using Curves creatively is experimentation. You can easily produce some wildly dramatic results by pulling sections of the curve at random.

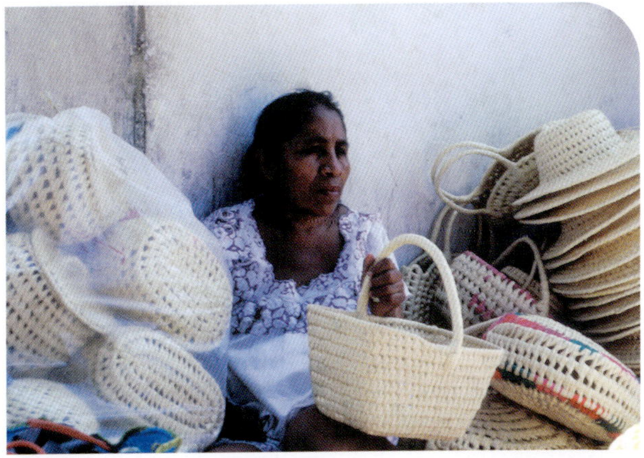

**06** The final result here is a best compromise. The lower (shadow) end of the curve has been lifted a little to lighten the shadow areas. The brighter midtones have also been lifted a small amount by adding the third anchor point and moving the curve upwards slightly. Finally, the extreme highlights have been darkened slightly to reduce contrast.

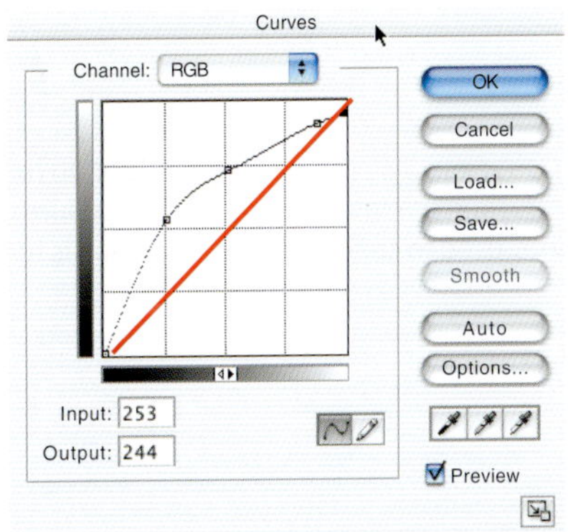


**navigator**
Using levels p64
Playing with color p92
Other color tools p68

**keep in mind**
You can remove anchor points you have added to the curve by dragging them off the graph in any direction.

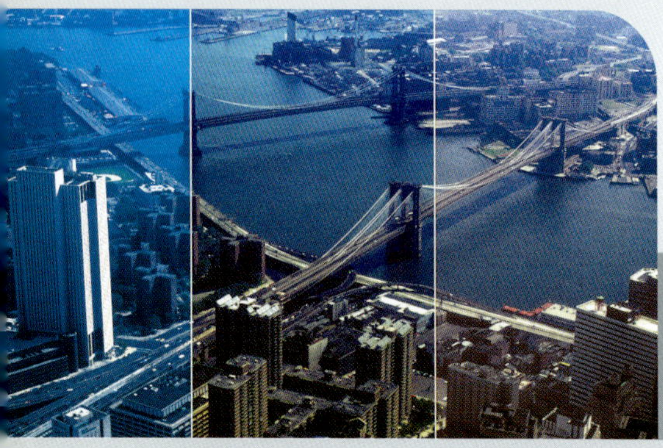

# Other color tools

**Although most everyday color corrections can be performed using Levels or Curves, there are plenty more weapons in the digital photographer's arsenal.**

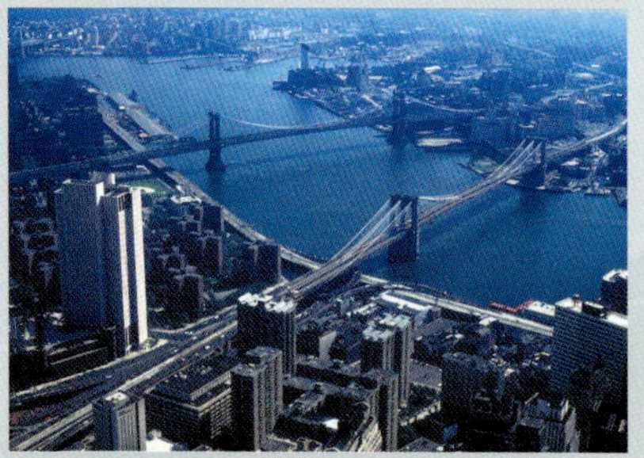

**01** Our starting shot this time is an aerial shot of New York City that has a distinct bluish hue. This kind of color cast is common when shooting at high altitude or in very bright sunshine. You can prevent it with most digital cameras using the manual white-balance settings, but as this is a scan of a 35mm transparency that simply wasn't an option. None of the automatic 'quick fix' functions could fix the image satisfactorily, perhaps as the color cast is so overwhelming.

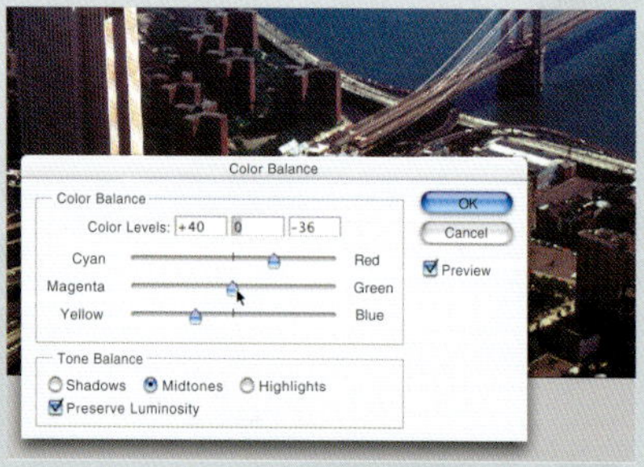


**02** Most applications offer a 'color balance' function, where the amount of the individual red, green and blue channels can be altered using sliders. Photoshop's Color Balance tool allows you to alter each channel in one of three rough tonal ranges- Shadows, Midtones and Highlights - which offers a remarkably fine level of control over the image. Here I've moved the Cyan-Red slider towards the Red and the Yellow-Blue slider towards the Yellow, working on the midtones.

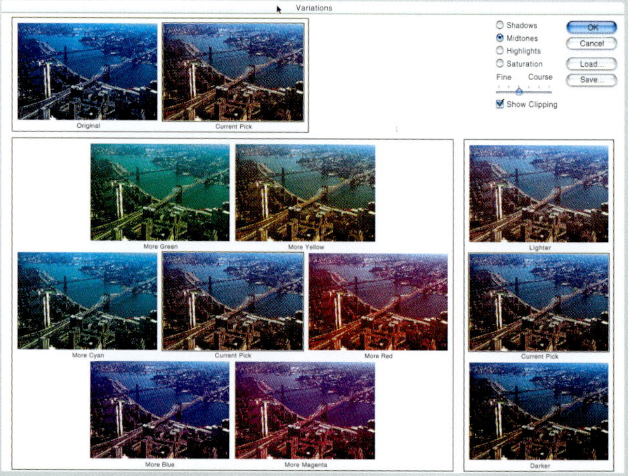


**03** Most color corrections require you to have some idea of what needs changing. Applications such as Photoshop's Variations also offer an easy, visual option. Click on the thumbnail nearest to the result you'd like and repeat until it is spot on. You can alter overall brightness as well as color balance.

**technical details**
Canon A1
24mm Canon lens
Fujichrome 100
Adobe Photoshop 6.0

**tools**
Hue/Saturation/
Lightness
Curves
Variations

**keep in mind**
You can apply any color alteration to a portion of an image by first making a selection or creating an adjustment layer.

## Hue and Saturation

A final tool for radically altering color is the Hue/Saturation and Brightness control. Let's use it on this image.

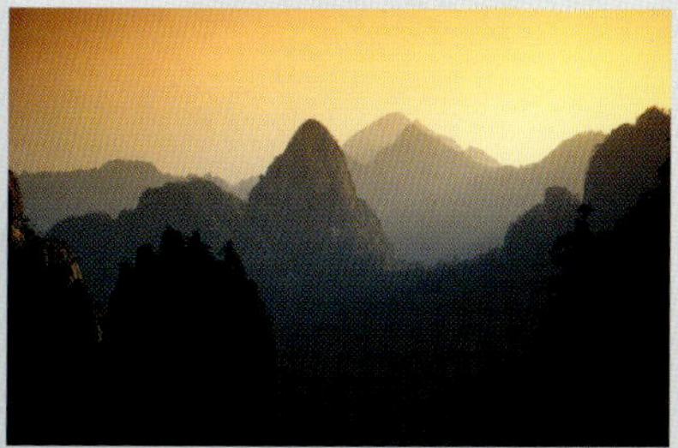

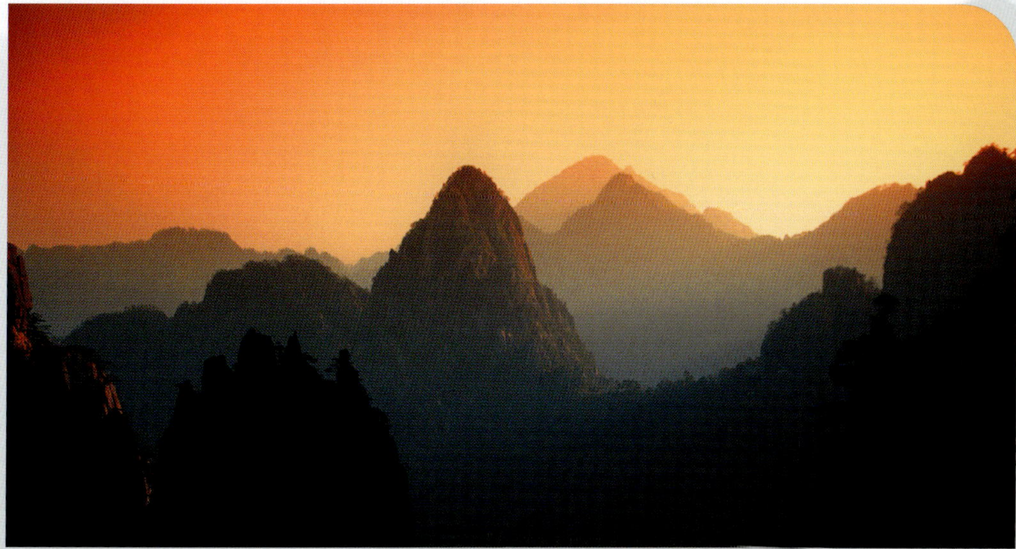

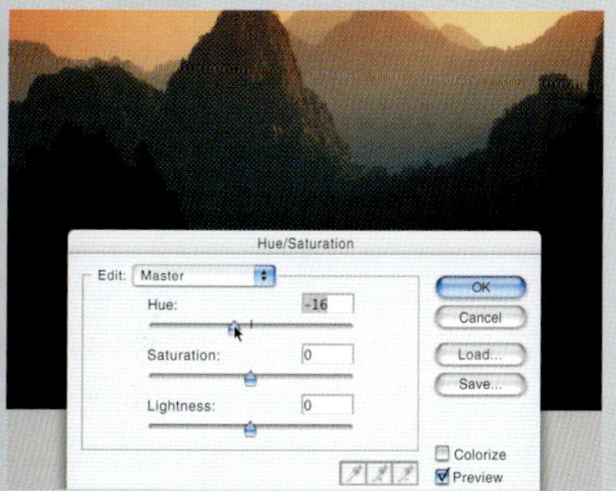


**01** There are three variables here; Hue (the overall color), Saturation (the 'strength' of the color) and Lightness. Open the HSL dialog and try moving the Hue slider from left to right. You will see the entire image radically shift hue as you do.

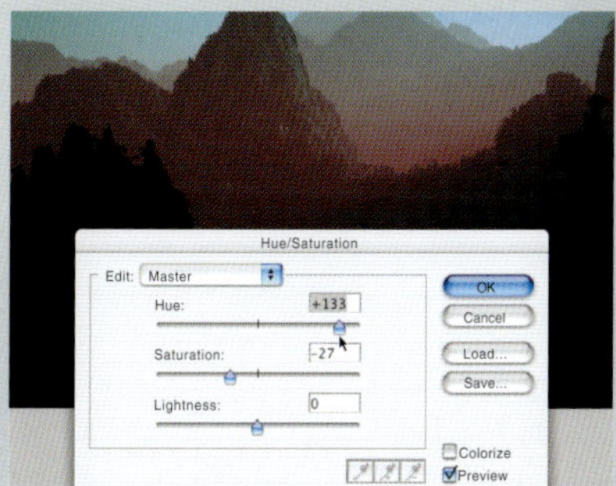


**02** If your image becomes noisy when you make an extreme hue change try reducing the saturation.

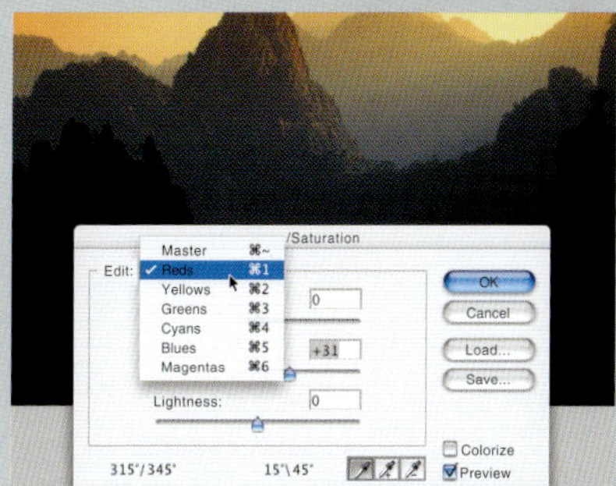


**03** You can usually alter the HSL settings for particular color ranges individually. Here, I have increased the saturation of the reds.

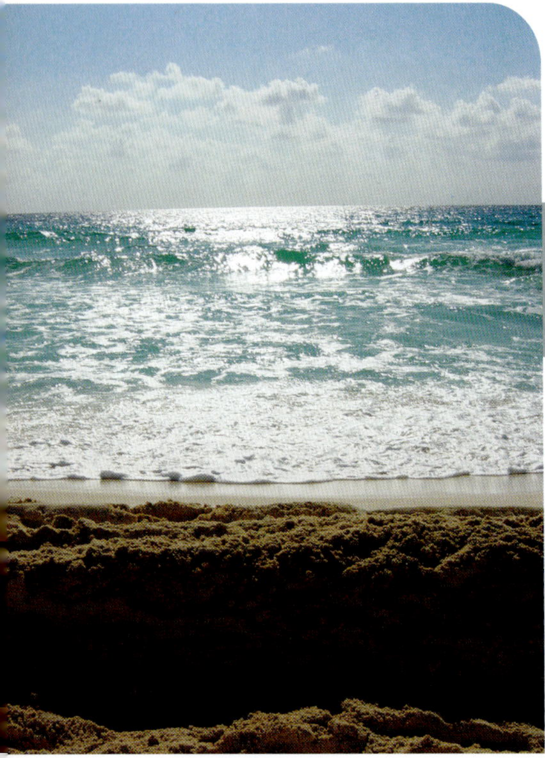

# Selective changes

Sometimes, no matter how hard you try, you can't find a single color or contrast adjustment that works – so you simply need to apply different effects to different areas of the image.

## input

**01** There's nothing wrong with this shot of the sea in Cancun, Mexico, *per se*; I just want to lighten and increase the contrast of the beach without losing tonal detail in the sea. I'd also like to add a little more 'oomph' to the sky if at all possible.

## process

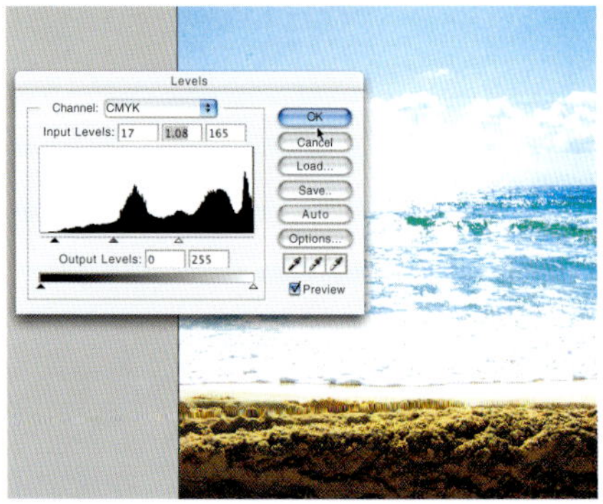


**02** Applying Levels (or any other adjustment) to the entire image simply doesn't work; to get the sand the way I want it I lose all but the darkest parts of the rest of the image. This is often the case when the brightness of the foreground and background (usually the sky) are massively different.

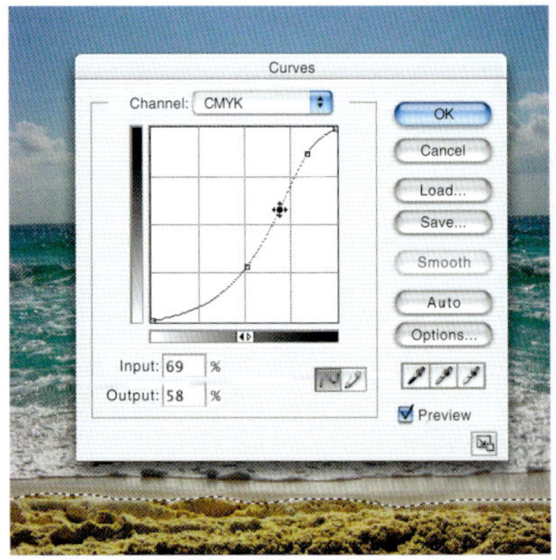


**03** The simplest solution is to select areas of the image and apply the required adjustment. Here, I've selected the sand and applied a quite radical Curves adjustment to lighten and increase contrast. The changes occur only inside the area selected. I then applied a different adjustment to the sky.

**technical details**
Sony DSC-P71
digital camera
Adobe Photoshop 7.0

**tools**
Selection tools
Levels
Quick Mask
Curves

**keep in mind**
It is always better to use masks and duplicate layers or adjustment layers than to apply adjustments directly to areas of your original image. That way you can always go back and tweak your alterations without having to start again from scratch.

**Adjustment Layers**

A few applications offer a special type of layer called an Adjustment Layer. These are basically layers containing a tonal adjustment with an associated Layer Mask that allows you to control which parts of the image are affected.



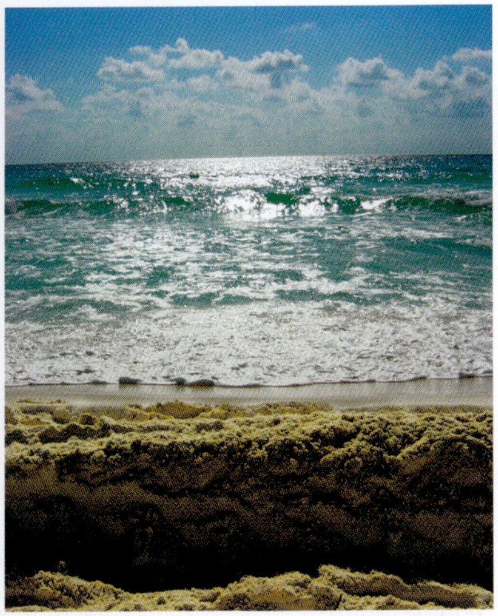

**04** The final result, with a different adjustment made individually to the beach, sea and sky areas.

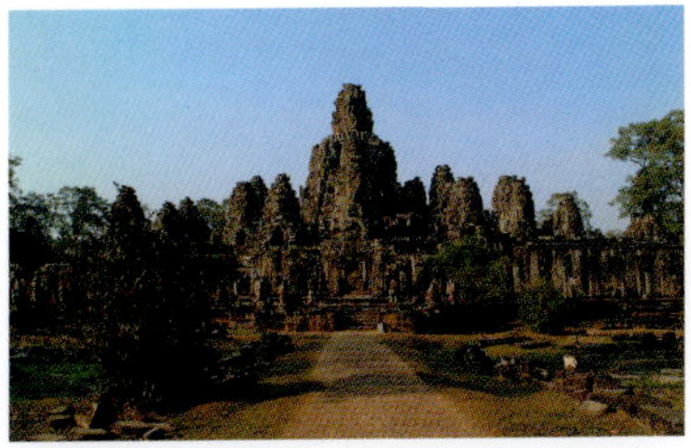

**01** We'll start with a typical scenic shot; the camera has slightly underexposed the foreground due to the large area of bright sky.

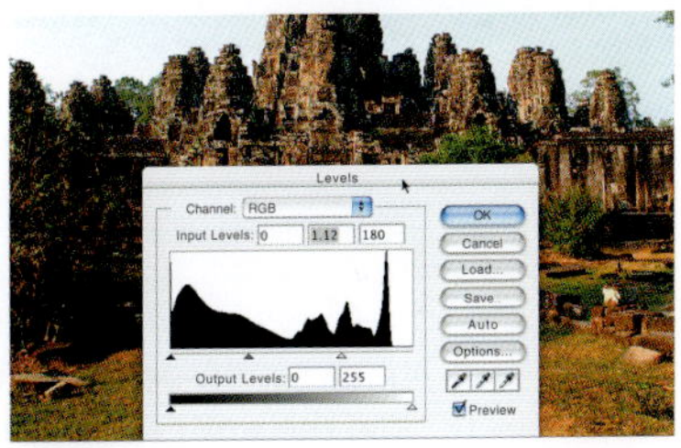

**02** There is plenty of detail in the shadowy building but, again, brightening the whole image means we lose that lovely blue sky.

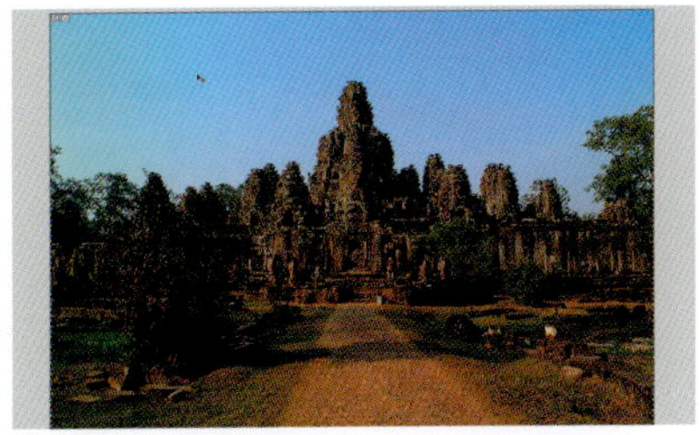

**03** The first step is to select the entire foreground area.

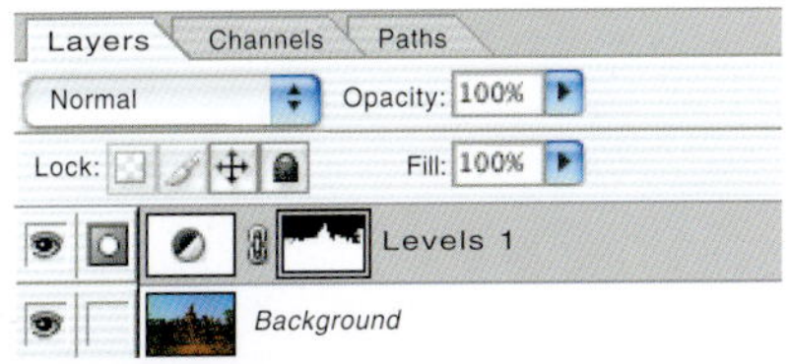


**04** From the Layers menu choose New> Adjustment Layer>Levels. This will create an Adjustment Layer with a mask based on the selection just made.

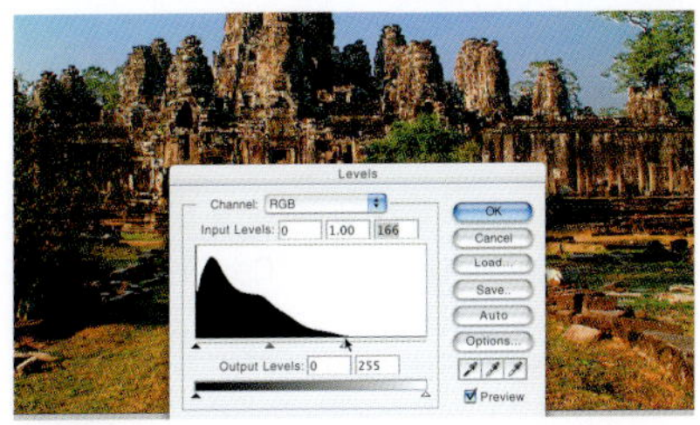

**05** As soon as you create the Adjustment Layer the Levels dialog will appear; you can now alter the brightness of the foreground on its own.

**navigator**



**keep in mind**
You can adjust the settings made to the Levels in step 05 at any time by double-clicking on the Adjustment Layer icon (shown here circled in red). You can also paint directly onto the mask, editing the areas affected by the adjustment.

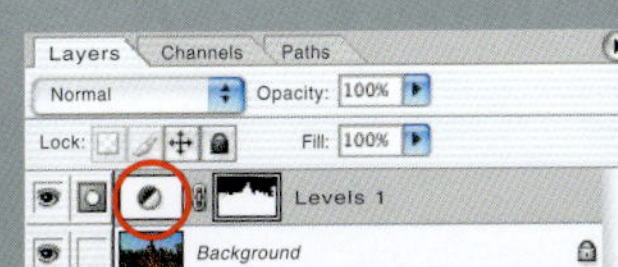

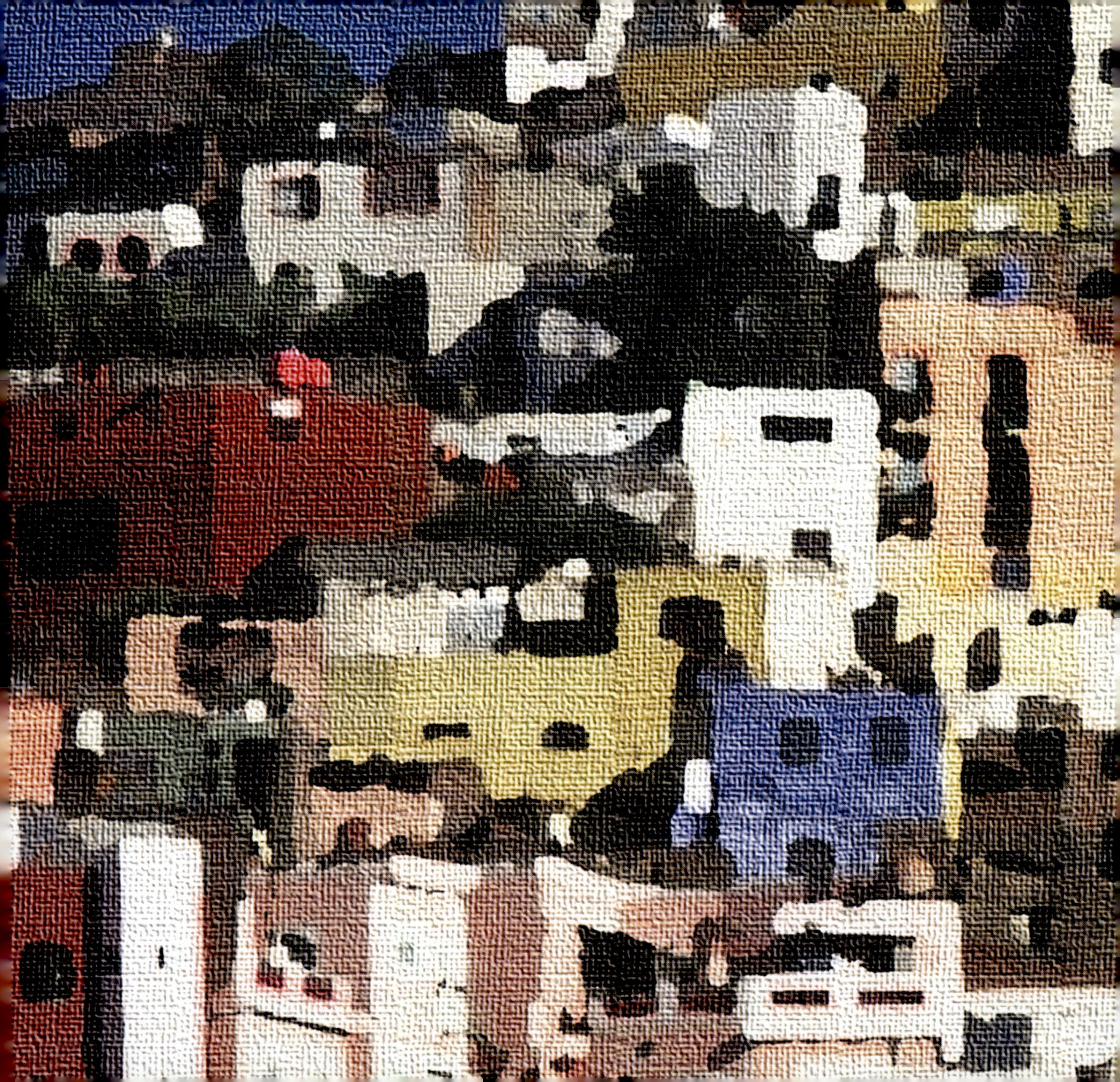

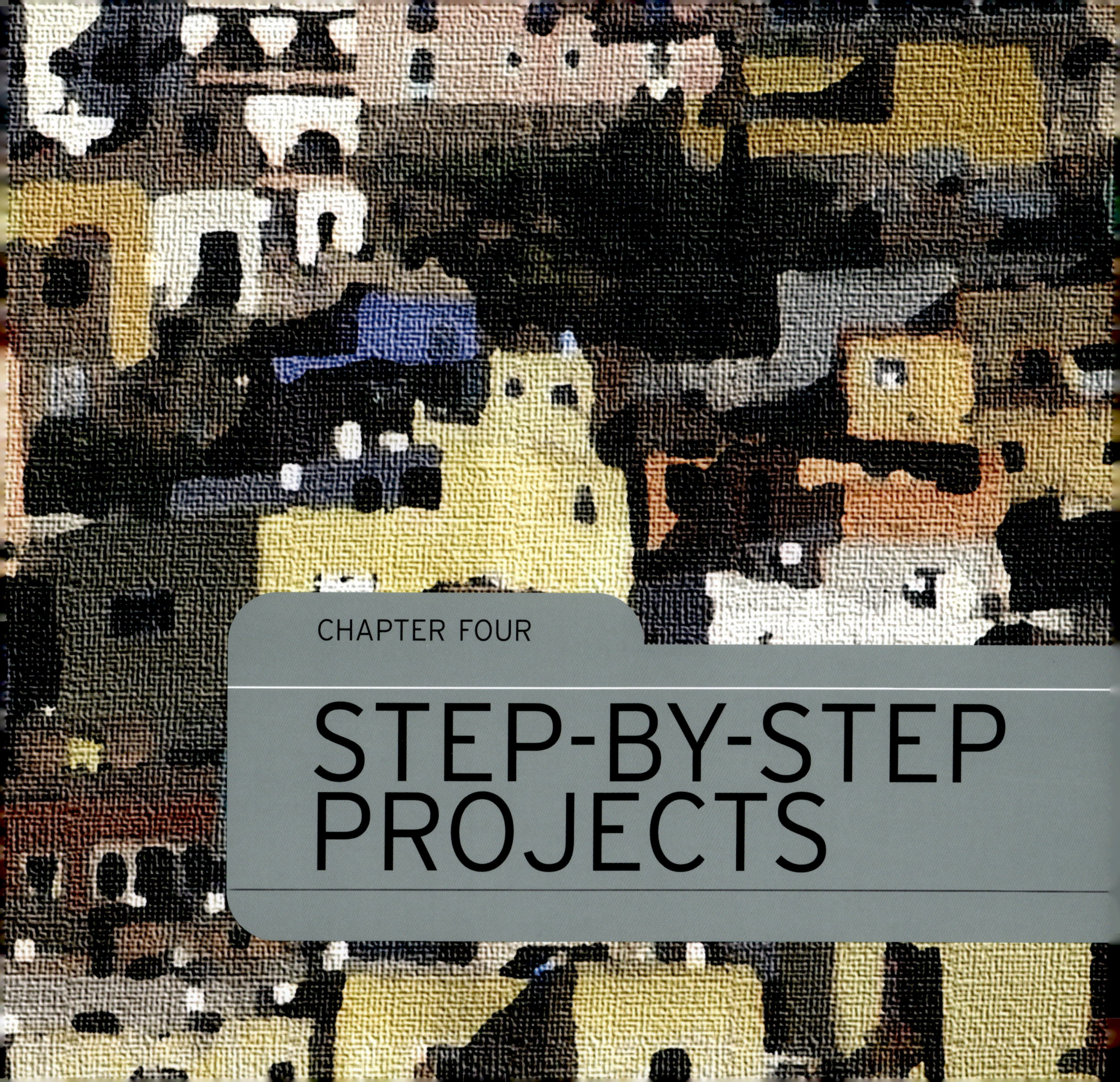

CHAPTER FOUR

# STEP-BY-STEP PROJECTS

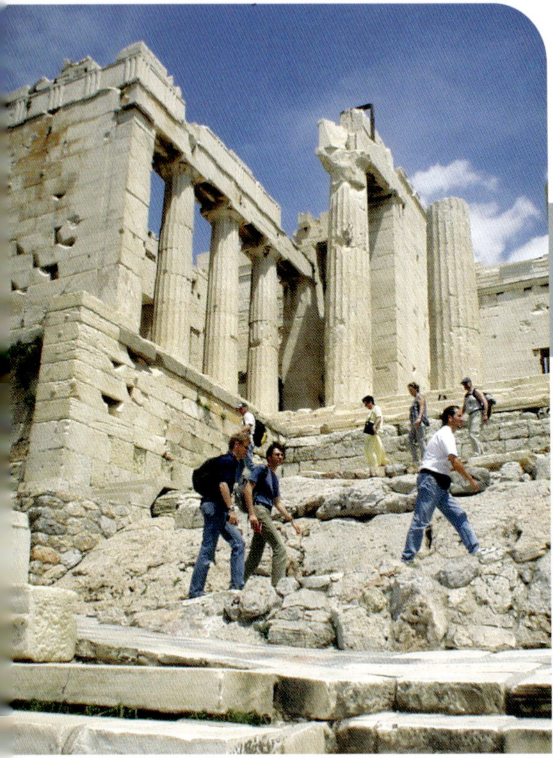

# Removing elements

No matter where you go or how long you wait, you'll inevitably find something that spoils an otherwise perfect scene. Here's how to remove anything you don't want in your picture.

input

**01** As usual in very popular areas it proved impossible to shoot anything without mobs of tourists spoiling every shot. Without the time to wait, I simply ignored the other visitors and snapped merrily away. The first step is to create a new transparent layer above the image.

process

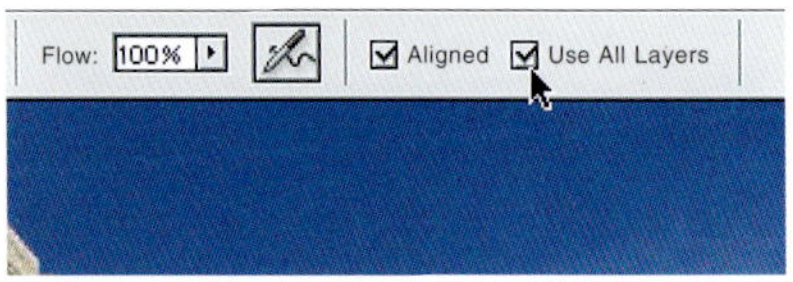


**02** Select the Clone or Rubber Stamp tool and, in the Tool Options palette, make sure the 'Use All Layers' option is turned on. This allows us to clone pixels from one layer (in this case the original image) onto another layer (the new transparent layer created in step 01). The advantage of working this way is that if things go wrong, we can simply erase what we've done. The corrections are all on a separate layer, and the original image remains untouched. If your image-editing application doesn't support cloning from one layer to another, don't worry, you'll just have to be very careful!

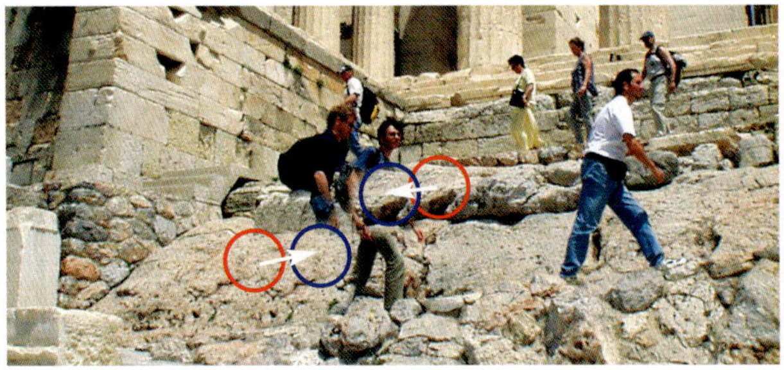

**03** Using the techniques described on page 59 start to use the Clone tool to paint over each person or whatever blemish you are trying to remove. Here I am using areas of stone (areas circled in red) to cover the two figures in the foreground (areas circled in blue).

**technical details**
Olympus C-200 digital camera
Fixed wide-angle lens
Adobe Photoshop 7.0

**tools**
Rubber Stamp

**keep in mind**
The size and softness of brush you use for cloning makes a huge difference; use soft edges wherever possible and choose a brush size that is smaller than the area you are trying to cover.

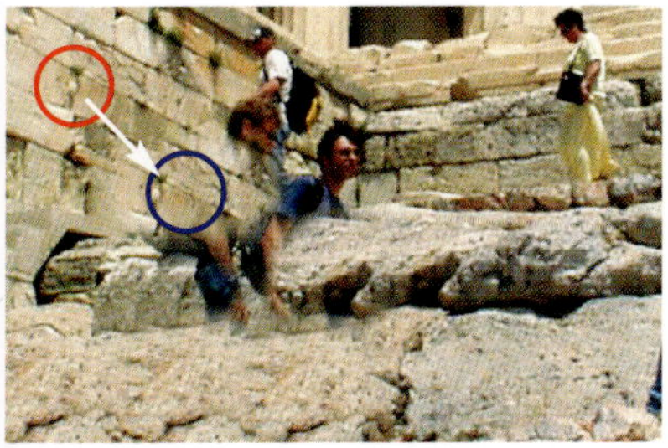

**04** The upper part of the left-hand figure's body is in front of the wall, so I need to use detail from the far left of the wall to cover him, being careful to align the bricks as well as possible. Again the source pixels are highlighted in red, the target area in blue.

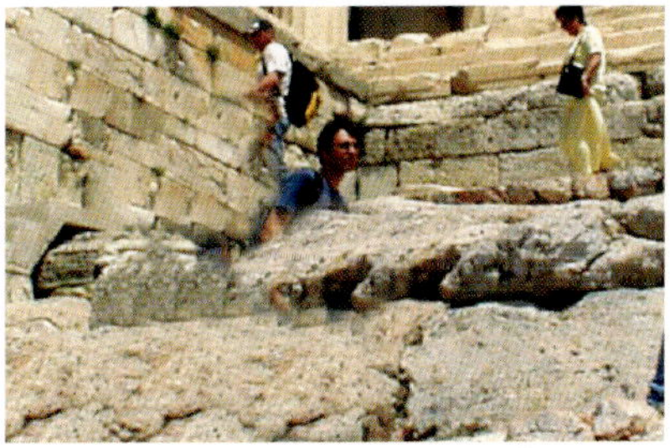

**05** With the figure on the left successfully removed, it's time to concentrate on his companion. I started by cloning part of the rock in front of him over his arm.

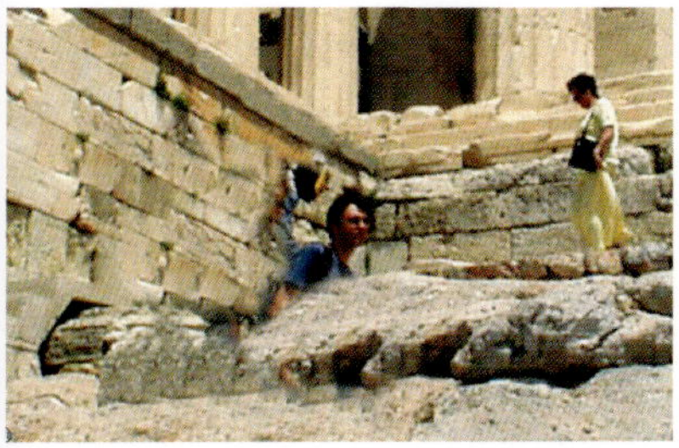

**06** The next bit is pretty tricky; removing the upper part of his body and the remains of the other figure to the left of the background.

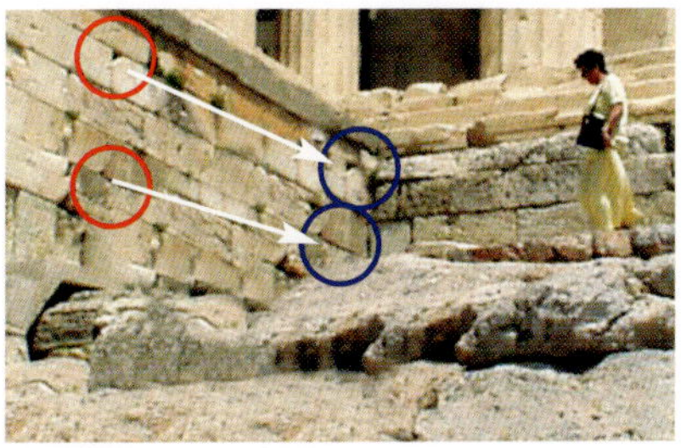

**07** Using a smaller brush - and after a lot of fiddling about - the corner of the wall is recreated using bricks from the left-hand side of the wall.

## Cloning tips

**Avoid repetition by covering your tracks**

The human eye is remarkably good at spotting patterns and repetition, something cloning inevitably produces. Try to cover your tracks by returning to areas you've produced using the Rubber Stamp and carefully cloning out any obvious repetition.

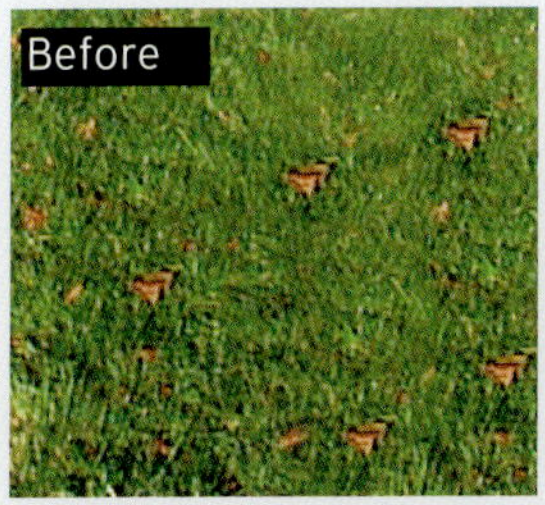


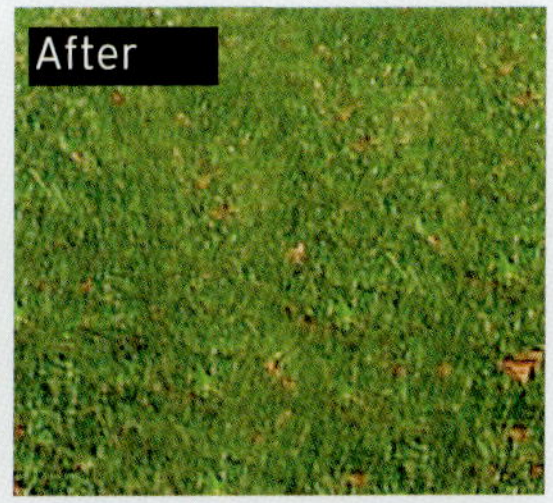


**Make sure edges line up**

Take great care when cloning an edge that you position the cursor in exactly the right place as you start to paint. With practice, you can ensure that any edge continues seamlessly, rather than 'jumping' as you start to clone.

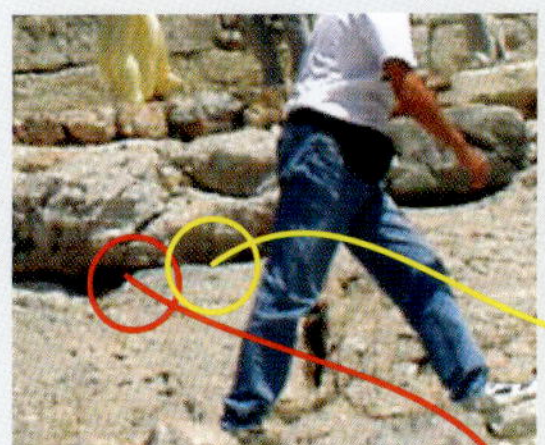

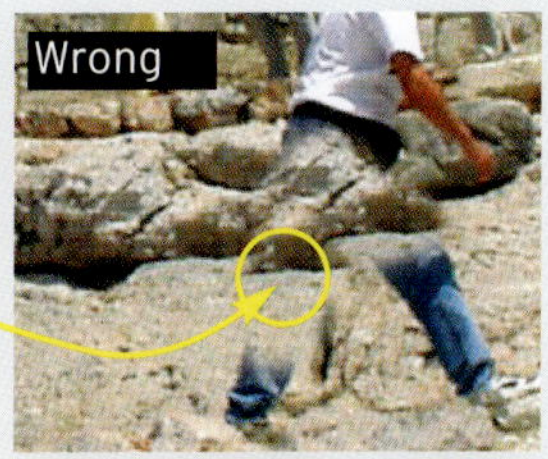


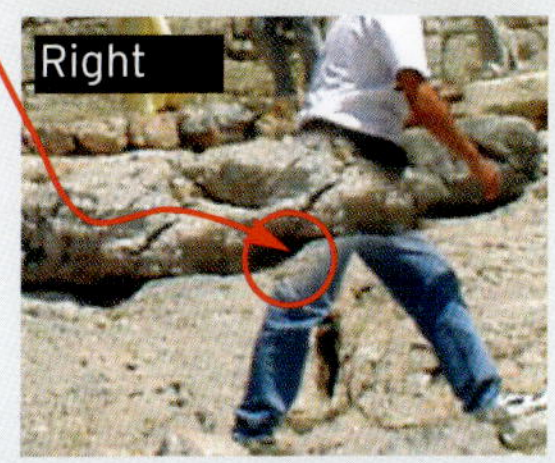


**It is also important to choose an edge to clone from that is at the same angle as the the edge you want to create.**

**Photoshop keyboard shortcuts**

| | |
|---|---|
| Rubber Stamp | S |
| Larger brush size | ] |
| Smaller brush size | [ |
| Change brush pressure: 1 for 10%, 2 for 20% and so on | |

output

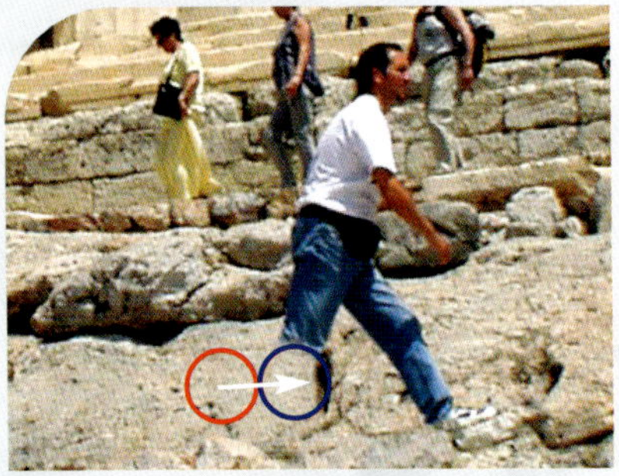

**08** Now to get to work on the figure to the left of the foreground. His lower half is relatively easy. For advice on cloning the edge of the rock turn back to page 75.

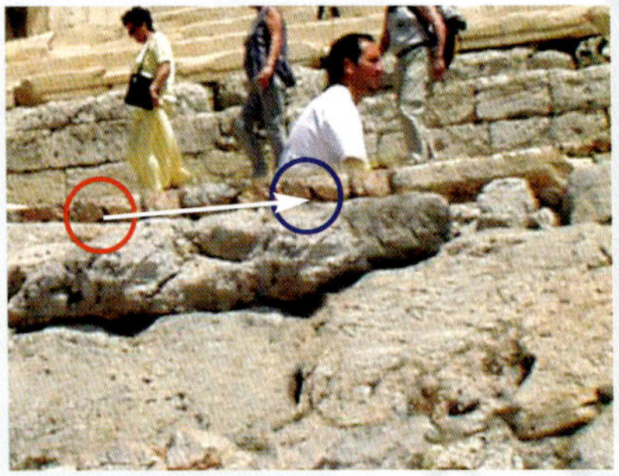

**09** Once again it gets a little trickier further up his body; there is a footpath and wall to recreate, both of which are partially obscured by other people.

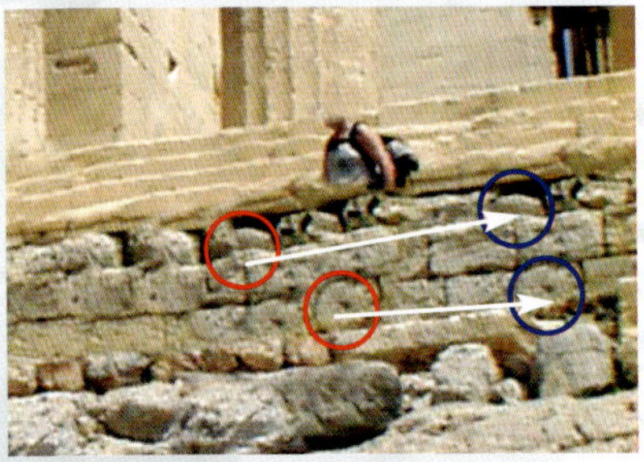

**10** What remains of the three figures in the background are quite easily covered using the surrounding wall and steps.

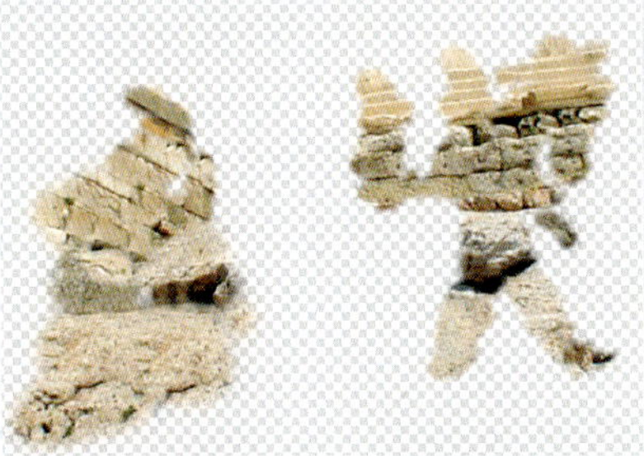

**11** Here's the 'Clone' layer viewed on its own. All that remains - if you are totally happy with your work - is to flatten the two layers and resave the image.

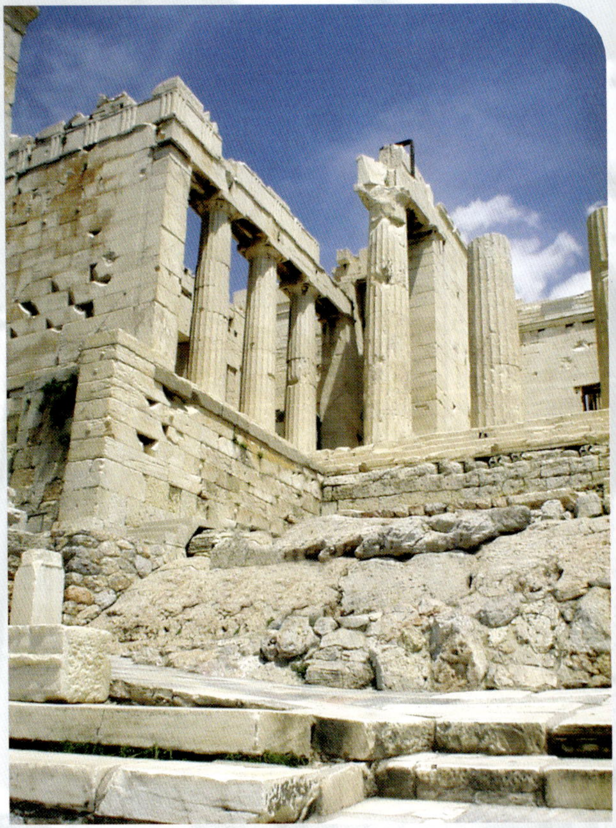

**12** The end result after a little final tweaking to cover the 'tracks' of the extensive cloning work. It may no longer be a faithful photographic record, but it is a picture I simply couldn't have taken in the time I had.

**keep in mind**
The Rubber Stamp acts in exactly the same way as any other painting tool; you can use any of the brush shapes and sizes, alter hardness and size at will and use any opacity from 1-100%.

**Aligned or non-aligned?**

The Clone/Rubber Stamp tool offers two modes of operation; aligned and non-aligned. But what's the difference?

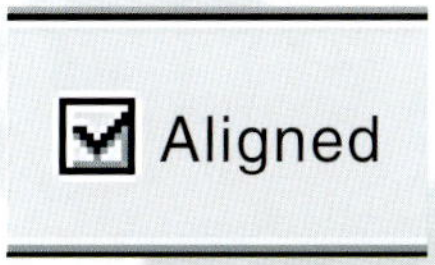


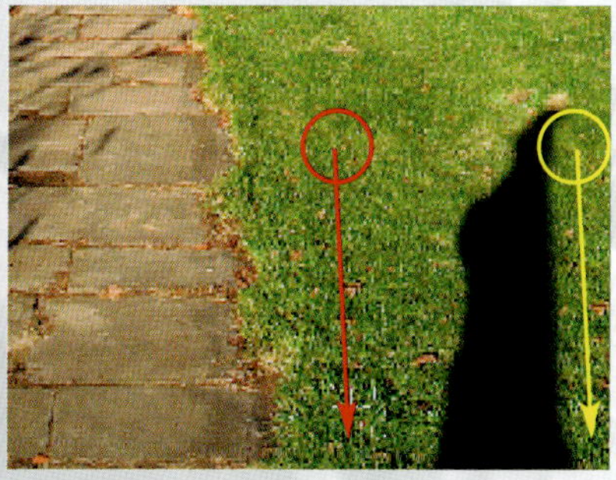

**01** Let's start by cloning an area of grass over the shadow in this image. I've alt-clicked in the red circle and painted a line indicated here in yellow.

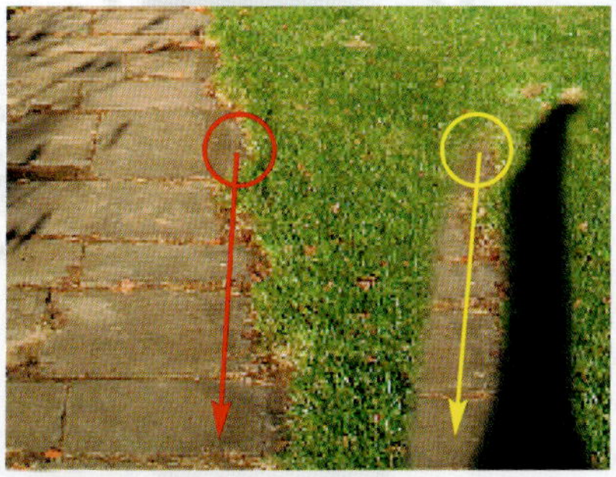

**02** In aligned mode if I paint again (without resampling) to the left of the shadow, my sample point moves the same distance, and uses pixels from the path.

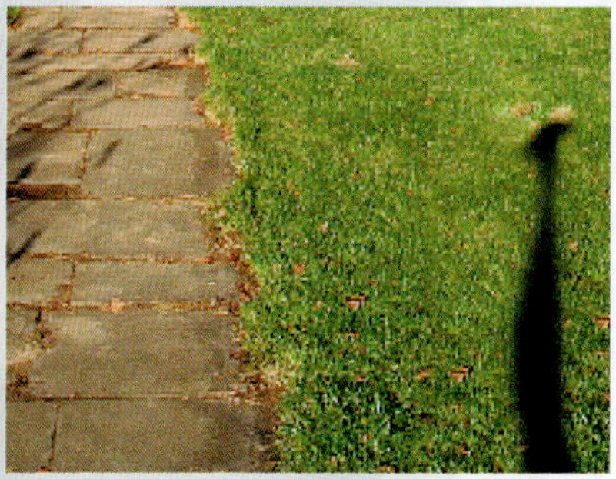

**03** In non-aligned mode the same action uses the same pixels from my original sample point. No matter where I paint, the source starting point will always be the same. The mode you use depends on the circumstances; non-aligned is particularly useful for covering large areas with a sample of the original , but can lead to repetitive patterns.

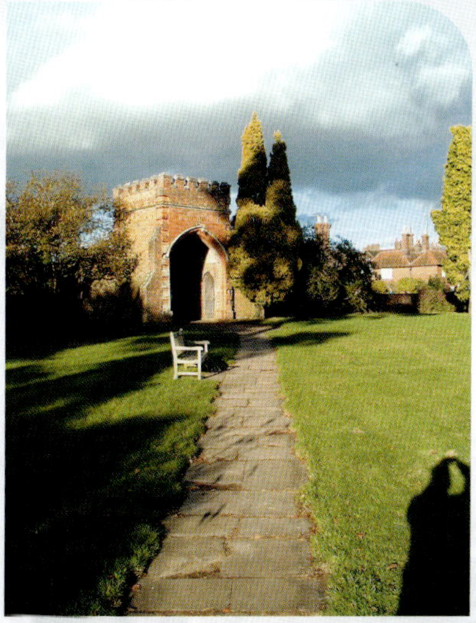

**04** This original had little wrong with it, but I wanted to remove my own shadow and the modern houses to the right of the central area.

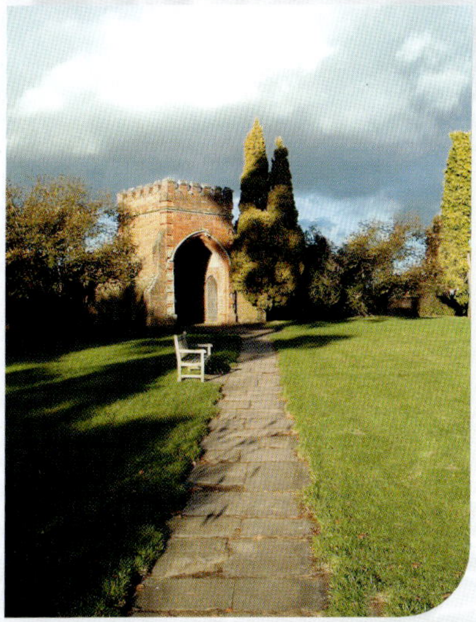

**05** The shadow was removed using a little non-aligned cloning of the grass directly to the right. The houses were covered using a much larger brush and detail from the trees to the right of the tower. In this case aligned mode was used to avoid repetition of detail.

**navigator**
Basic corrections p58

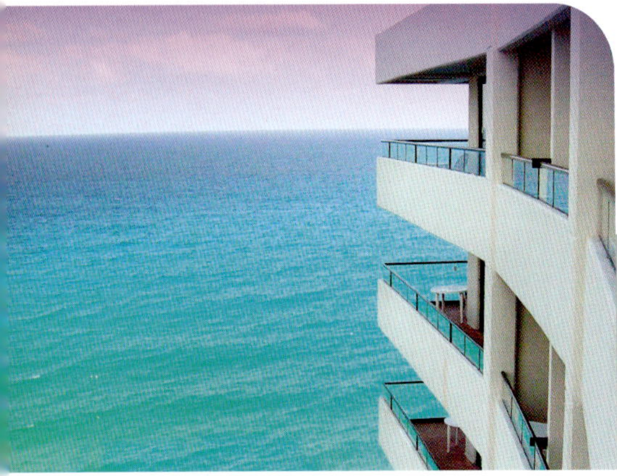

# Graduated filter

The use of a color graduated filter is one of the oldest tricks in the photographer's arsenal when confronted with dull, featureless skies. Fortunately for the digital photographer, there is no need to invest in a whole set of colored filters – we just apply it later!

## input

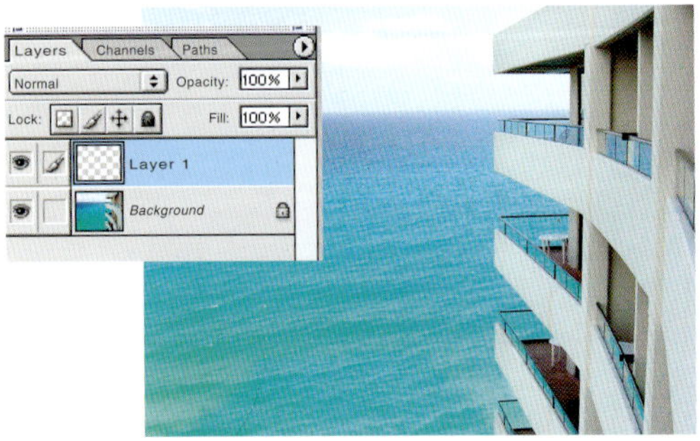


**01** We're going to put our colored gradient onto a separate layer as this means we don't have to commit to any changes until we are totally happy with the result. Create a new blank layer above your original picture. It will be transparent by default.

## process

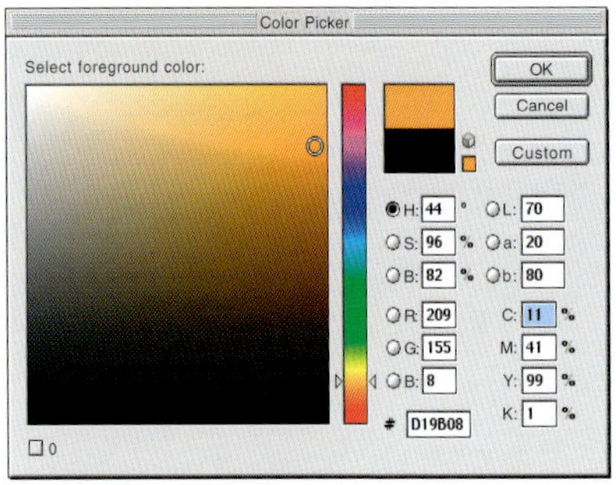


**02** Now to choose a color for our graduated tint. Click once on the foreground paint color at the bottom of Photoshop's toolbar and select a color. I'm starting with a dull orange (similar to the 'Tobacco' filters commonly used by photographers). Don't worry about your choice of color too much – you can change it later.

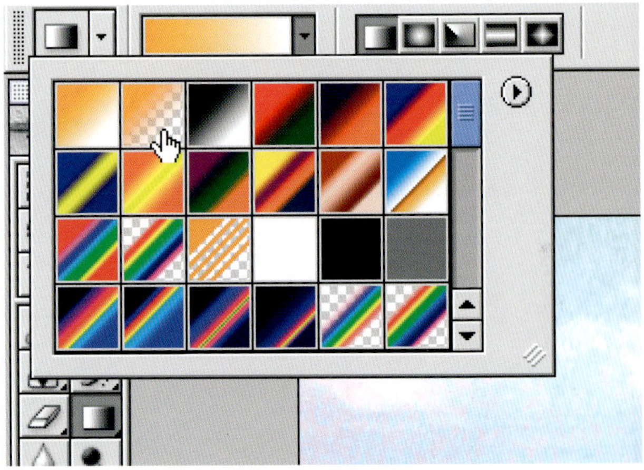

**03** Click on the gradient tool and choose the 'foreground to transparent' option from the pop-up options menu (as shown above).

**technical details**
Sony DSC-P71
digital camera
Wide end of zoom lens
Adobe Photoshop 7.0

**tools**
Layers
Gradient tool
Transform
Hue/Saturation

**keep in mind**
If your image-editing application doesn't support gradients with transparency, use a gradient from your chosen color to white and use Darken or Multiply as the blending mode.

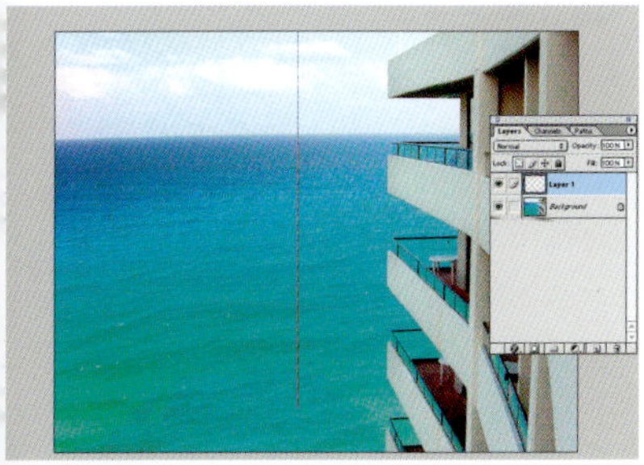

**04** Click at the top of the frame and drag a straight line to near the bottom of the frame. Again, don't worry too much about how far you drag the gradient as we can change it later.

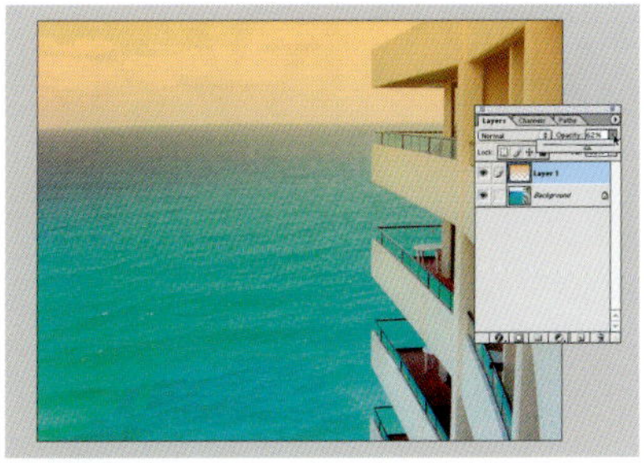

**05** Change the opacity of the upper (gradient) layer to around 50-60%. You can also experiment with different Layer blending modes for different effects.

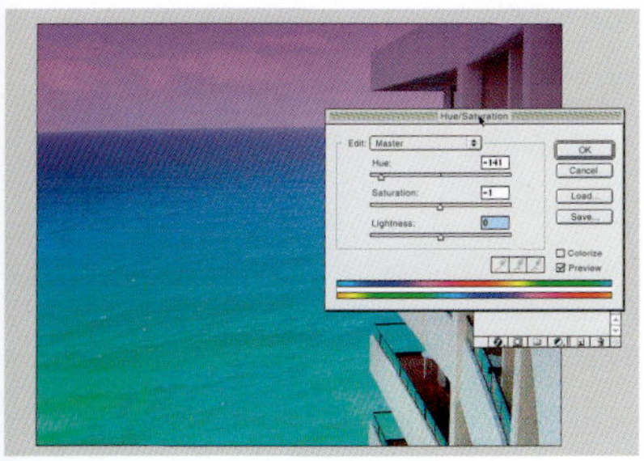

**06** If you want to change the color of your graduated filter, simply shift the hue using the Hue/Saturation controls (under the Image>Adjust menu).

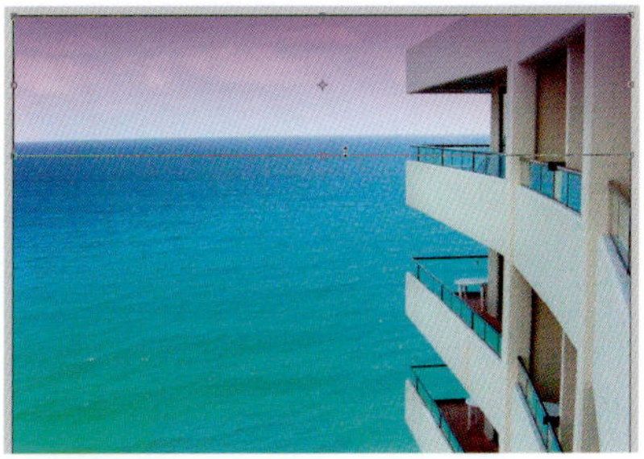

**07** Finally, you can alter how far down the filter comes by stretching or sqashing the entire upper layer (Edit>Transform).

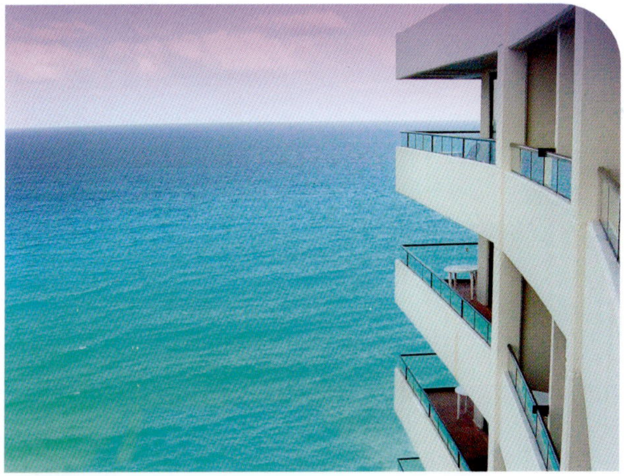

**08** The end result. As with all things photographic, subtlety is the key to success.

**Quick blue sky**

One of the favourite uses of colored graduated tint filters in conventional photography is to make an overcast sky blue. The same idea can be used pretty successfully in digital photography using the techniques described on these pages.

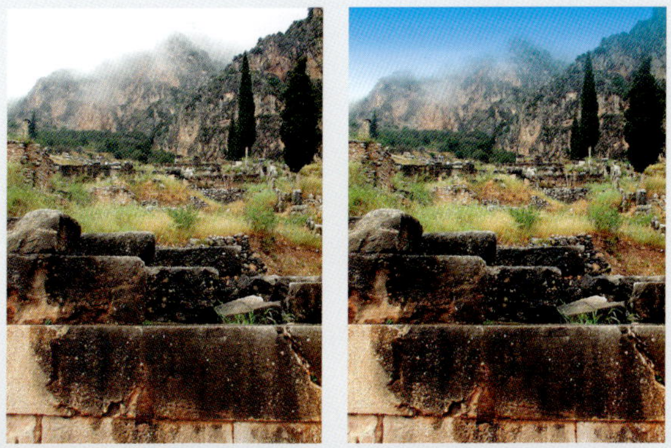

**navigator**
Playing with color p92
Basic corrections p58
A new sky p80

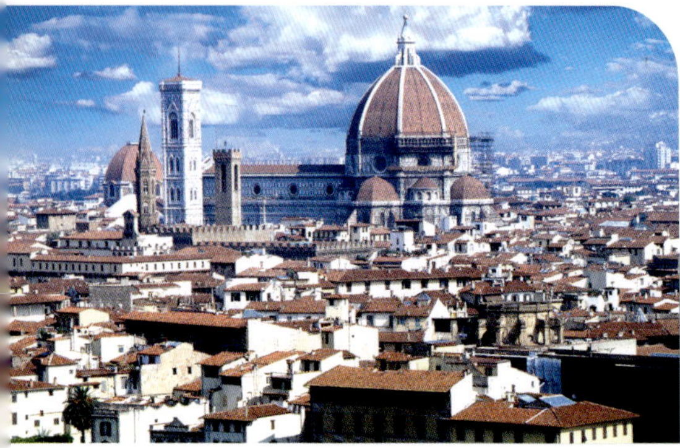

# A new sky

**One of the digital photographer's favourites; don't let a murky day spoil your shot; simply drop in a new blue sky once you get home.**

input

process

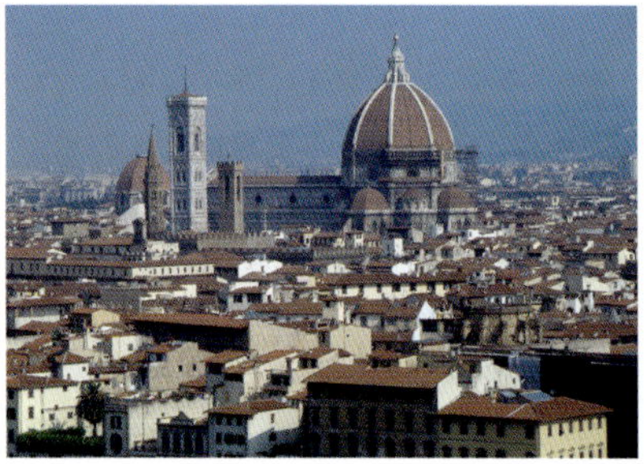

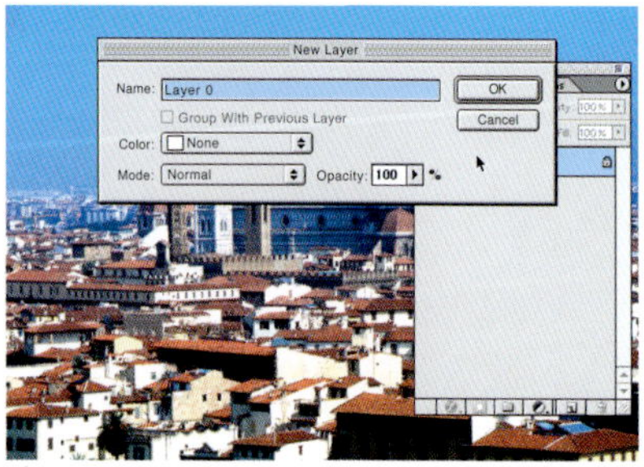


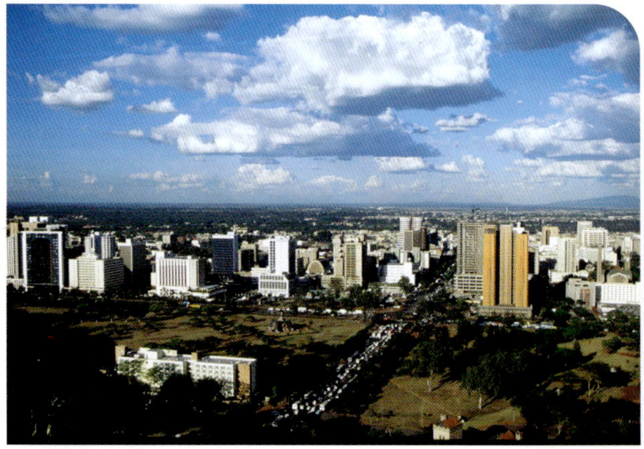

**01** This shot of Florence is typical; it may have been a nice warm day but it was also overcast, resulting in a muddy, uninspiring sky and overall muted tones. Try and cheer the image up as much as possible by increasing the contrast and saturation a little.

**02** We're going to use a layer mask to hide the old sky (the new sky will sit in its own layer directly below). We first need to turn the background into a 'normal' unlocked layer (the background layer cannot be masked, and cannot have any layers below it).

Double click on the Background Layer thumbnail in the Layers Palette and click OK when you see the window above appear.

**03** Now to choose your new sky. This otherwise uninspiring shot taken in Kenya has a lovely sky and is taken from a similar position using a similar focal length lens. It is always worth shooting skies wherever you go as they can come in handy.

**technical details**
Nikon F4
35-70mm f2.8 Nikkor
Fujichrome 100
Adobe Photoshop 7.0

**keep in mind**
There are two key things to getting this kind of project right; a seamless join (which comes down to the accuracy of your masking) and finding a new sky that doesn't look completely out of place. You may need to distort the new sky if the perspective doesn't match, and if the color or contrast is too different to the original scene it simply won't look real.

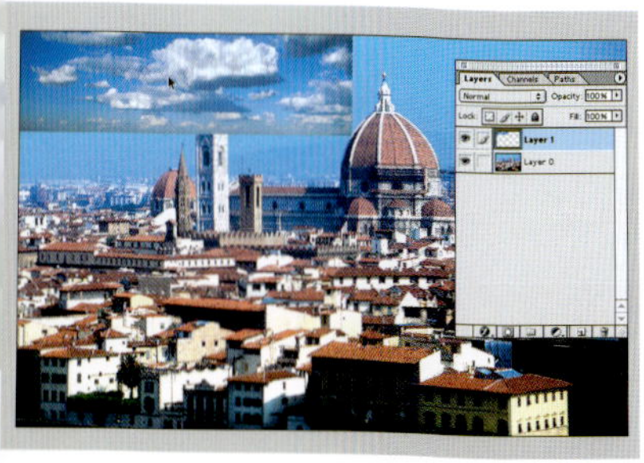

**04** With both documents open select the sky area and drag it onto the original picture using the Move tool.

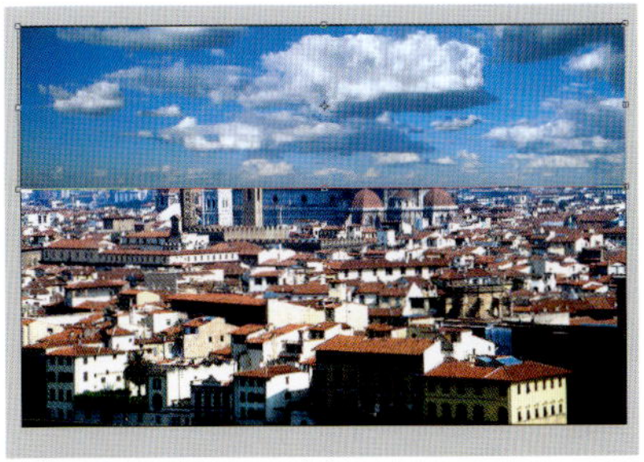

**05** You'll need to rescale the new layer to fit the sky in your original image (in Photoshop, the Edit>Transform command).

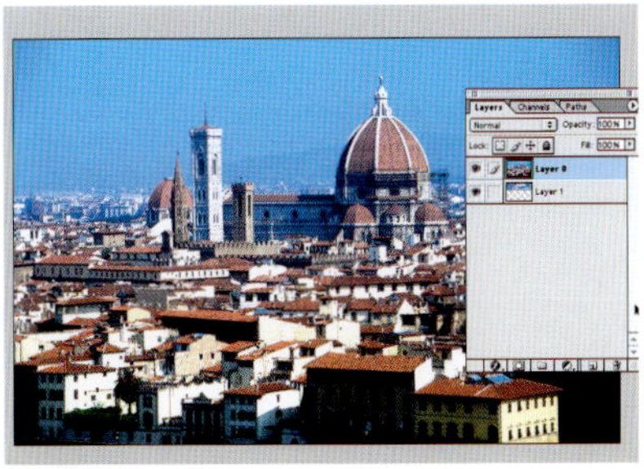

**06** Move the new layer (containing the sky) to underneath the layer containing your original photograph using the Layers palette.

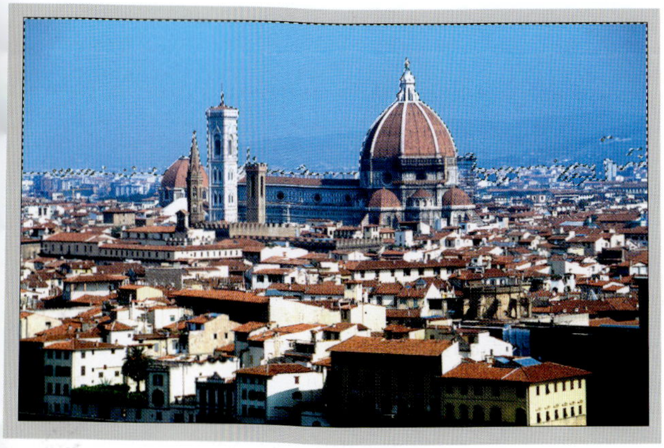

**07** Now to remove the original sky so our new one can show through. Start by making a rough selection - here I've used the Magic Wand on the sky.

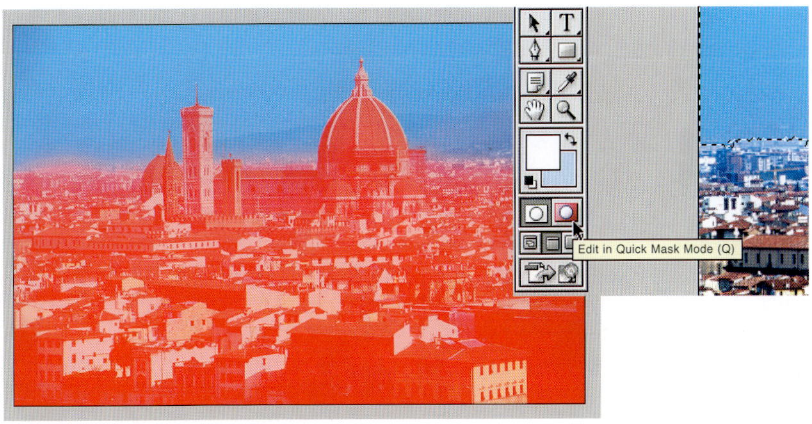


**08** Unless the selection made in step 06 is perfect, switch to Quick Mask mode and use the Paint tools to clean up the edges.

**navigator**
Basic corrections p58
Removing elements p74
Graduated filter p78

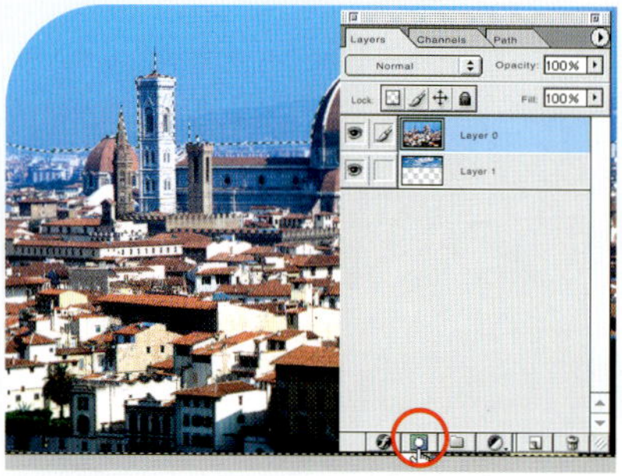

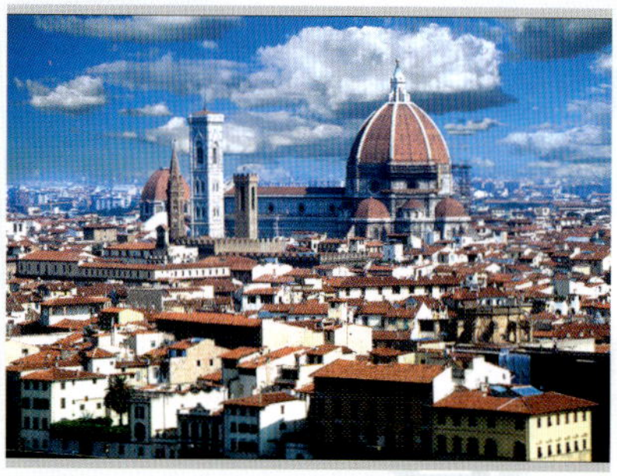

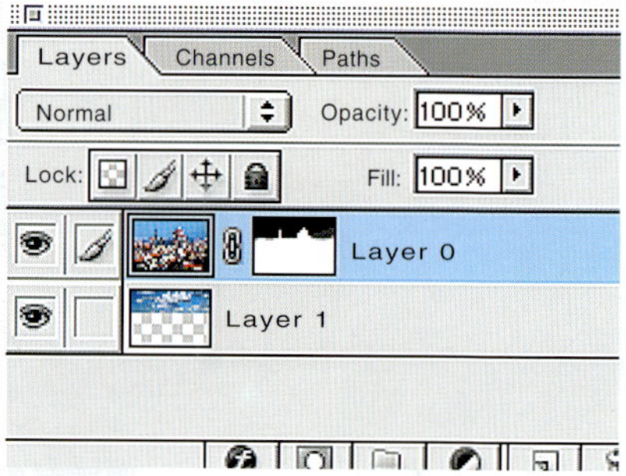


**09** Invert the selection (Select> Inverse) so it surrounds everything but the sky area. Click on the 'Make Layer Mask' icon (circled here in red) at the bottom of the Layers palette or choose 'add layer mask' from the Layers menu.

**10** If you've followed the previous steps correctly you will now see your new sky peeping through the areas masked off in step 09.

**11** The Layers palette now shows the layer mask attached to the layer containing your original photograph.

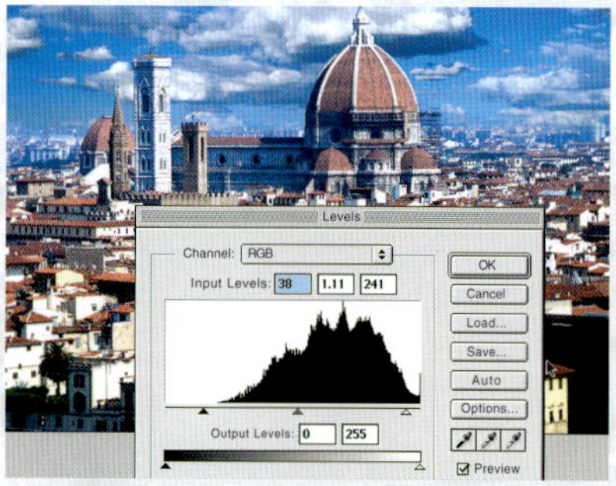


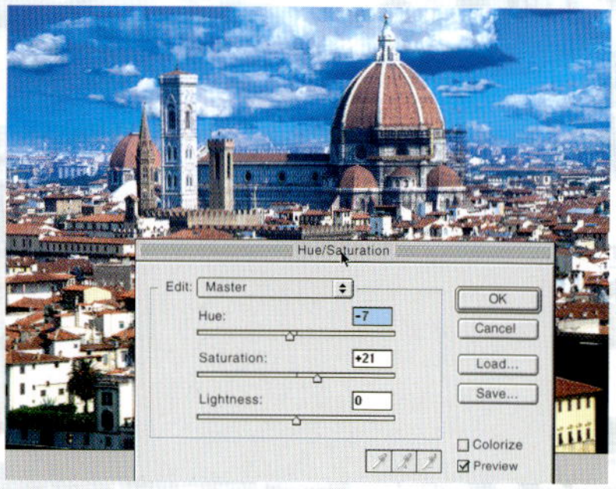


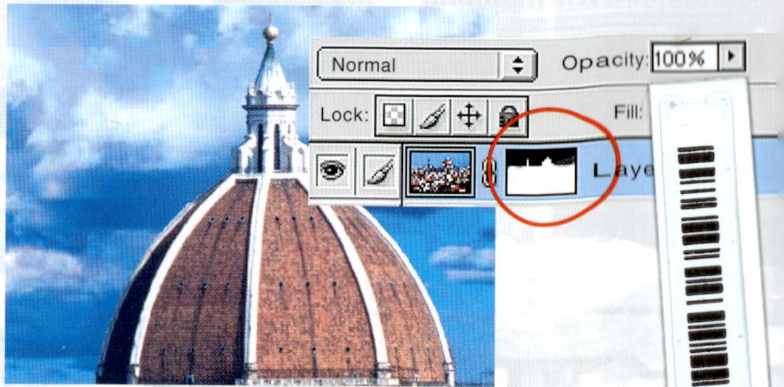




**12** You'll probably need to tweak the sky's levels to match the brightness and contrast of your original scene.

**13** In this case I'm also cooling down the foreground a little to take out the warmth of the original scene, which was shot at a different time of day.

**14** At this stage it makes sense to zoom in and examine the edges of your mask. To edit the mask click on its thumbnail in the Layers palette.

**Photoshop keyboard shortcuts**

| | |
|---|---|
| Magic Wand | W |
| Hue/Saturation | ctrl-H/⌘-H |
| Levels | ctrl-L/⌘-L |
| Swap foreground and background colors | X |

**tools**
Layers
Layer Masks
Hue/Saturation
Levels

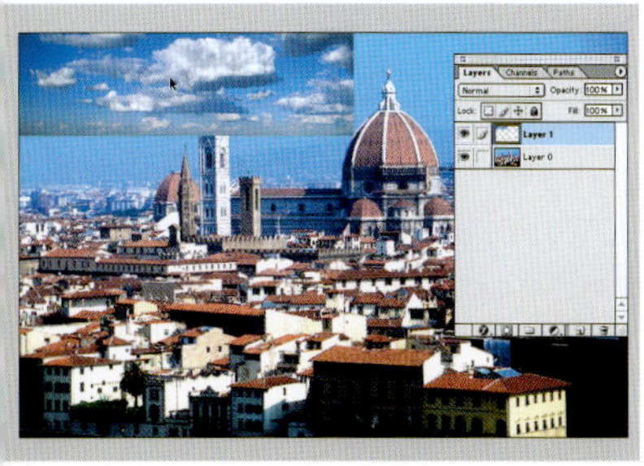

**04** With both documents open select the sky area and drag it onto the original picture using the Move tool.

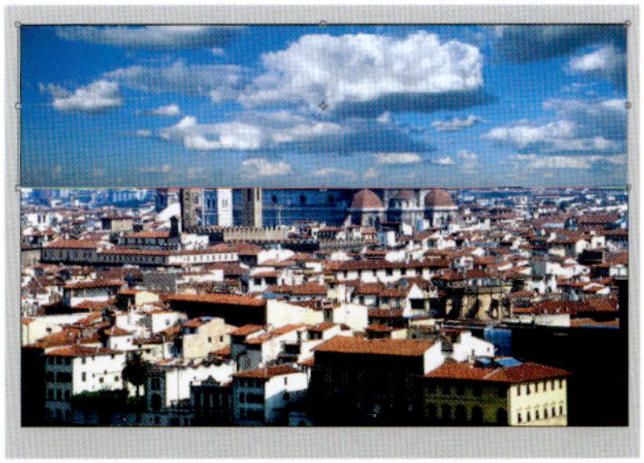

**05** You'll need to rescale the new layer to fit the sky in your original image (in Photoshop, the Edit>Transform command).

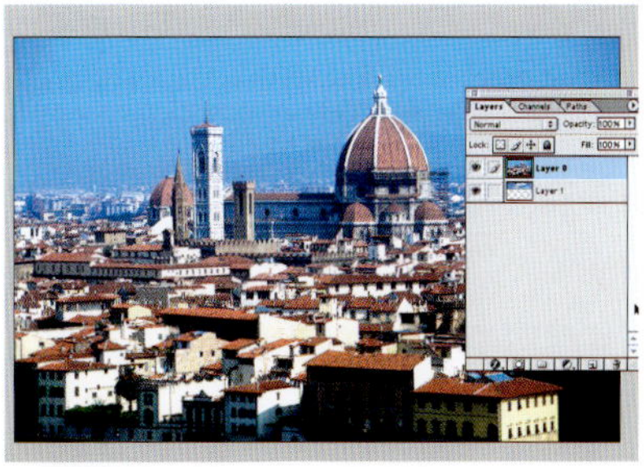

**06** Move the new layer (containing the sky) to underneath the layer containing your original photograph using the Layers palette.

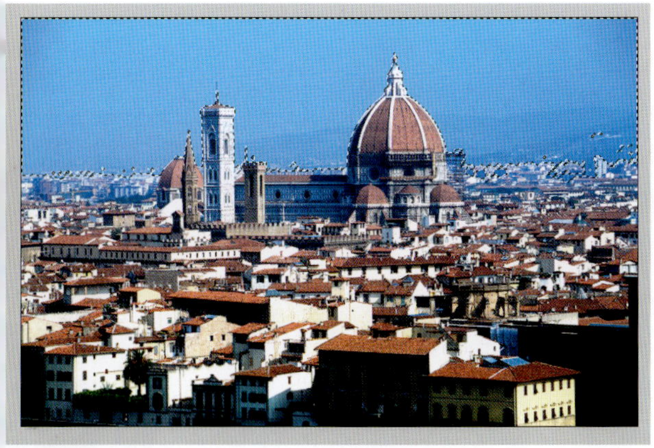

**07** Now to remove the original sky so our new one can show through. Start by making a rough selection - here I've used the Magic Wand on the sky.

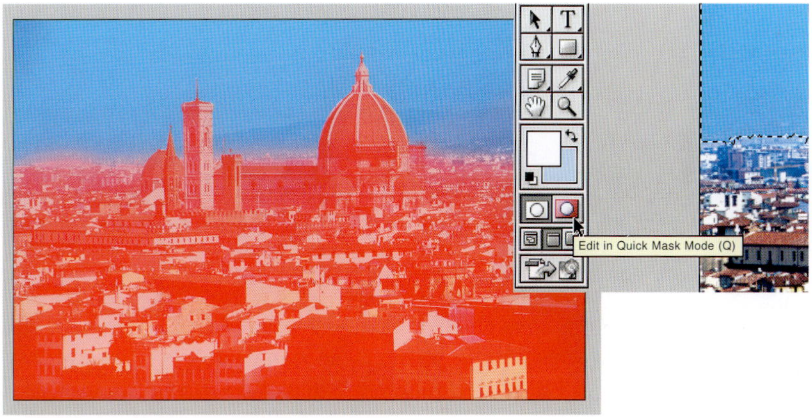


**08** Unless the selection made in step 06 is perfect, switch to Quick Mask mode and use the Paint tools to clean up the edges.

**navigator**


Basic corrections p58
Removing elements p74
Graduated filter p78

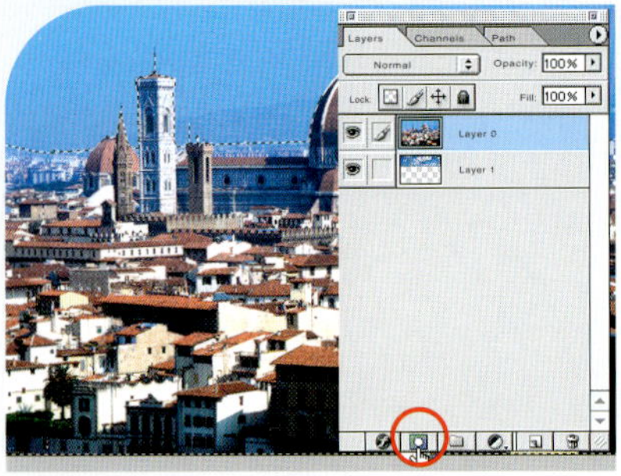

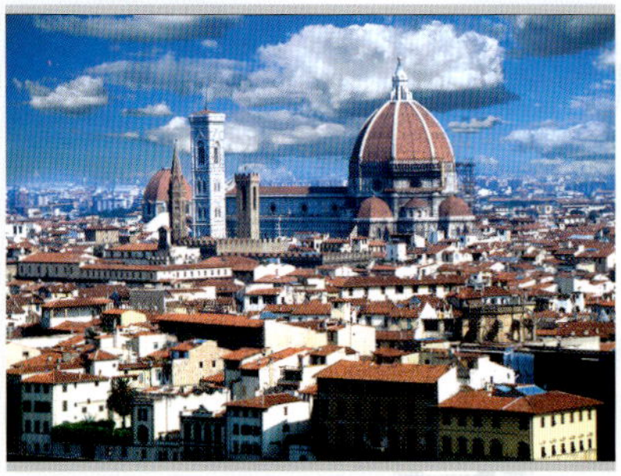

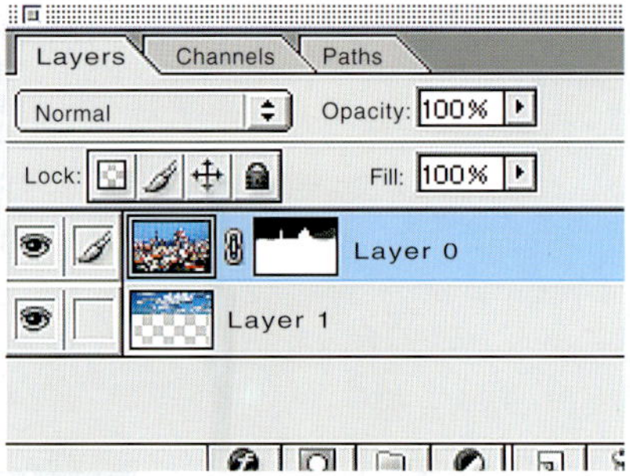


**09** Invert the selection (Select> Inverse) so it surrounds everything but the sky area. Click on the 'Make Layer Mask' icon (circled here in red) at the bottom of the Layers palette or choose 'add layer mask' from the Layers menu.

**10** If you've followed the previous steps correctly you will now see your new sky peeping through the areas masked off in step 09.

**11** The Layers palette now shows the layer mask attached to the layer containing your original photograph.

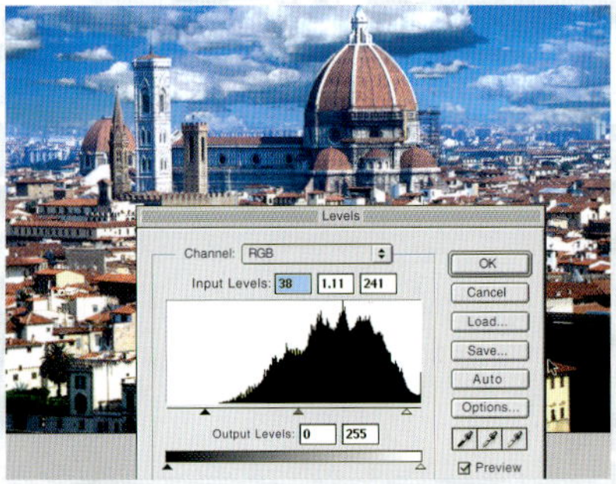


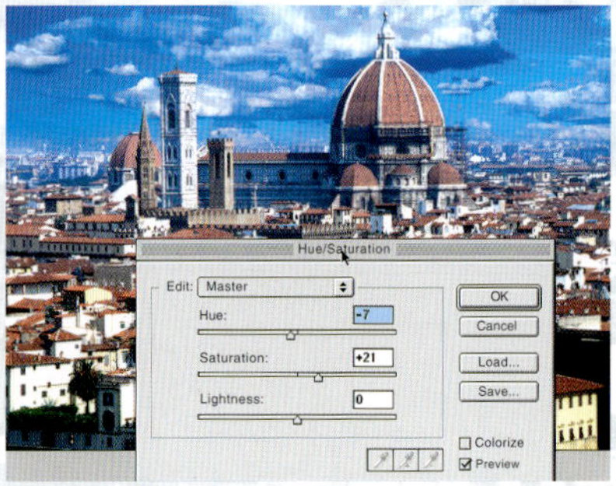


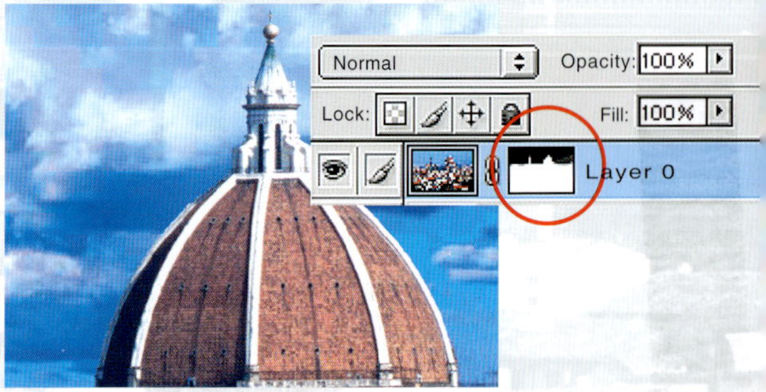


**12** You'll probably need to tweak the sky's levels to match the brightness and contrast of your original scene.

**13** In this case I'm also cooling down the foreground a little to take out the warmth of the original scene, which was shot at a different time of day.

**14** At this stage it makes sense to zoom in and examine the edges of your mask. To edit the mask click on its thumbnail in the Layers palette.

**Photoshop keyboard shortcuts**

| | |
|---|---|
| Magic Wand | W |
| Hue/Saturation | ctrl-H/⌘-H |
| Levels | ctrl-L/⌘-L |
| Swap foreground and background colors | X |

**tools**

Layers
Layer Masks
Hue/Saturation
Levels

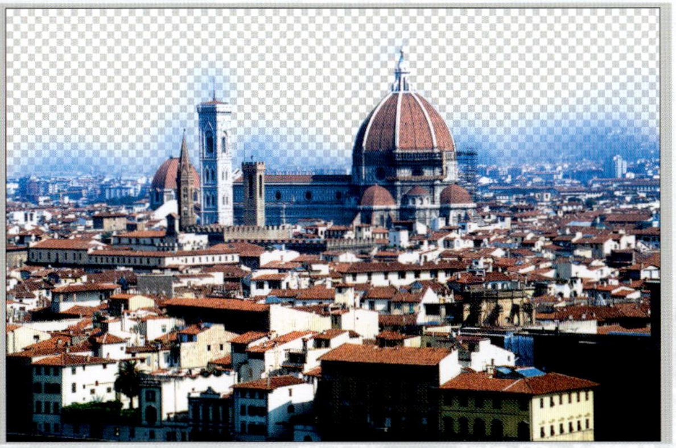

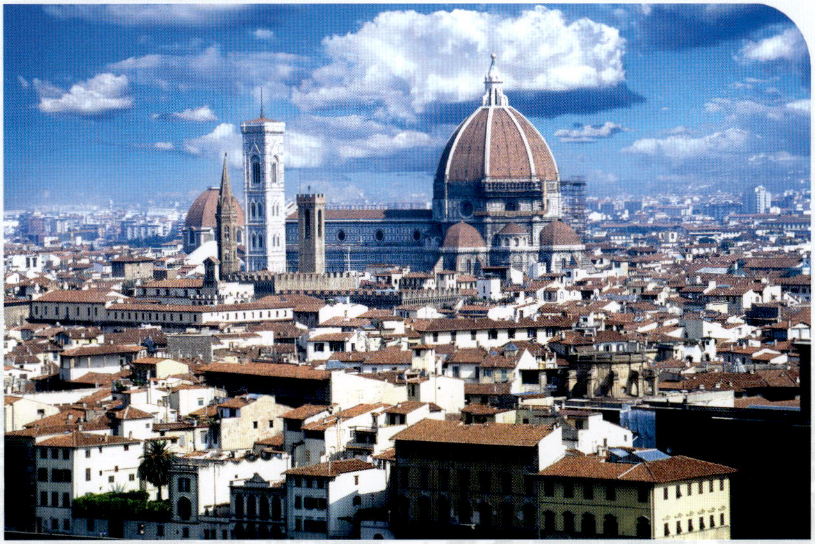

**15** Use the Paint tools on the mask to 'hide the join'. Black hides more of the original scene whilst white reveals more. I've used a large soft-edged brush along the horizon (except the top of the Dome) as the original scene is quite misty.

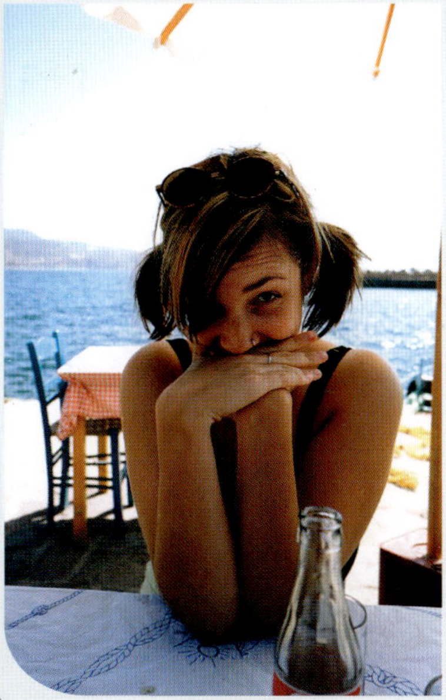

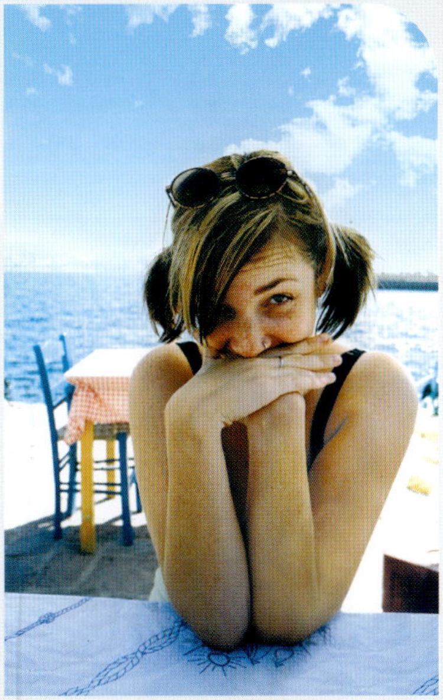

**A complete transformation**

The addition of a new sky has formed part of this complete transformation of a typical holiday snap. Other work involved the removal of the bottle in the foreground (using the techniques described on pages 74-77) and some overall alteration of color and contrast to give a bright, 'pop' feel to the shot.

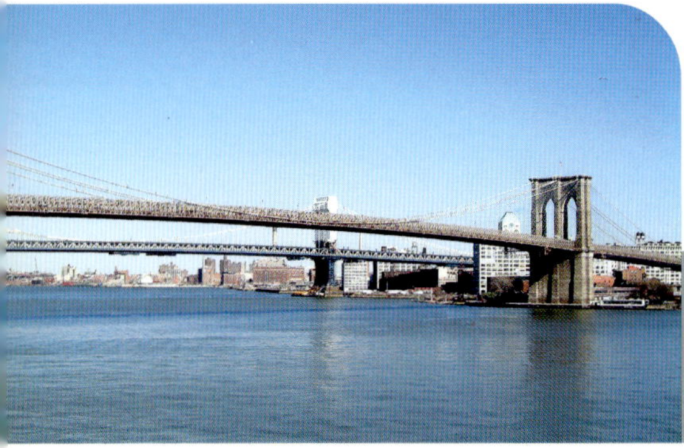

# Stitched panorama

The ability to seamlessly stitch together two or more shots into a single scene means panoramic photography no longer needs specialist equipment. Here's how it's done.

**input**

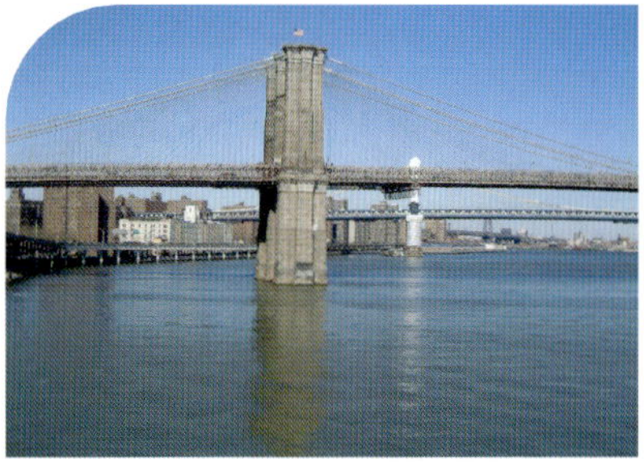

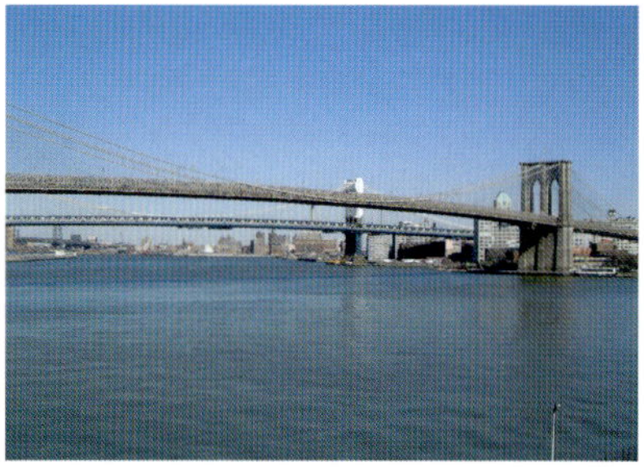

**01** We'll start with these two shots taken of the Brooklyn bridge.

I didn't use a tripod, but rested the camera on a ledge.

**process**

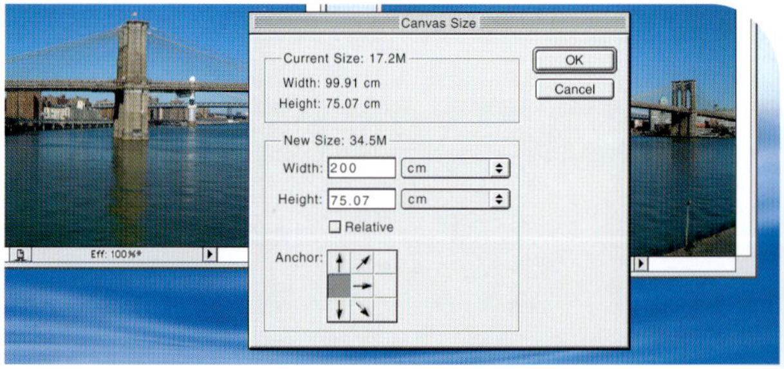


**02** Double the width of the canvas of one of the images.

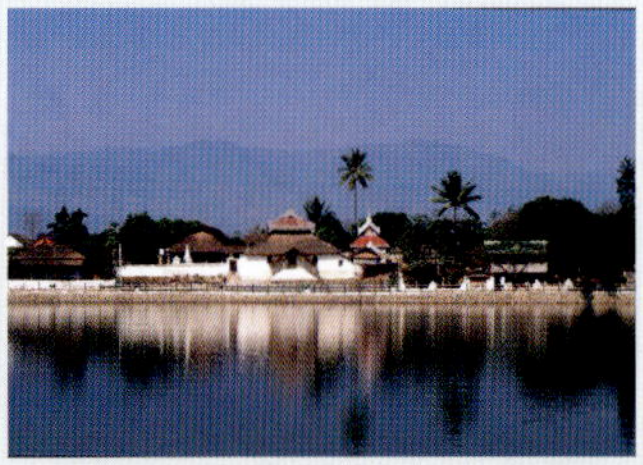

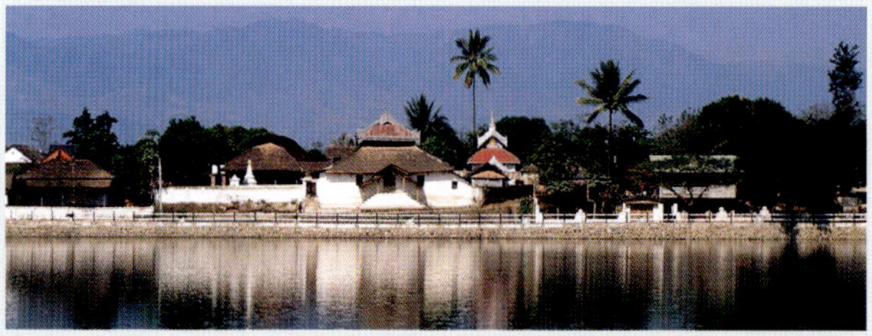

### Panoramic cropping

It is possible to produce very effective panoramic shots with a wide lens and some severe cropping. See page 62 for more cropping ideas.

**technical details**
Fuji FinePix 6800 Zoom digital camera
Wide end of zoom
Adobe Photoshop 6.0

**tools**
Canvas size
Transform tool
Levels
Eraser

**keep in mind**
Although this technique can be very effective, it is rather laborious. Some applications, such as MGI PhotoSuite and Photoshop Elements, have tools that will automate the whole process, cutting the time involved down to minutes. Standalone stitching programs are also available.

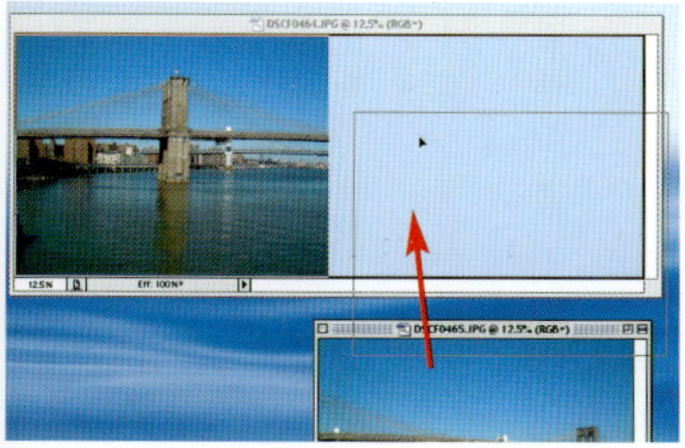

**03** Using the Move tool drag the second image onto the one you increased in size in step 02. It will appear as a new layer.

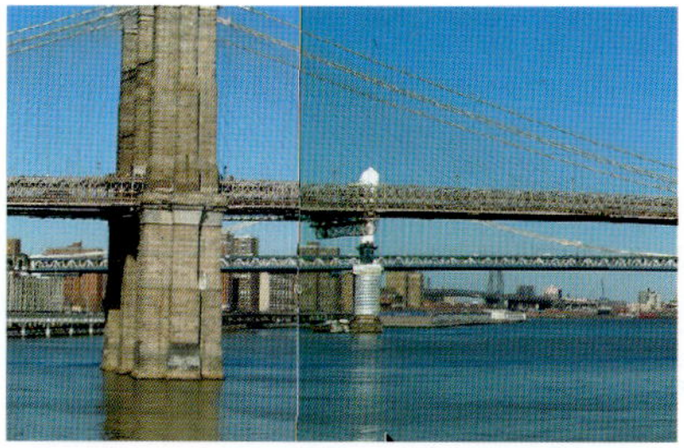

**04** You now need to get the two halves of the picture to line up as closely as possible. This is easier if you allow about 15-20% overlap when you shoot the frames in the first place. Use the Distort and Rotate tools to make the two halves match as well as you can from top to bottom. This bit can take some time!

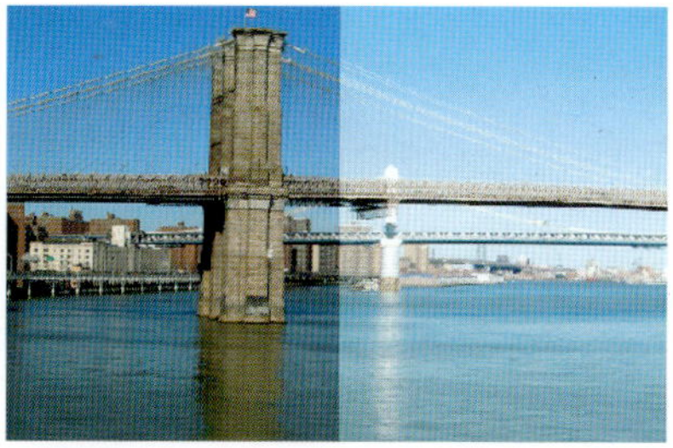

**05** It can help to temporarily switch the blend mode of the upper layer (the one you are moving around) to 'Screen'. You will be able to see the areas of overlap more clearly. Switching to 'Difference' mode, incidentally, can be useful with closely matched pictures (it turns black when the alignment is perfect). Inevitably, no amount of layer transformations or nudging will produce a seamless join. Alter the color and contrast of the individual layers to ensure a perfect match.

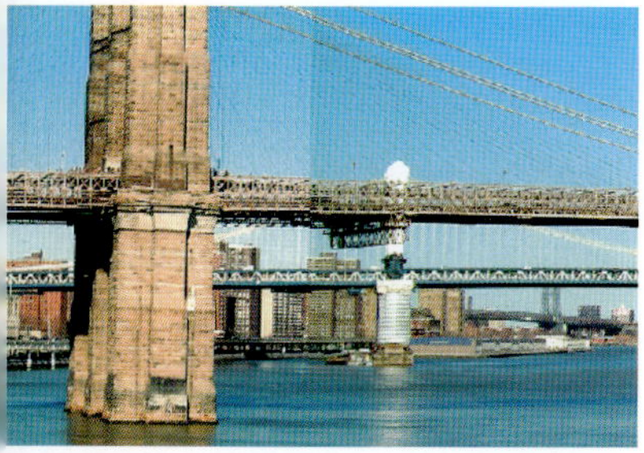

**06** Finally, use the Eraser tool with a large, soft brush and around 50% opacity and remove the hard edge of the upper layer (where it overlaps) to smooth the join. You may also need to do a little cloning work to hide any problem areas.

## output

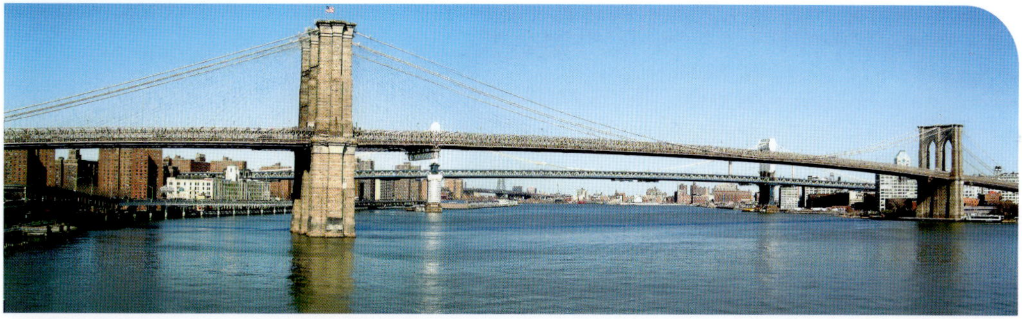

**navigator**



**tips for shooting for panoramas**

The key is keeping the camera at exactly the same angle for each shot to avoid the horizon 'jumping' at each join. The safest way to ensure this is to use a tripod (ideally with a spirit level attached), but resting the camera on a secure surface can be enough for a two-shot stitch. Unless you have specialist stitching software, don't use a very wide-angle lens as the distortion is simply too difficult to fix using this technique.

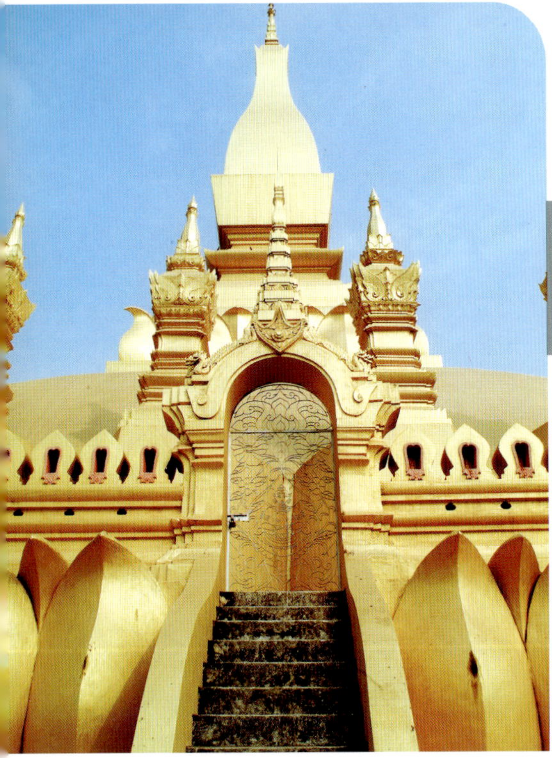

# Converging verticals

Shoot anything tall with a wide lens and – unless you have some pretty specialised equipment – you'll find the verticals converging towards the top of the frame. Here's how we fix it.

process

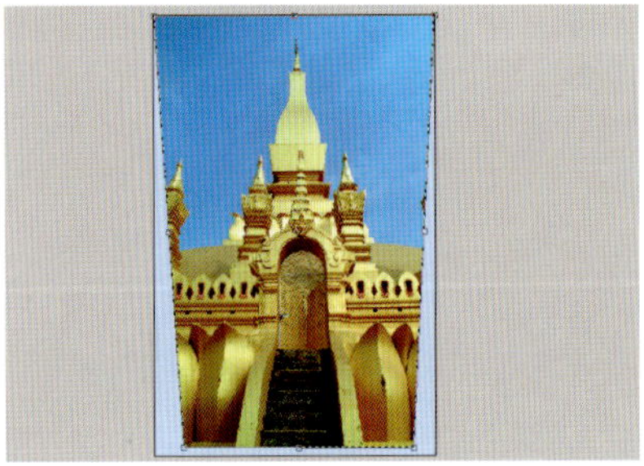

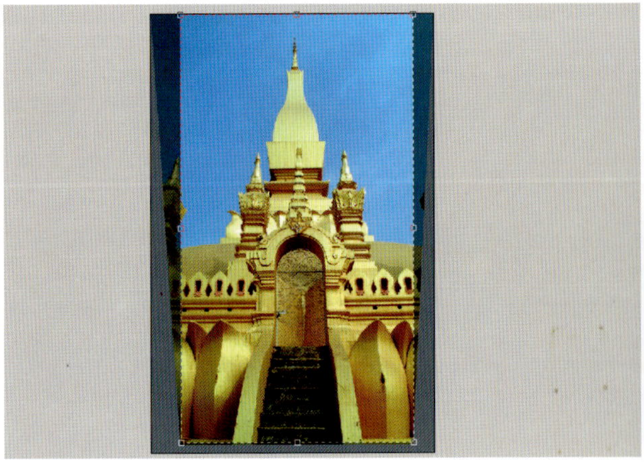

input

**01** This shot of a temple is typical of the kind of alarming convergence of verticals you find whenever you tilt the camera upwards to shoot a tall building. Although the phenomenon can be used to great effect, in this case I'd rather the picture showed a little less distortion. The first step is to correct the brightness, contrast and sharpness.

**02** Select the entire image (Select>Select All) and use the Free Transform (Edit>Free Transform) command to drag in the bottom corners of the image as shown above. In Photoshop you need to hold down the control key (apple key on a Mac) as you click and drag to move individual 'handles' at the corners.

**03** Once you are happy that the image looks as distortion-free as you want, use the crop tool to remove the triangles that appeared in the bottom left- and right-hand corners in step 02.

**technical details**
Fujifilm S1 Pro digital SLR
24-70mm Sigma lens
Adobe Photoshop 6.0

**tools**
Select All
Free Transform
Crop tool
Cloning

**keep in mind**
You always lose some of the left- and right-hand edge of the picture when using this technique so, if possible, leave a little extra around your subject when you shoot in the first place; don't crop too closely.

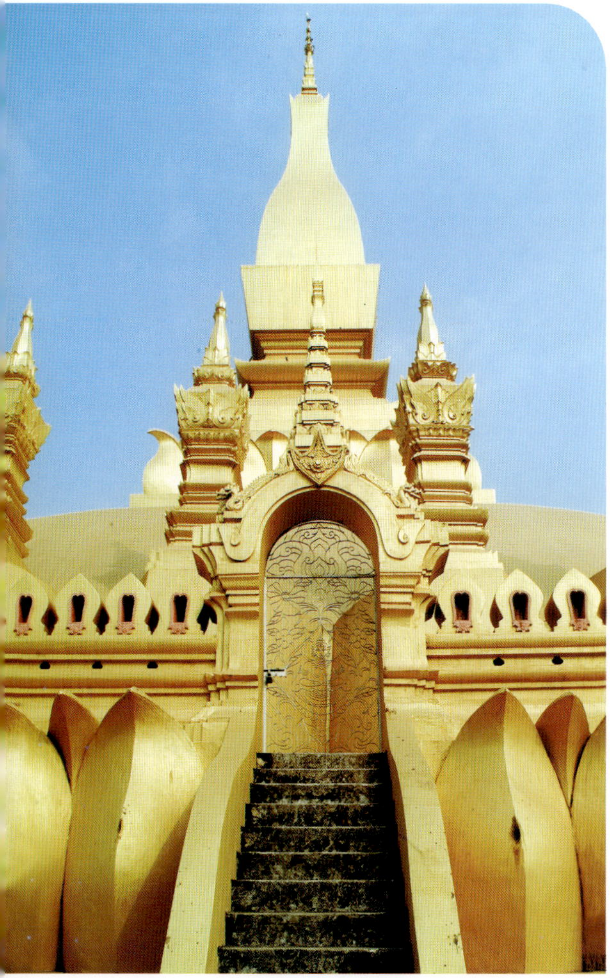

**04** In this example I minimized the amount of the picture I had to crop out by filling in the missing areas using the cloning techniques described on pages 74-77.

### Barrel distortion tips

Barrel distortion – the other big problem faced by photographers using very wide lenses – is pretty difficult to remove effectively. There is, however, one quick technique that is always worth a try.

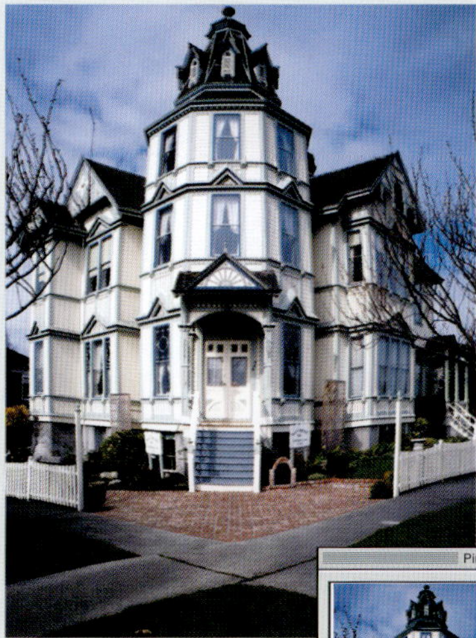

**The original image looks as though it is reflected in the back of a spoon, so bad is the barrel distortion. Run Photoshop's Pinch filter (found under the Filter> Distort menu).**

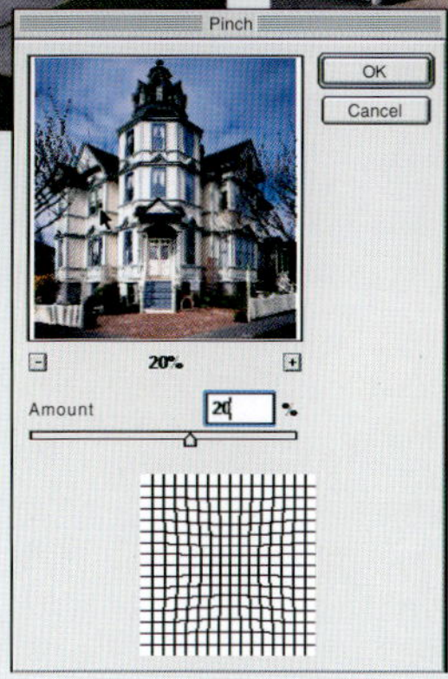


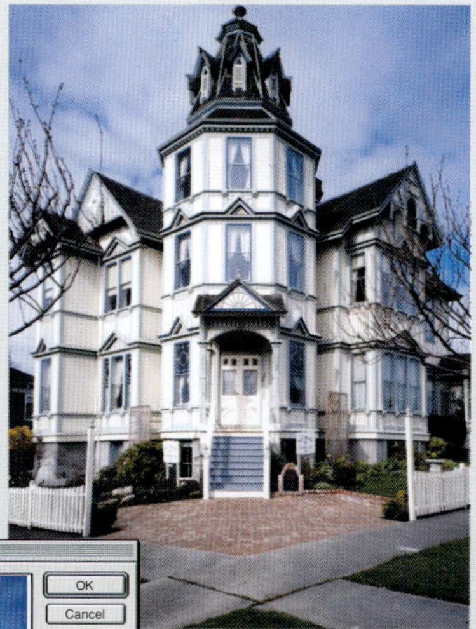

**The success of this technique is slightly unpredictable, but on occasion, as here,a little experimentation with the Pinch settings produces a remarkably good result.**

**navigator**
Basic corrections p58
Cloning tips p59
Cropping and rotating p62

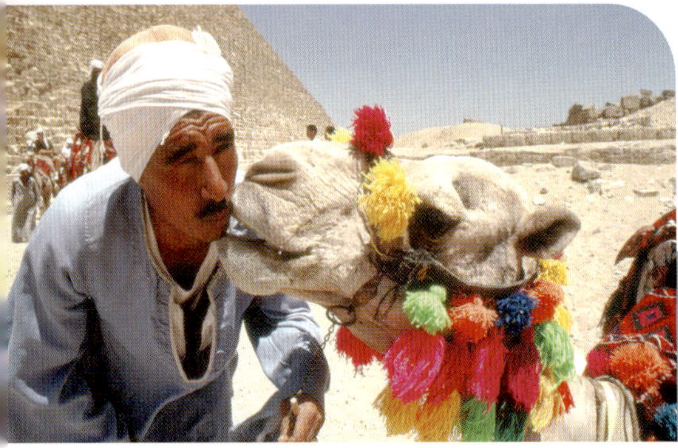

# Fisheye effect

**In the last project we looked at removing wide-angle distortions. Now we'll go the other way to recreate the ultimate wide-angle shot – the fisheye – and all without any expensive optics!**

## process

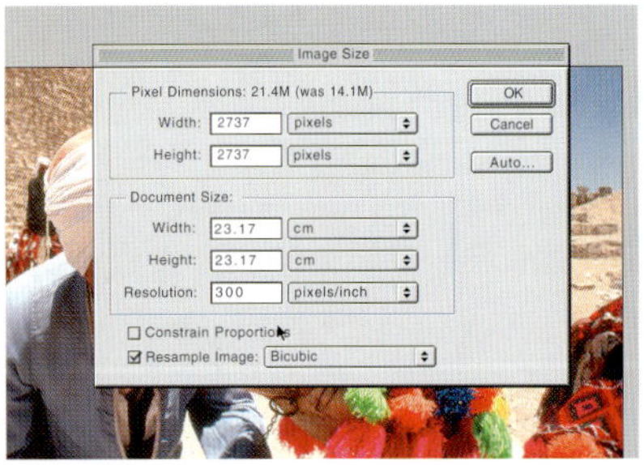


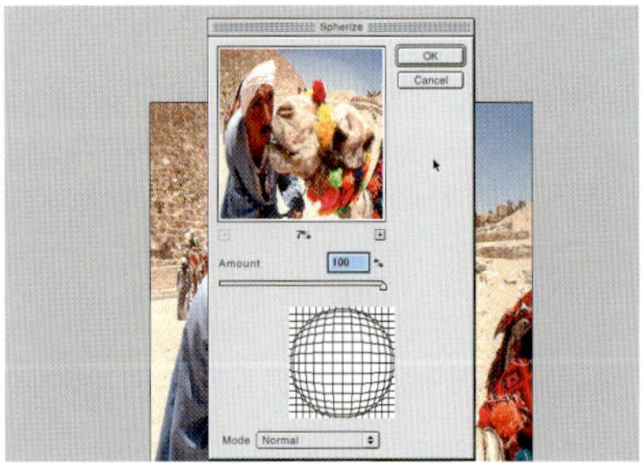


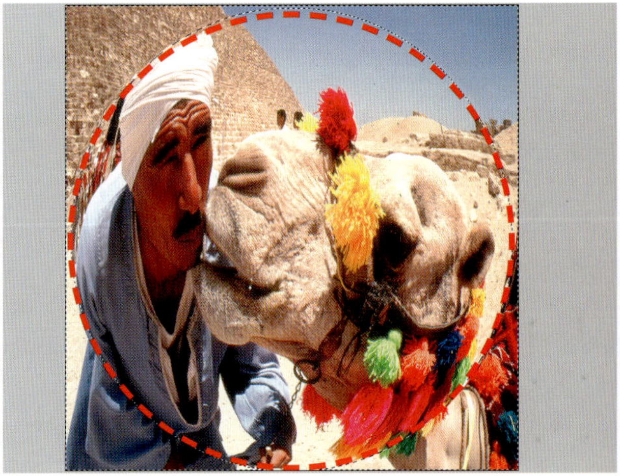

**01** You should ideally start with a wide-angle shot where the main subject is as near to the lens and to the centre of the frame as possible. If your image is rectangular (which most are), use the Image Size command to squash it into a square. Turn off the Constrain Proportions option (circled here in red) and change the longer dimension (in this case the width) to match the shorter one (the height).

**02** Select the entire image and choose the Spherize filter (from the Filter>Distortions menu). Set the amount to 100%, choose Normal as the mode and click on OK.

**03** You now need to make a circular selection as shown above in red. Hold down the shift key to ensure the Eleptical Marquee tool produces a perfect circle and the Transform Selection option to make it fit the square exactly.



**technical details**
Canon A1 SLR
24mm Canon lens
Kodachrome 64
Adobe Photoshop 6.0

**tools**
Image Size
Spherize filter
Circular Marquee
Lens Flare filter

**keep in mind**
The best subjects for the fisheye treatment are those that already exhibit characteristic wide-angle distortions.

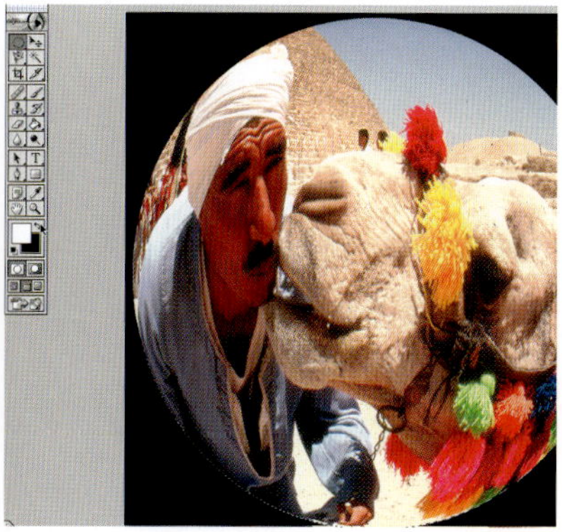

**04** Make sure your background color is black (press D, then X) and hit the Delete key.

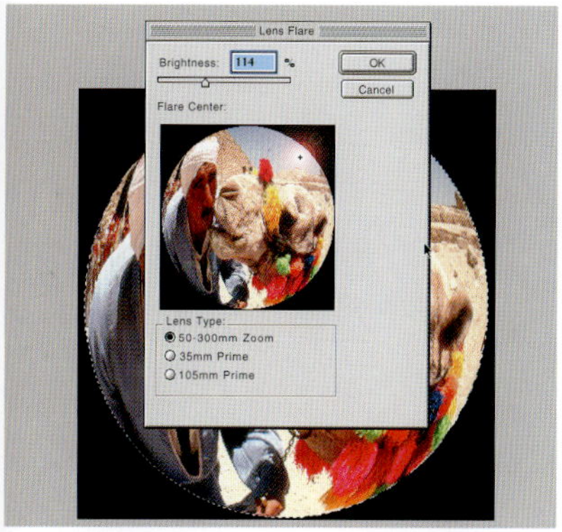


**05** For an added touch of realism, invert the selection again and use the Filter>Render>Lens Flare command to add some lens flare.

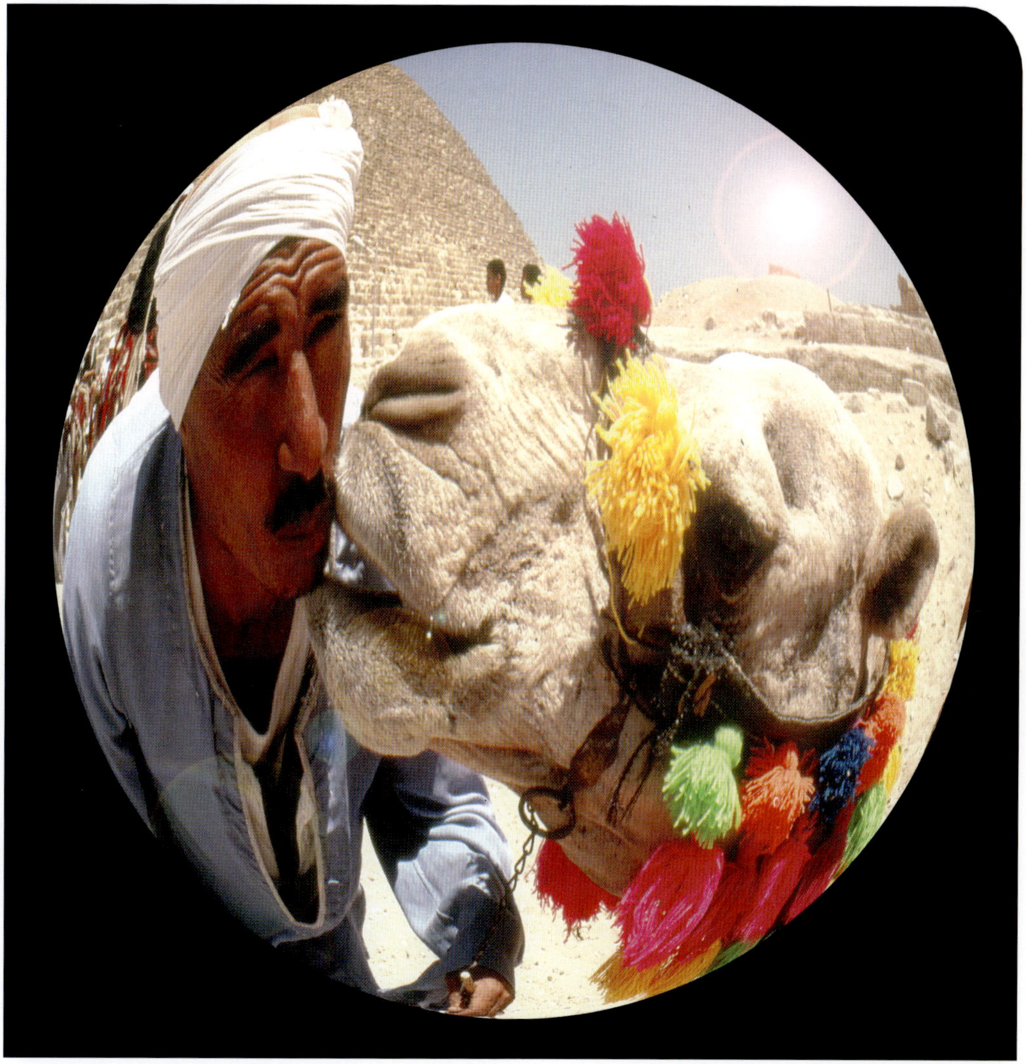

**navigator**
Converging verticals p86
Basic corrections p58
The right lens p36

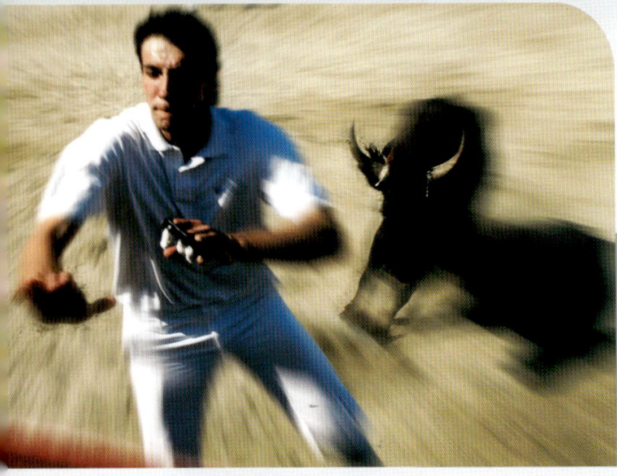

# Zoom blur

Photographers regularly allow a certain amount of motion blur into their pictures in order to add some dynamism. One technique – zooming the lens during exposure – is difficult to master in-camera, but very easy in software.

## input

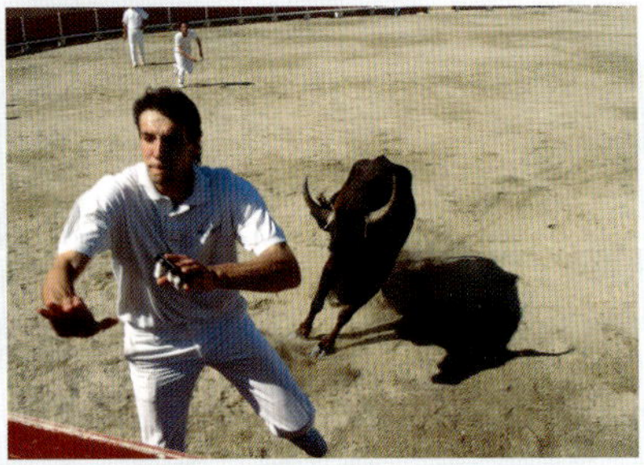

**01** This technique is best suited to shots such as this one, where the subject is moving directly towards the viewer. Perform any necessary color, contrast and sharpening corrections before you move on to the next step.

## process

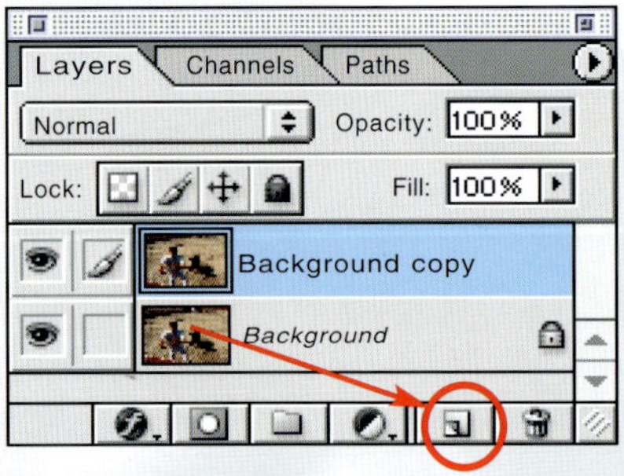


**02** As with all major manipulations it is sensible to work on a copy of your image. In this case we need a duplicate of the image in a new layer too. In Photoshop the quickest way to duplicate a layer is via the Layers palette. Simply drag the Layer thumbnail to the 'New Layer' icon (circled here in red) to create a duplicate.

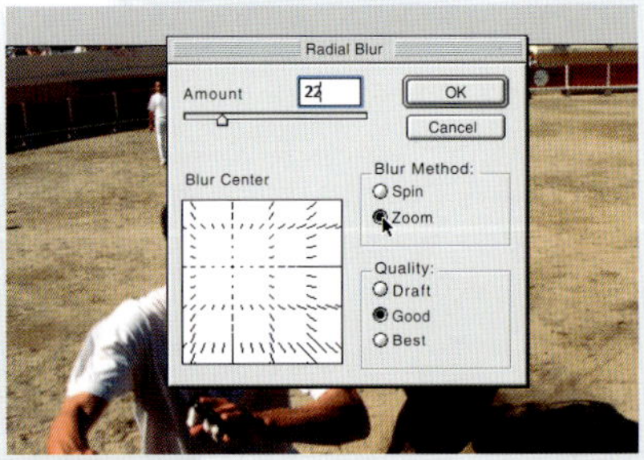


**03** With the new (upper) layer active choose the Radial Blur filter from the Filter>Blur menu. In the Blur Method section choose Zoom, and click and drag the blur centre to the main subject of your shot – in this case the bullfighter to the left of centre. Set the amount to about 25% and click on OK. If the zoom effect is too weak or strong simply undo and try another amount setting.

**technical details**
Nikon F4
35-70mm f2.8 Nikkor
Fujichrome 100
Adobe Photoshop 7.0

**tools**
Layers
Zoom Blur filter
Layer Mask

**keep in mind**
You can use this type of technique to give the impression of the camera travelling forwards at speed – through a tunnel or along a freeway for example.

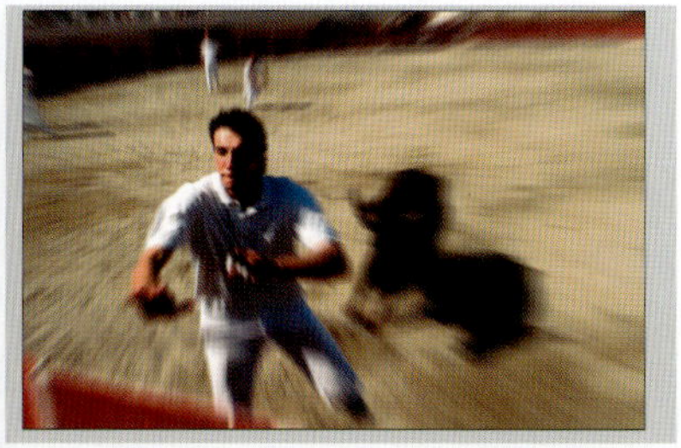

**04** If you have placed the zoom centre in the right place, you should see the effect as shown above.

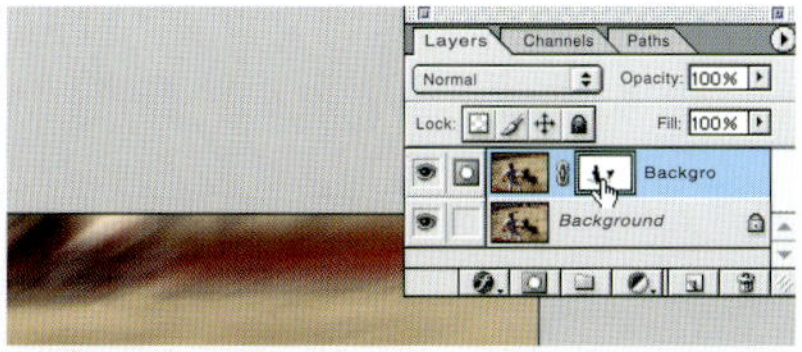


**05** I wanted to remove the effect from some areas of the scene so that more of the fighter and bull were unaffected. Add a Layer Mask to the upper (blurred) layer and paint away the effect with a soft brush and black paint.

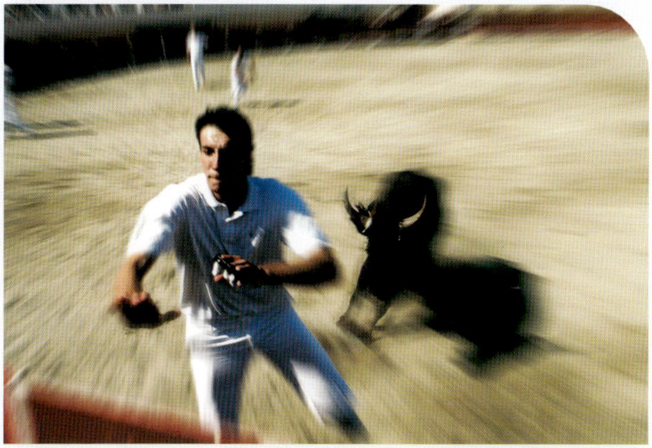

### Blurring tips

**(Below) Using a Gaussian Blur duplicate layer and a Layer Mask you can quickly reduce the depth of field in an image in order to add emphasis to the main subject.**

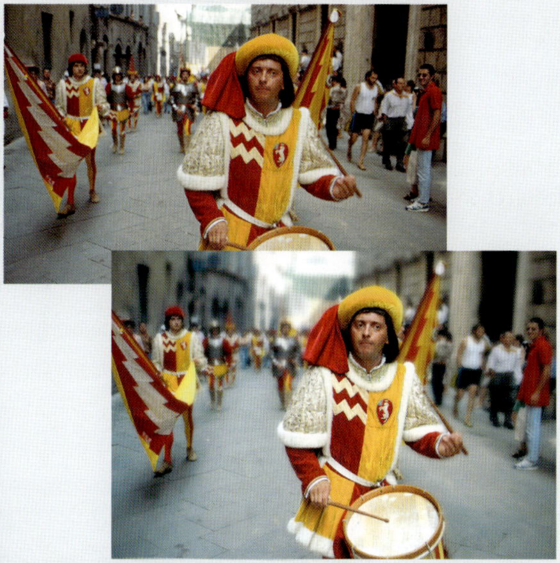

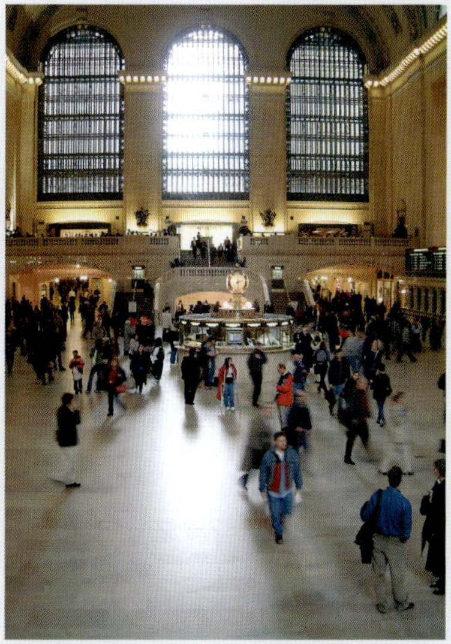

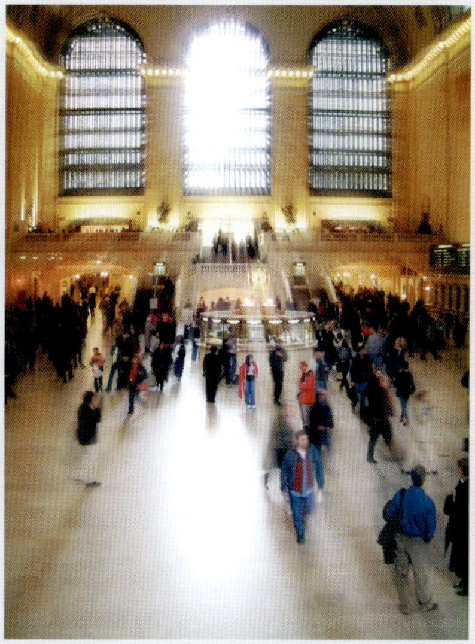

**(Above) Add blur to a duplicate layer and experiment with different layer blending modes for subtle, yet dramatic effects. Here the Zoom Blur filter has been used on a duplicate layer set to Screen mode, giving the impression of light flooding into New York's Grand Central Station.**

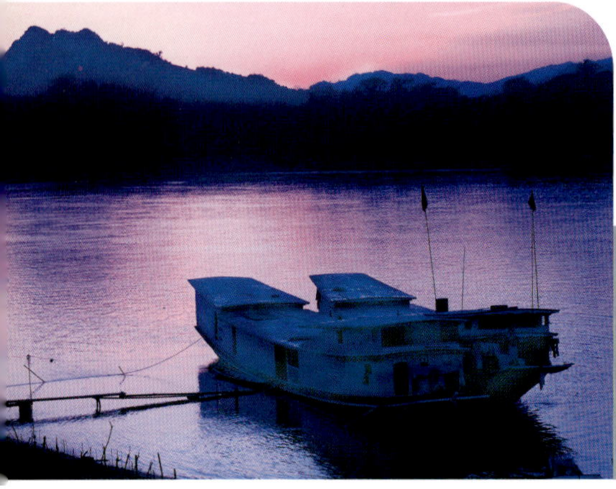

# Playing with color

Most of the work we've done so far with color has been concerned with reality; getting as natural and neutral a result as possible. With the powerful tools at our disposal in the digital darkroom, however, we should always look to experiment with 'breaking the rules'.

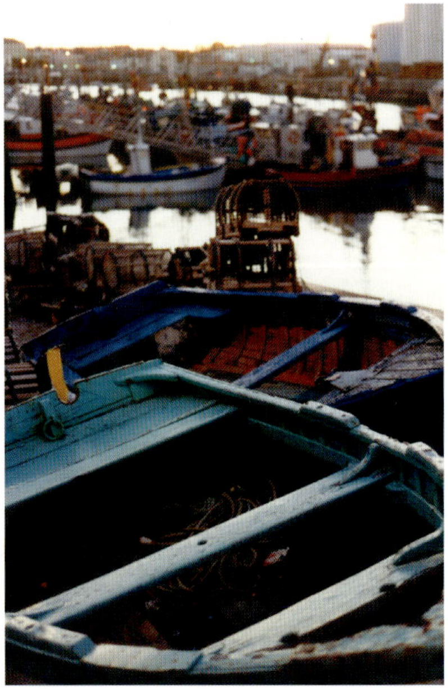

**01** There's nothing wrong with this shot – it simply lacks punch.

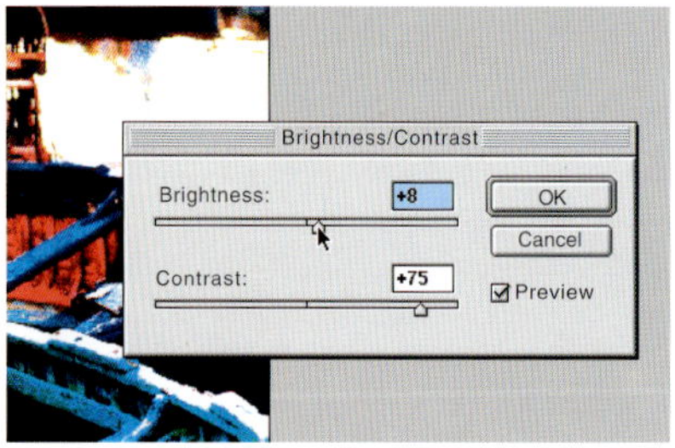


**02** The most basic color alterations are Brightness and Contrast. By dragging the Contrast slider way over to the right (massively increasing contrast) we can transform the image in a second. By removing virtually all midtones we end up with a vivid, graphic picture. Note that in this case the brightness was also edged up slightly – use the on-screen preview to judge the effect of your changes and, remember, there is no right or wrong as long as you are happy with the result.

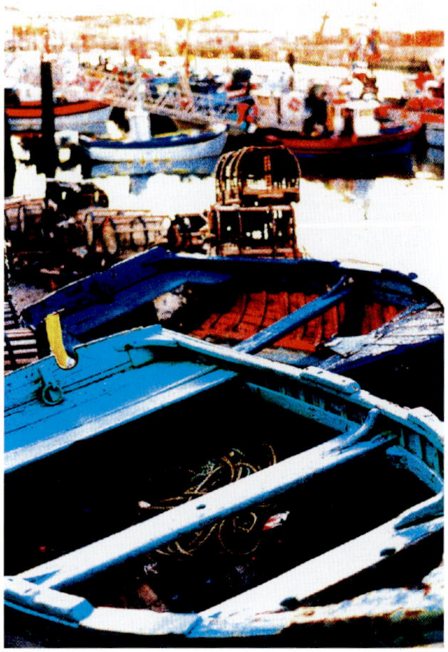

**03** Et voilà : a radically different interpretation of the scene!

**technical details**
Nikon F301 + 50mm f1.8 lens
Kodacolor print film
Microtek ScanMaker 8700
Adobe Photoshop Elements

**tools**
Brightness and Contrast
Levels
Curves

**keep in mind**
The key to learning how to work creatively with color is to experiment and try everything once; you could be surprised at the results you get.

## Using Levels for color adjustment

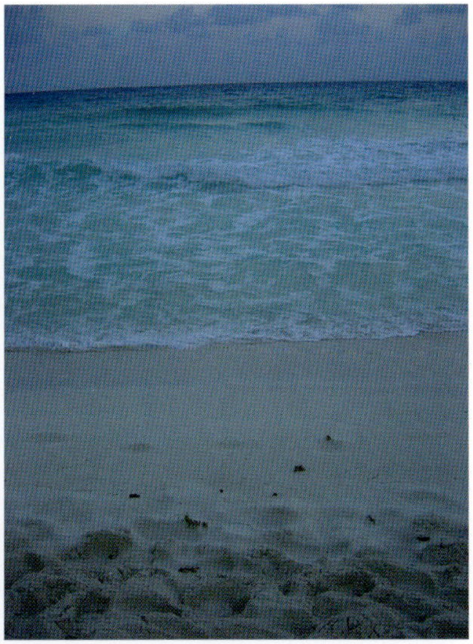

**01** We'll start with this digital camera shot of a beach at dusk in Cancun, Mexico.

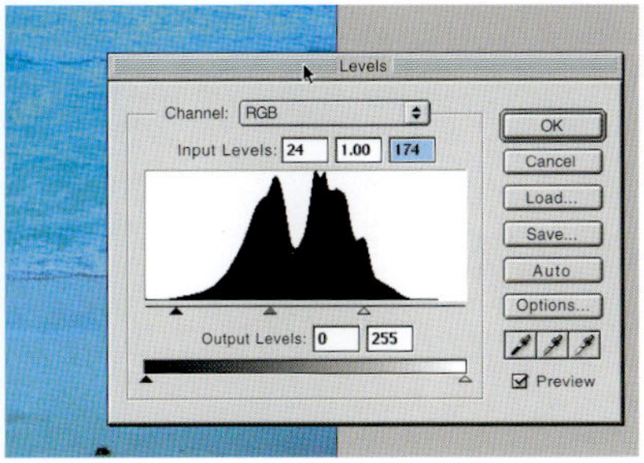


**02** First step is to increase the contrast using the Levels sliders.

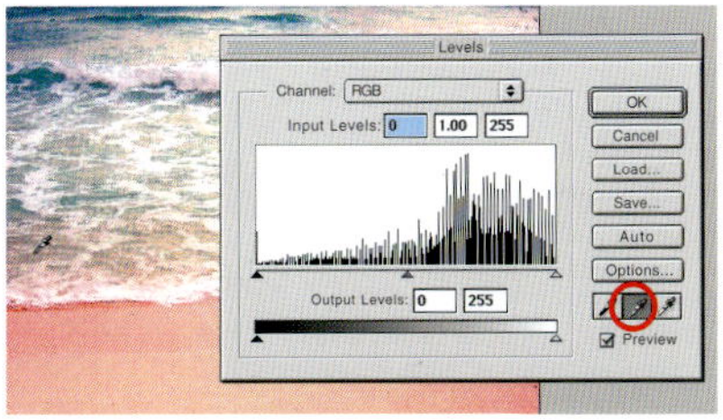


**03** Click on the grey eyedropper (circled in red) and around the image to set the grey point: the image colors change dramatically as you do.

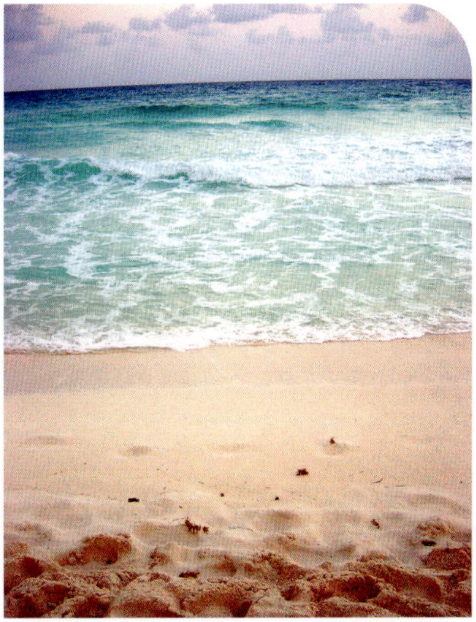

**04** Keep experimenting, clicking in different areas of the image until you find an overall color you like.

## Throwing a curve

By radically altering the curve (see page 66 for details of the Curves command) you can make dramatic color changes. The 'U' shape used here produces a pseudo-solarized effect.

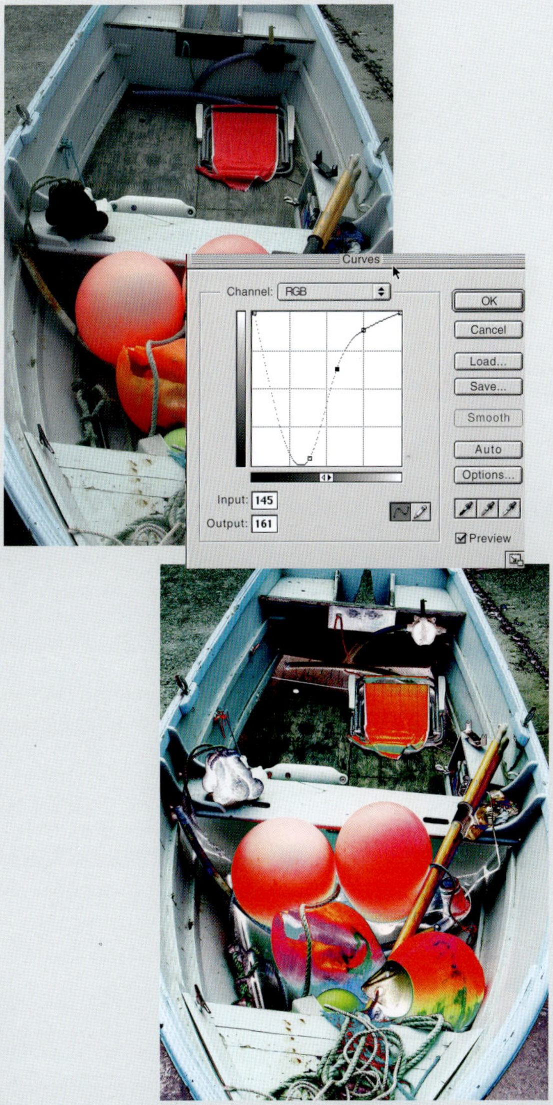


**navigator**
Using levels p64
Using curves p66
Hue and Saturation p94

## Hue and Saturation

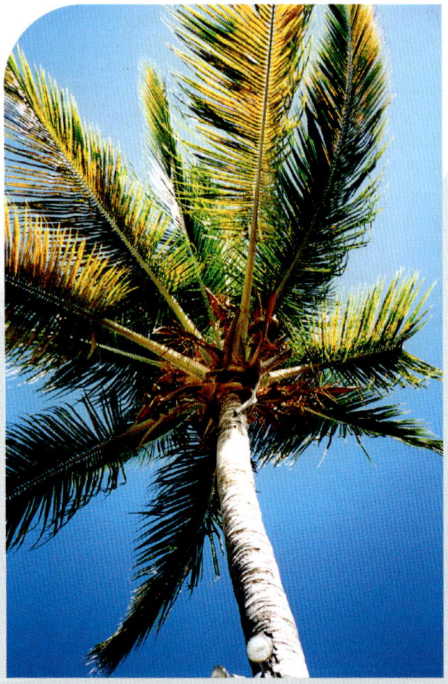

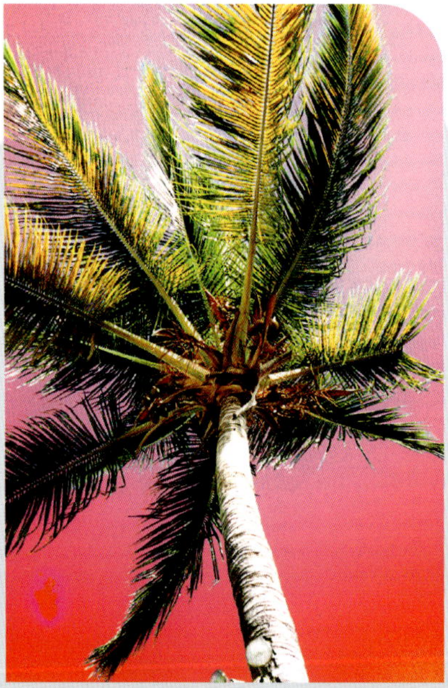

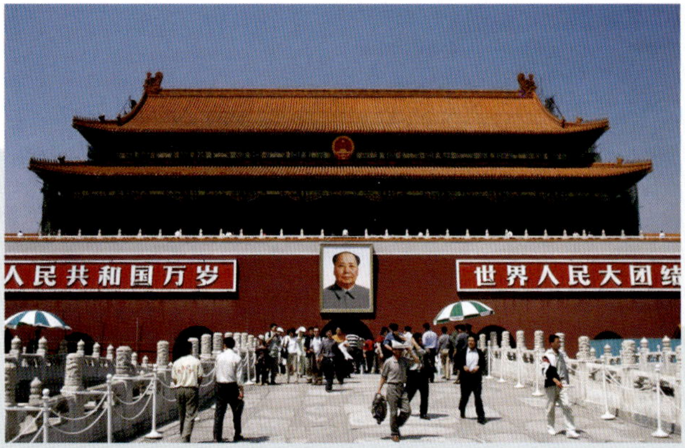


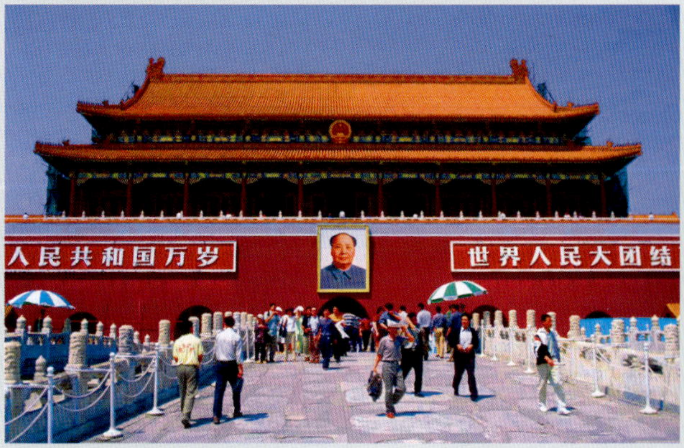


**01** Hue and Saturation give very powerful control over the overall color of an image. Start by playing with the Hue and Saturation sliders.

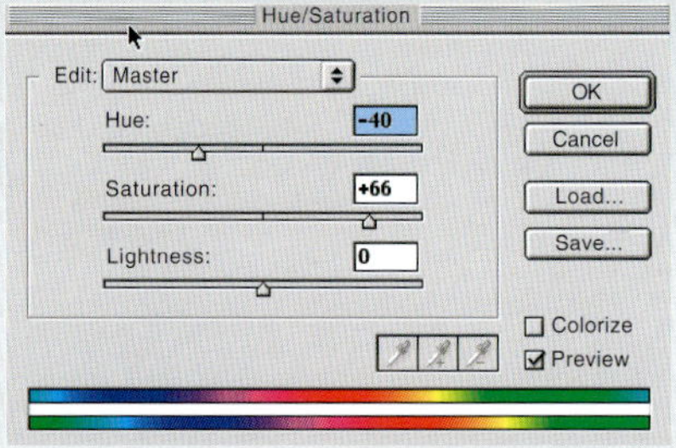


**02** Most applications allow you to alter the Hue and Saturation settings for specific colors. In the example above the Hue of the blues and Cyans was shifted and the Saturation increased. To restrict the effect to certain colors click on the Edit drop-down menu at the top of the Hue/Saturation dialog box.

**03** This shot, taken in China, has taken on the look of a 'hyperreal' 1950s postcard after a heavy increase in the Saturation.

**Photoshop keyboard shortcuts**

| | |
|---|---|
| Hue/Saturation | ctrl-H/⌘-H |
| Levels | ctrl-L/⌘-L |
| Color Balance | ctrl-B/⌘-B |
| Curves | ctrl-M/⌘-M |

**keep in mind**
It is sometimes more effective to remove the color from an image and then add a tone than to radically alter the original colors. See page 100 for toning techniques.

## Color balance

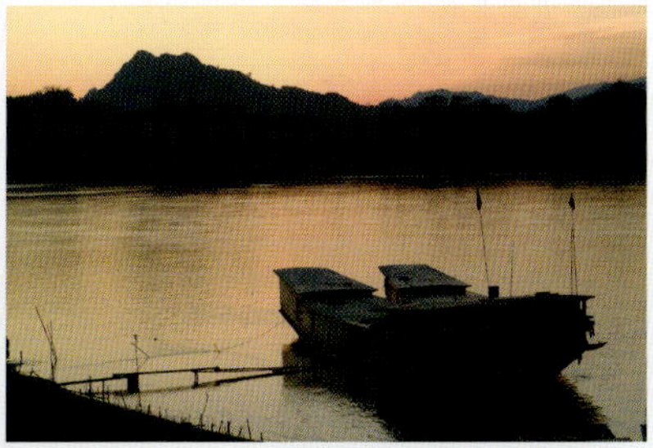

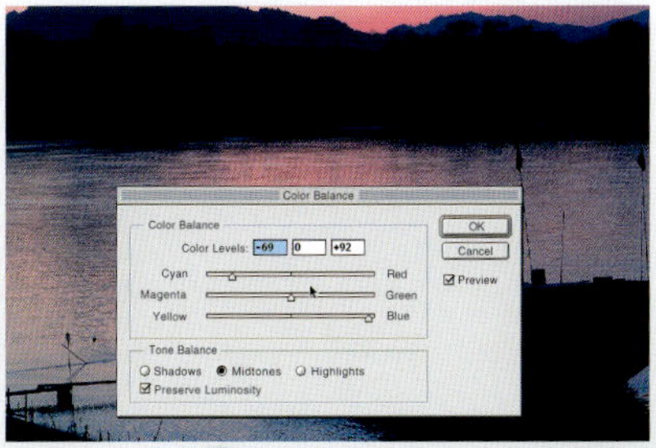


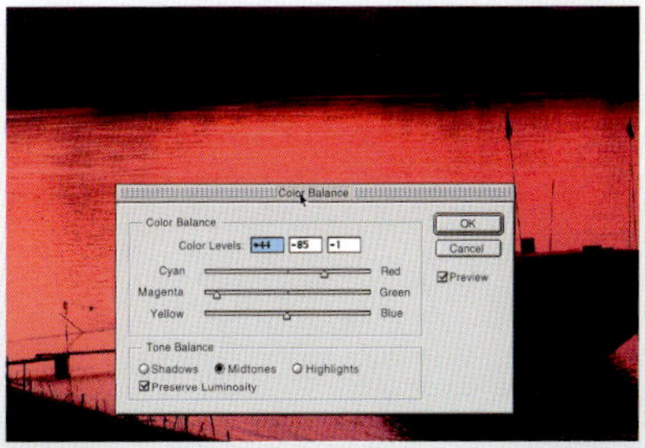


**01** Sunsets are often virtually monochrome, and lend themselves very well to radical color shifts; after all, sunset and sunrise skies come in a wide variety of colors.

**02** The most dramatic effects usually come about if you click on the Midtones option in the Tone Balance section. Just play with the sliders using the on-screen preview.

**03** An image like this one can take even extreme color changes without looking totally unnatural .

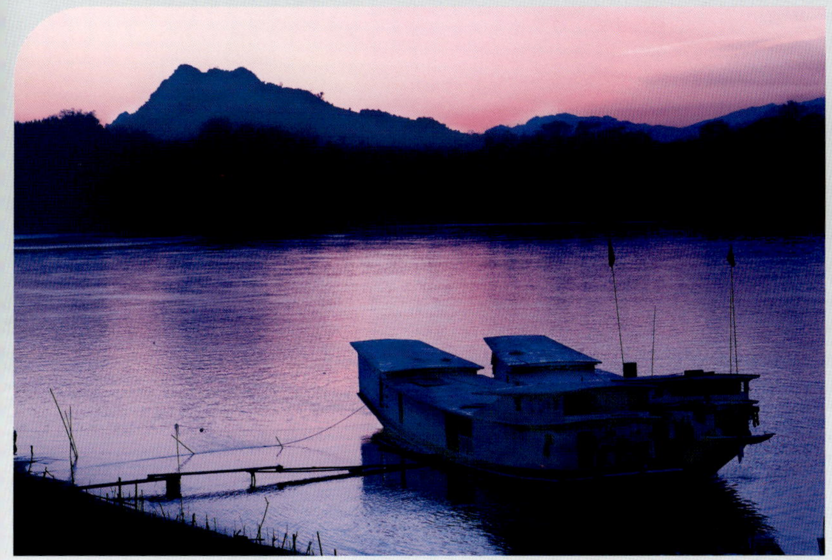

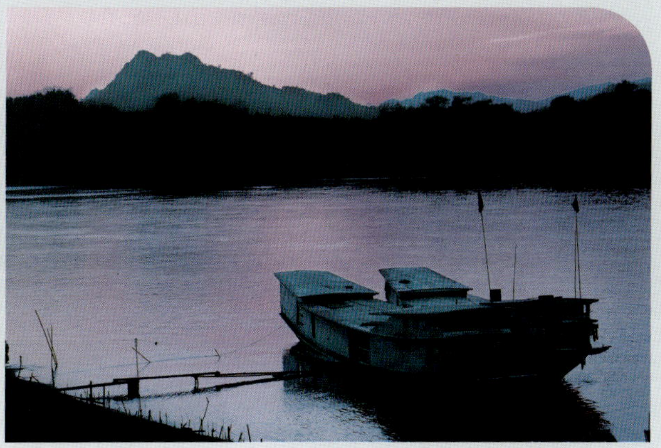

**04** The final image, above, is the result of some judicious dodging and burning of the initial result of the settings shown in step 02 (reproduced on the left).

**navigator**
Channel mixer p98
Hue/Saturation p69
Basic corrections p58

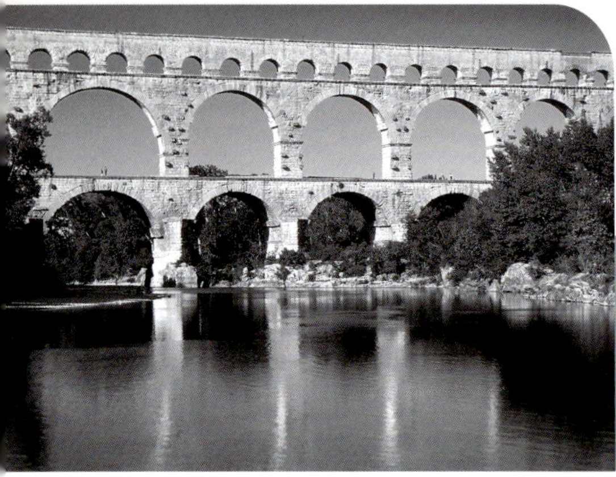

# Black-and-white

**The oldest type of photography is also one of the most powerful and evocative. And the digital photographer has the tools to make a great black-and-white shot from any original.**

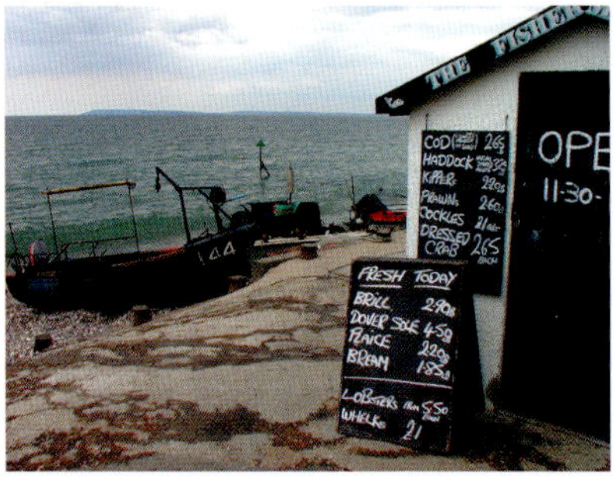


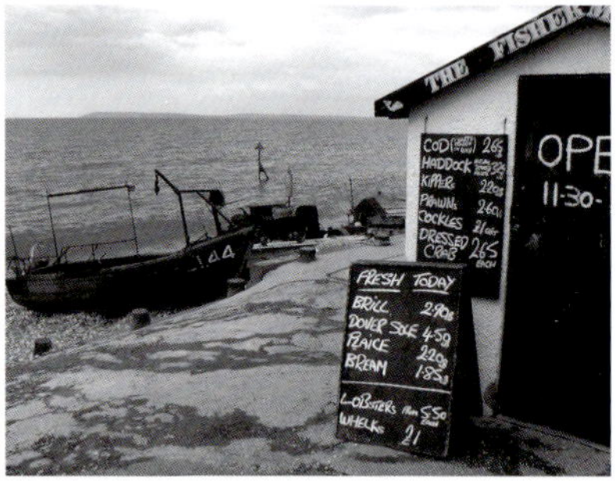


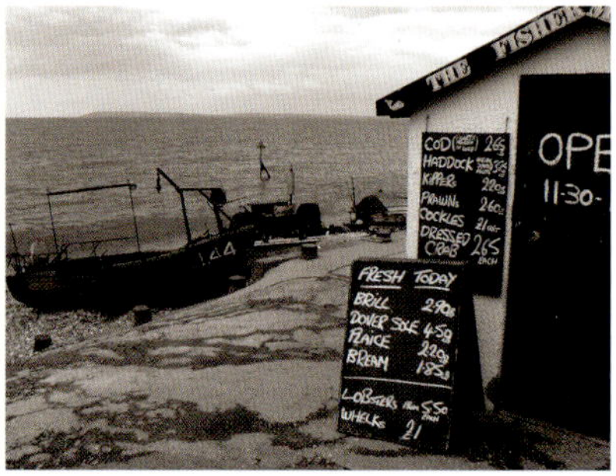


**01** Although you can use virtually any shot as the basis for a black-and-white print, scenes with good contrast and strong detail work better than those which rely on color for their impact. The beauty of digital photography is that you never have to choose between color or black-and-white; that's all done once you get home.

**02** There are many ways to convert a full-color image to black-and-white (or Grayscale as it is usually called in digital imaging). The quickest and easiest is to change the mode from RGB Color to Grayscale (in Photoshop you'll find this under the Image>Mode menu). The result is usually a little flat.

**03** An alternative is to 'desaturate' the image. You can do this by using the Hue/Saturation controls (simply reduce the saturation to zero). Photoshop also has a Desaturate command under the Image>Adjust menu. The difference in the end result is often minimal; in this case a small amount of color remained in the image. The main reason for desaturating rather than converting to Grayscale is that the image remains in RGB Color mode; useful if you intend to add a tone or hand-coloring.

**technical details**
Olympus C-2000L
digital camera
Adobe Photoshop 5.5

**tools**
Mode change
Desaturate
Levels

**keep in mind**
There are a thousand different black-and-white images inside each color shot, so – as ever – keep experimenting!

## Check out the channels

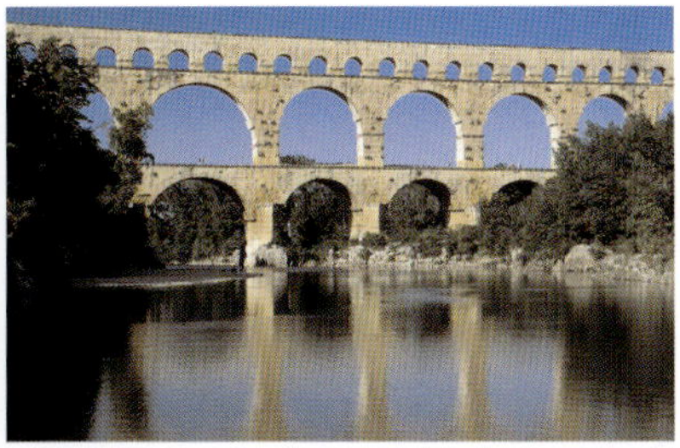

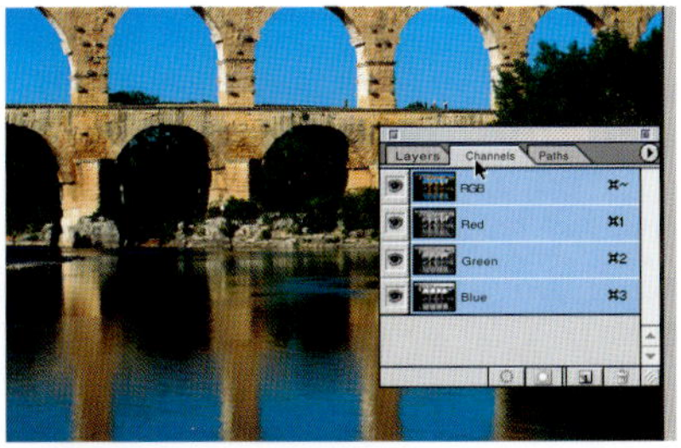

**01** In order to produce a more dynamic black-and-white print we need to excercise a little control over the process.

**02** Every color image is made up of three Grayscale channels (red, green and blue); you can see them by opening the Channels palette.

Each channel has its own unique characteristics, with the red channel usually the best for landscapes. The result is similar to shooting conventional black-and-white using a red filter. You can split the color image into three new Grayscale images using the Image>Adjust >Split Channels command.

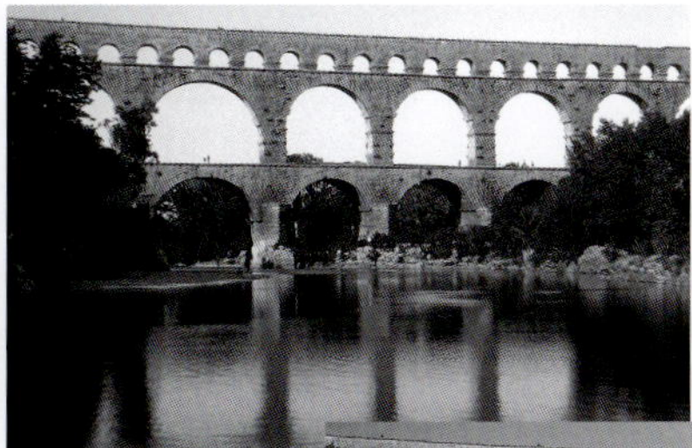

**Blue**

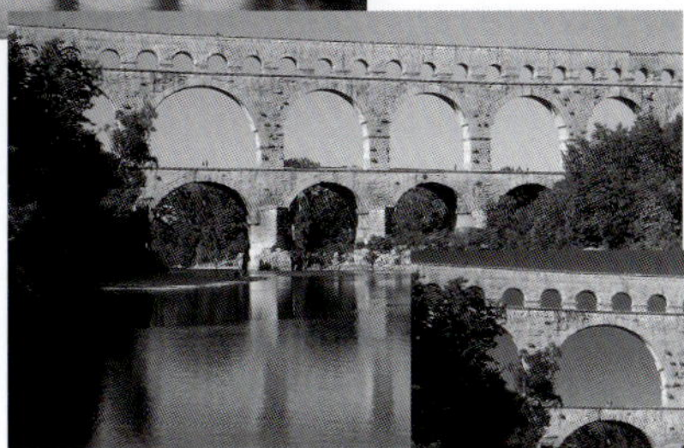

**Green**

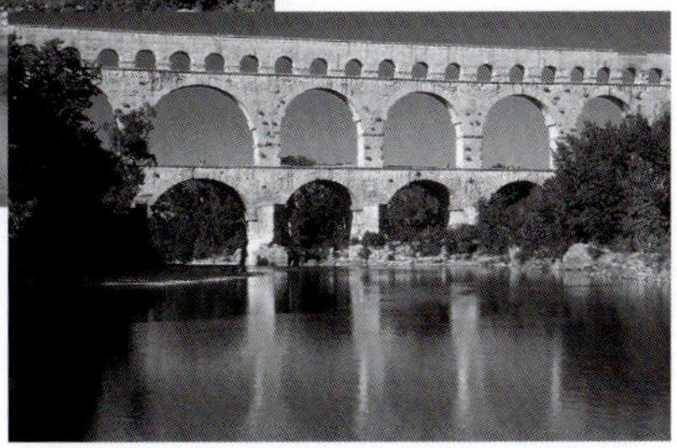

**Red**

### Dodging and burning tips

The Dodge and Burn tools allow you to selectively lighten and darken areas of the image in the same way that an experienced darkroom printer does.

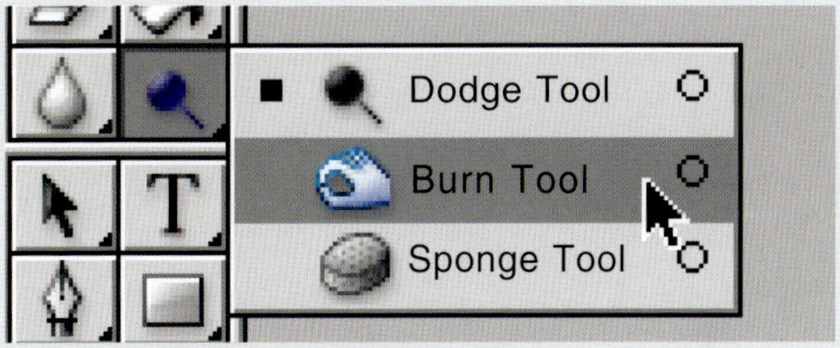


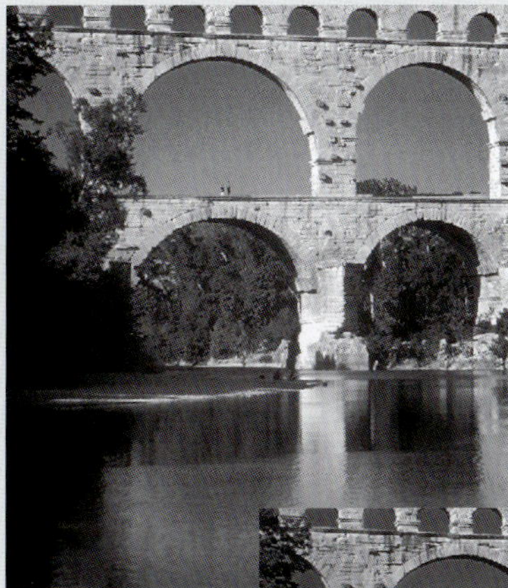

**The original image. I want to increase the contrast without losing any image detail.**

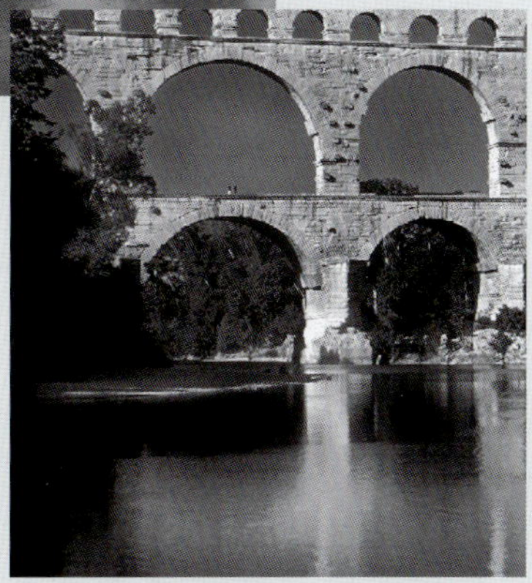

**The same scene after a few minutes' dodging and burning.**

**channel viewing**
In Photoshop you can view the individual channels by holding down the control key (apple key on a Mac) and pressing 1 (red), 2 (green) or 3 (blue). Press control ~ (the tilde key) to view the full RGB image again.

## Channel Mixer

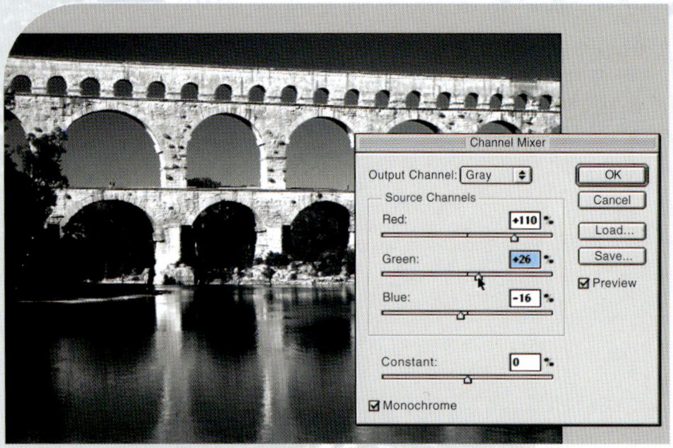


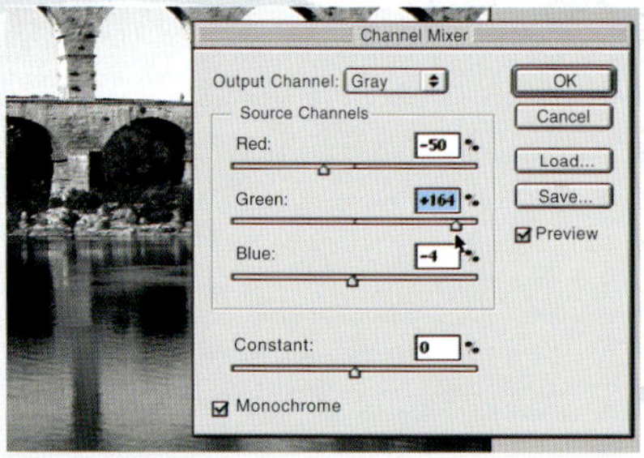


**01** A more sophisticated tool is the Channel Mixer, which allows us to fine-tune how the final Grayscale image is produced. Click on the Monochrome option and you can choose how the three channels are mixed to produce the monochrome image.

You should ensure that the percentages of the three channels add up to 100 or the overall brightness of the image will be changed (for the same reason it is rarely necessary to move the 'Constant' slider).

For scenic shots, I usually start with the red set to around +110%, and experiment with the green and blue quantities until I am happy with the overall tonal balance. The result of the settings shown above is reproduced to the right.

**02** Reducing the red and increasing the green and blue produces a totally different effect, with a much paler sky.

output

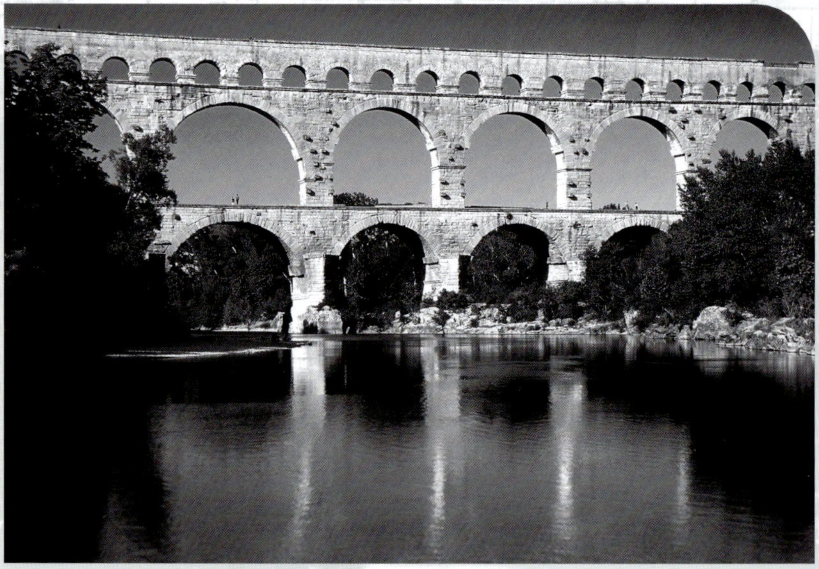

**Photoshop keyboard shortcuts**

| | |
|---|---|
| Levels | ctrl-L/⌘-L |
| Curves | ctrl-M/⌘-M |
| View red channel | ctrl-1/⌘-1 |
| View green channel | ctrl-2/⌘-2 |
| View blue channel | ctrl-3/⌘-3 |
| View composite RGB | ctrl-~/⌘-~ |

**tools**

Channel Mixer
Channels Palette
Levels
Curves
Gaussian Blur

## Contrast adjustments

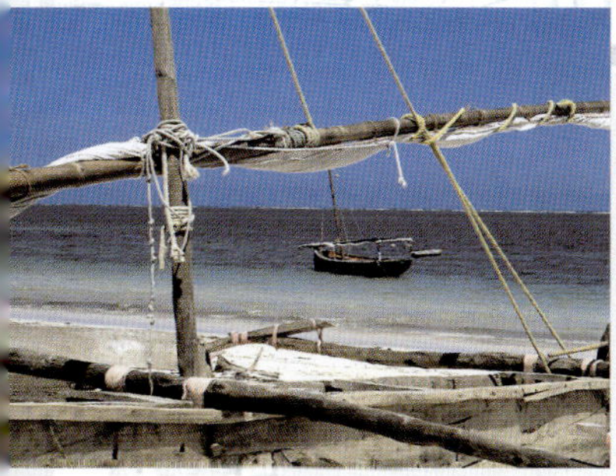

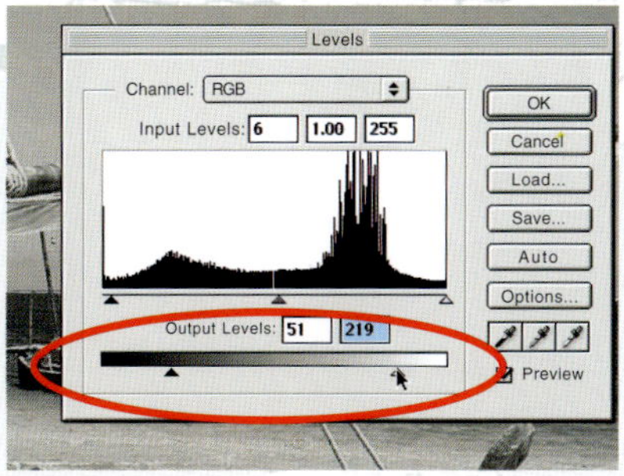


**01** Start with any color photograph and convert it to Grayscale (using any of the methods I have mentioned previously).

**02** Reducing contrast is a simple case of opening the Levels dialog and moving the Output Levels sliders towards the centre.

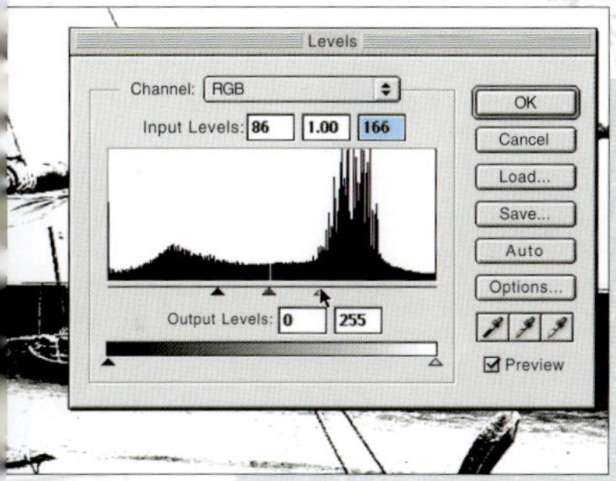


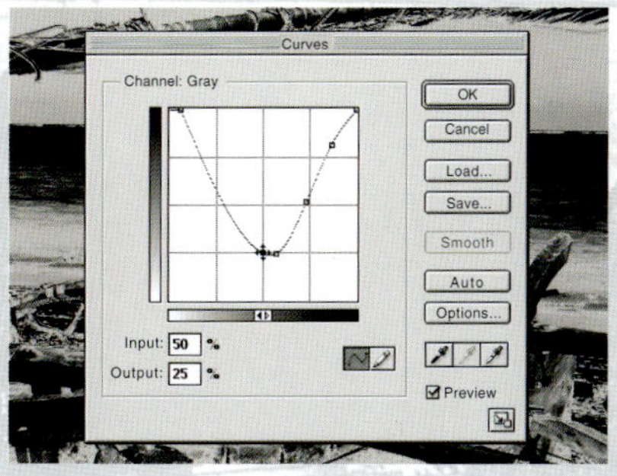


**03** To increase contrast move the black-and-white point sliders in towards the centre. If you go far enough you'll end up with a 'lith' effect as shown here.

**04** By playing with the curves you can get an amazing array of effects. As with color pictures a U-shaped curve produces an effect similar to solarization in conventional photography.

### Putting it all together

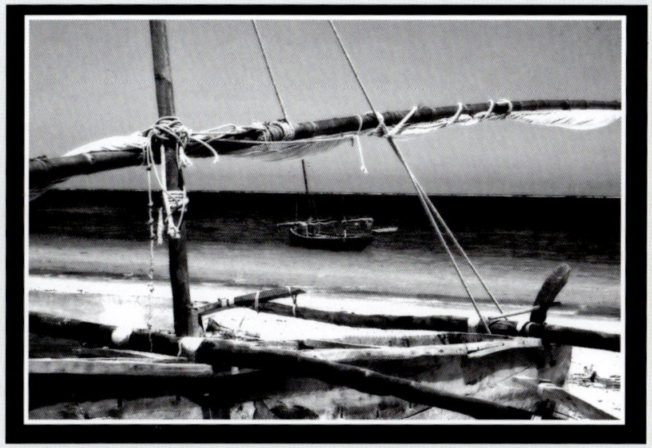

You can really get creative with digital black-and-white; the image above is the result of four separate processes. First, I did some channel mixing (with a heavy red bias), and dodging and burning (to selectively increase the contrast). Next, I created a copy layer, which was then Gaussian blurred and changed to a blend mode of Multiply. This gives a similar result to printing through a soft filter, with the shadows bleeding into the highlights for a subtle, almost eerie effect. The final step was to add a keyline and a black border.

**navigator**

Using levels p64
Using curves p66
Zoom blur p90

**black-and-white printing**
Most color inkjet printers struggle to produce a totally neutral Grayscale print. The solution is to buy specialist black-and-white print cartridges (the most popular are manufactured by Lyson Inks) or, to give your image a color tone, see page 100.

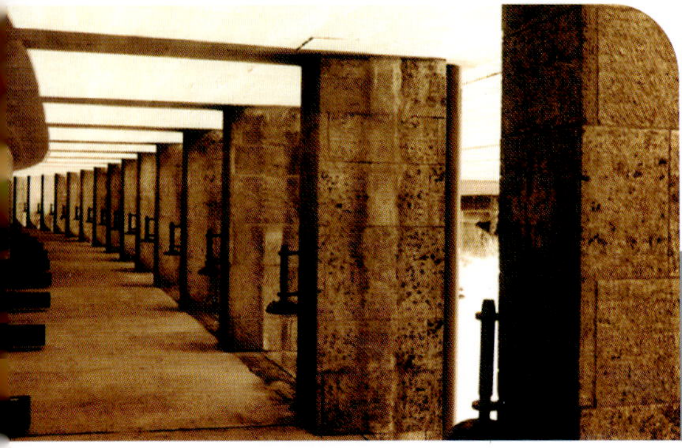

# Color toning

Imaging software such as Photoshop allows us to apply an almost infinite variety of tones to Grayscale images, adding a great deal of atmosphere along the way.

input

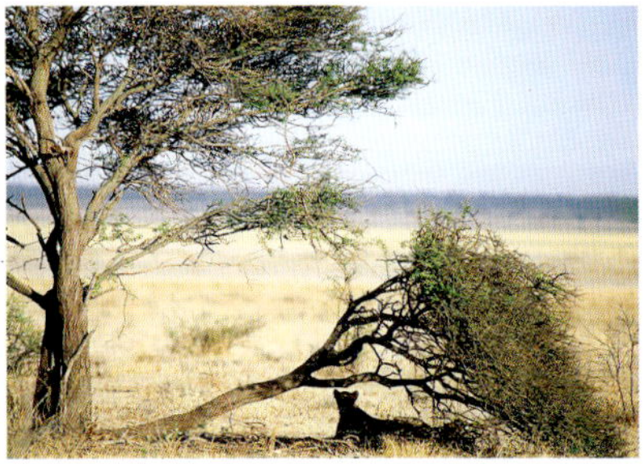

**01** Our starting point for this project is a fairly uninspiring snap showing - just visible - a lioness, resting in a Kenyan safari park. It will work well in black-and-white as it has plenty of detail in the trees and good contrast between the forground and background, but I'm only really using it here as an example.

The whole image has been cleaned up and sharpened whilst still in full-color mode.

process

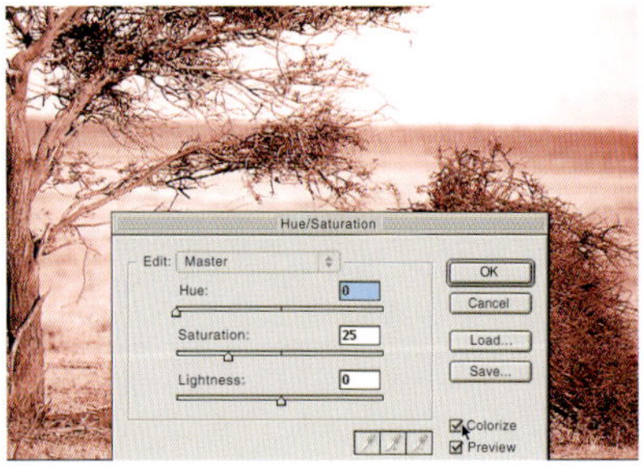


**02** By far the easiest, and most controllable, way to add tone to an image is via the Hue/Saturation and Lightness command. In Photoshop, in the bottom left of the dialog (it may be elsewhere in other applications), you'll find a option marked 'Colorize'; make sure it is checked. Immediately, you will see your photograph turn into a toned monochrome image.

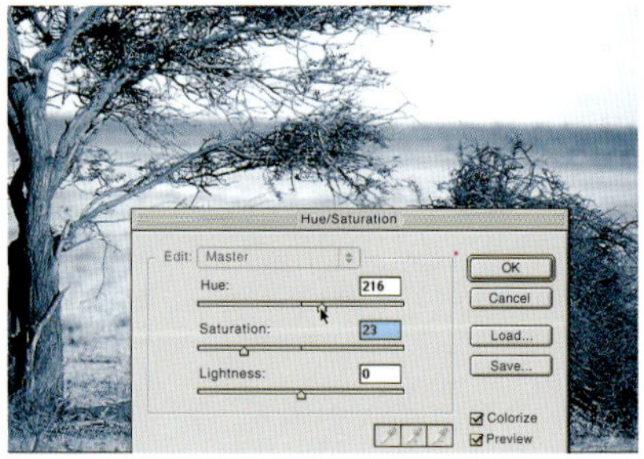


**03** By moving the Hue slider from left to right you can quickly experiment with a wide range of different colours. If the result looks a little gaudy - and it usually does - reduce the Saturation setting; about 20-30 is usually a good starting point.

**technical details (main image)**
Nikon D1X digital SLR
28-70mm Nikkor lens
Adobe Photoshop 6.0

**tools**
Hue/Saturation/
Lightness
Curves

**keep in mind**
Even a very subtle tone (using a low saturation) can alter the overall 'feeling' of an image, so don't feel the need to go over the top every time.

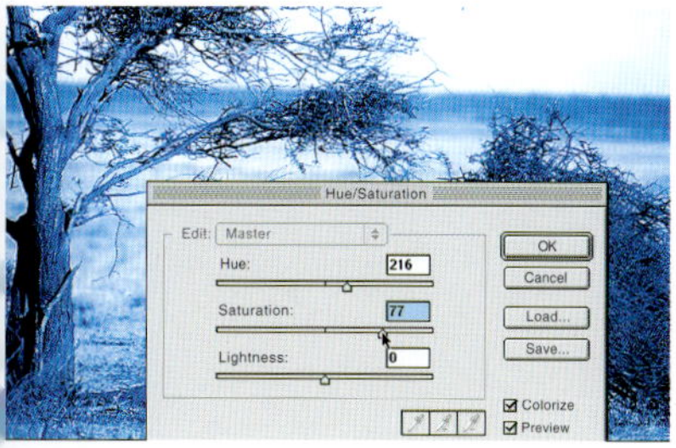


**04** Alternatively, for a bold graphic effect increase the saturation. You will lose some fine detail as the midtones start to fill in, but the results can be very striking.

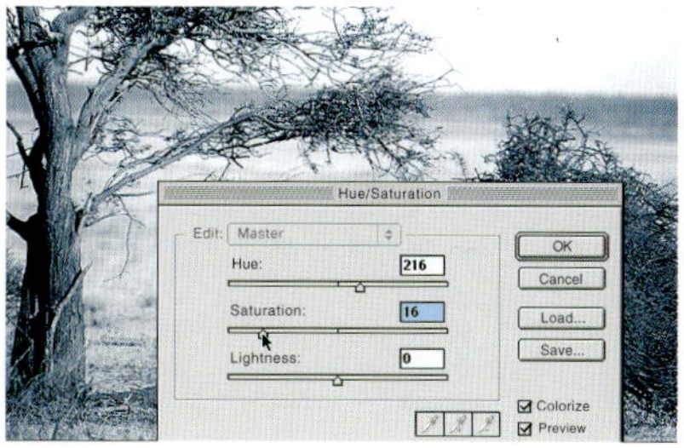


**05** For this image I want a much more subtle effect, so I've reduced the saturation considerably - to 16. As different printers produce very different results with the same colour settings you will need to use a little trial and error before you get exactly the result you want on paper.

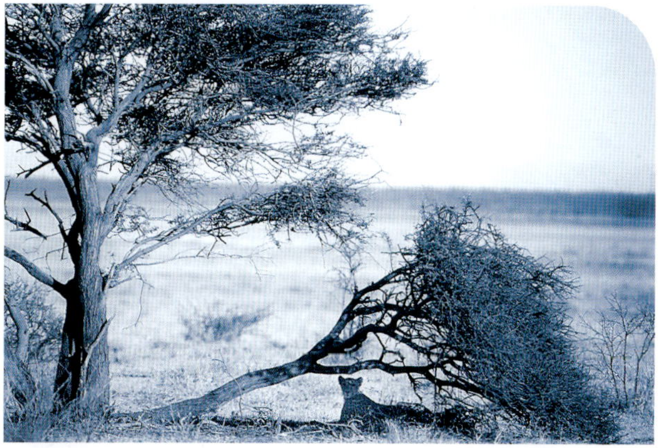

**06** The end result. A more advanced technique is to use a Hue/Saturation Adjustment Layer, which allows you to go back and change the tone at any point in the process.

### Matching tone to your subject

It makes sense to choose a tone that is sympathetic to your subject. As ever, the key here is to experiment until you find exactly the right treatment.

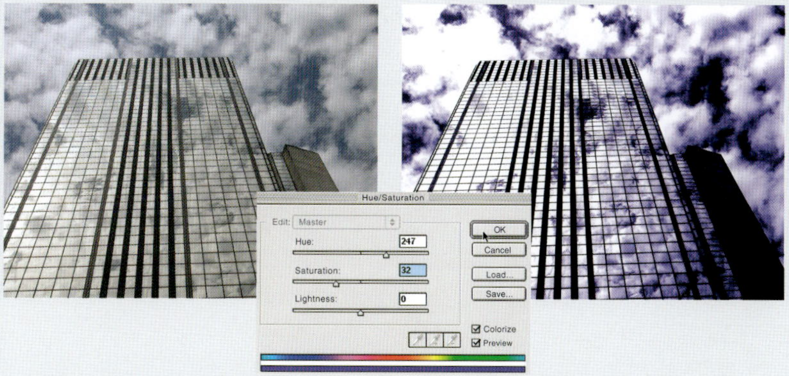


**This stark modern building in Brussels is well suited to a bold, cool approach. Here, I've increased the contrast using Curves and used a deep blue that doesn't look out of place applied to the expanse of sky.**

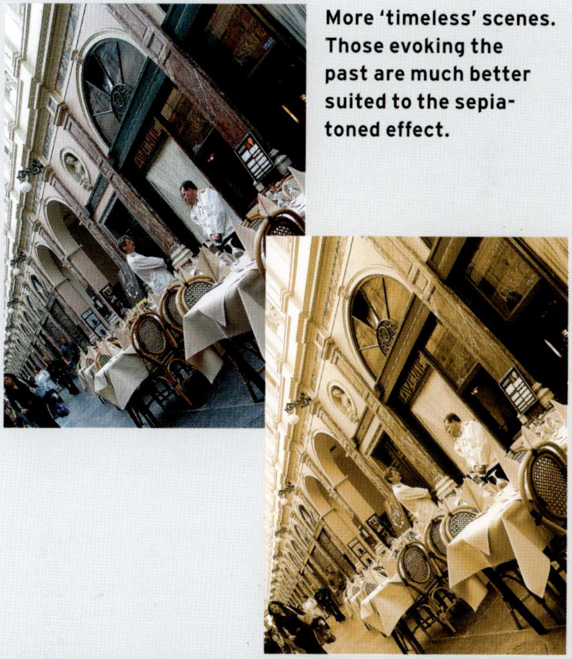

**More 'timeless' scenes. Those evoking the past are much better suited to the sepia-toned effect.**

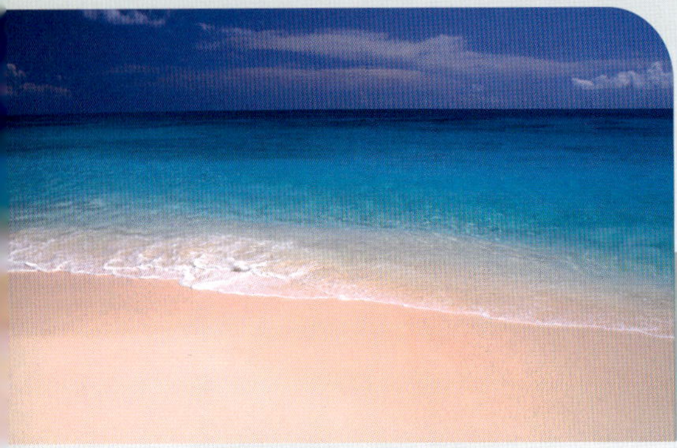

# Borders and edges

**Adding a border, or a cool edge effect, to an image can be just the lift it needs to turn something merely adequate into something special.**

## process

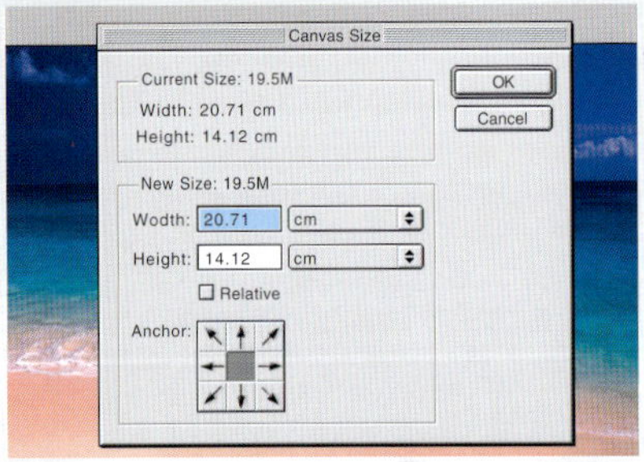


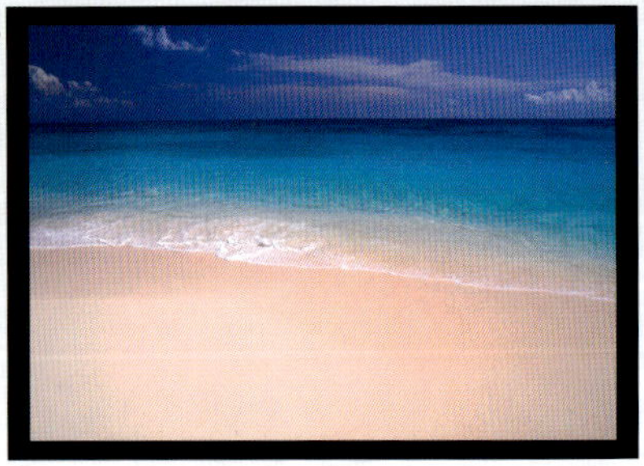

**01** First we'll look at a simple colored border. This couldn't be easier. Open your image and from the Image menu choose Canvas Size. Increase the width and height of the canvas by double the size of border you want. For example, if you want a 5mm border all round, increase both dimensions by 10mm. Leave the 'Anchor' point in the centre of the canvas as shown above.

**02** And there you have it. The colour of the border is defined by the current background colour, so if you want black (the most common choice) press D (to restore the default background and foreground colors), then X to swap foreground for background. You can, of course, choose any background color using the toolbar.

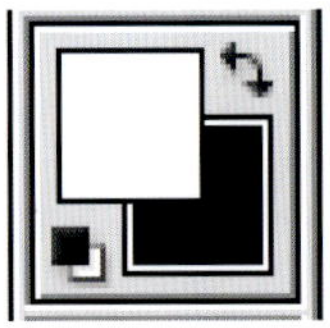

## output

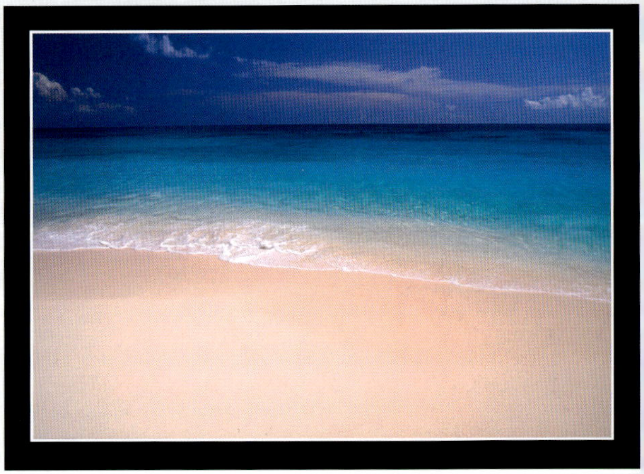

**03** In this case I've added a keyline to separate the image from its border. To do this simply perform step 01 twice; first with a white background and a small Canvas Size increase, then with a black background color and a larger increase.

**technical details**
Canon PowerShot G2 digital camera
Adobe Photoshop 5.5

**tools**
Canvas Size
Foreground and Background colors

**keep in mind**
Black borders suit virtually any image, but other neutral colors can also be effective.

**Adding a textured edge**

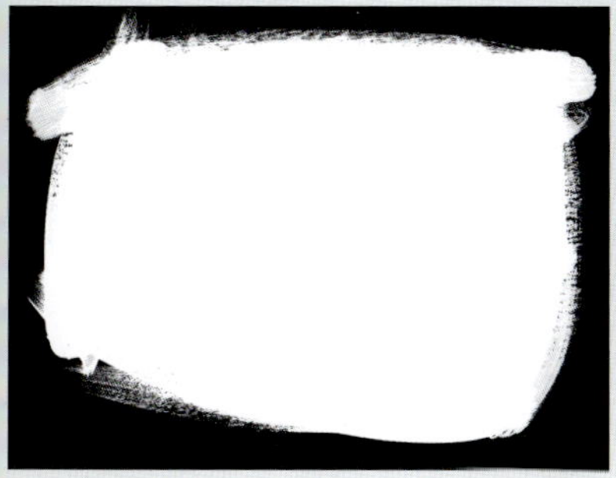

**01** Start by scanning a torn sheet of paper roughly the same shape as your image. You need to use Levels to make the central part white and the outside area completely black.

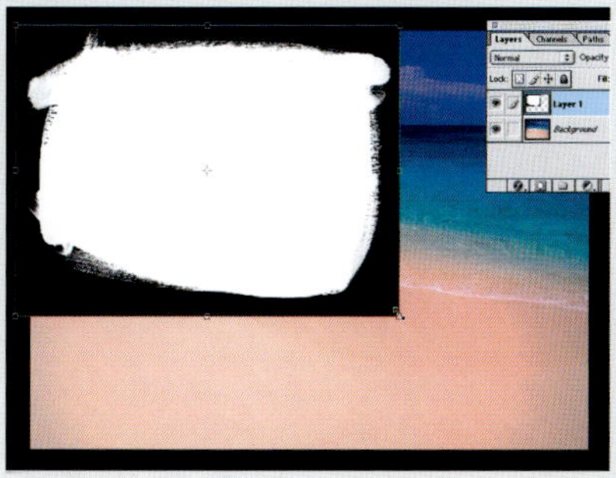

**02** Drag the image created in step 01 onto your target photograph using the Move tool. It will appear as a new layer. Use the Transform command to stretch it to fit the underlying picture.

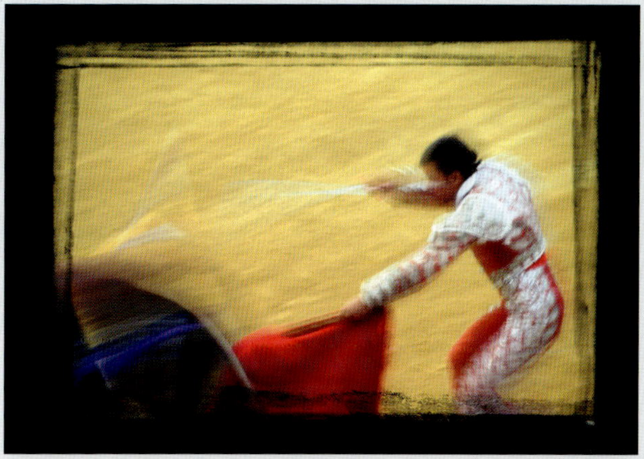

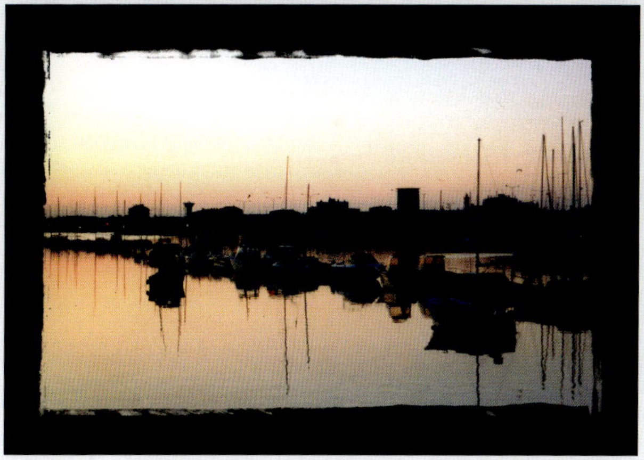

**04** The images above were created using commercially available masking frames, and exactly the same process described opposite.

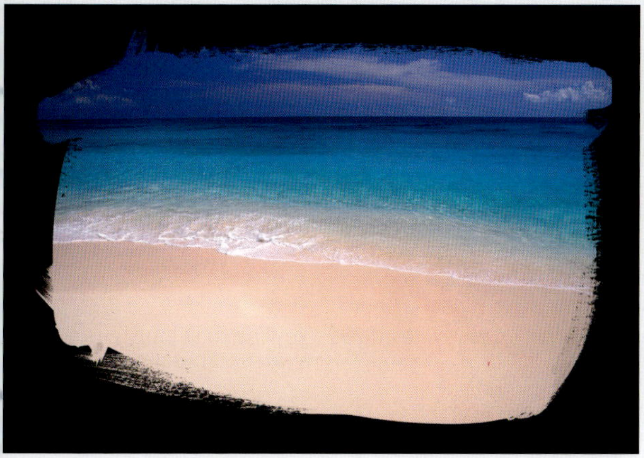

**03** Finally, change the Blend mode of the upper (torn paper) layer to Darken. Any white parts of the upper layer will allow your original picture to show through.

**keep in mind**

You can create natural-looking edges using almost anything you can get onto your flatbed scanner. Just remember that for your original image to be masked properly the scan needs to be adjusted to ensure the areas to 'show through' are white, and the rest black.

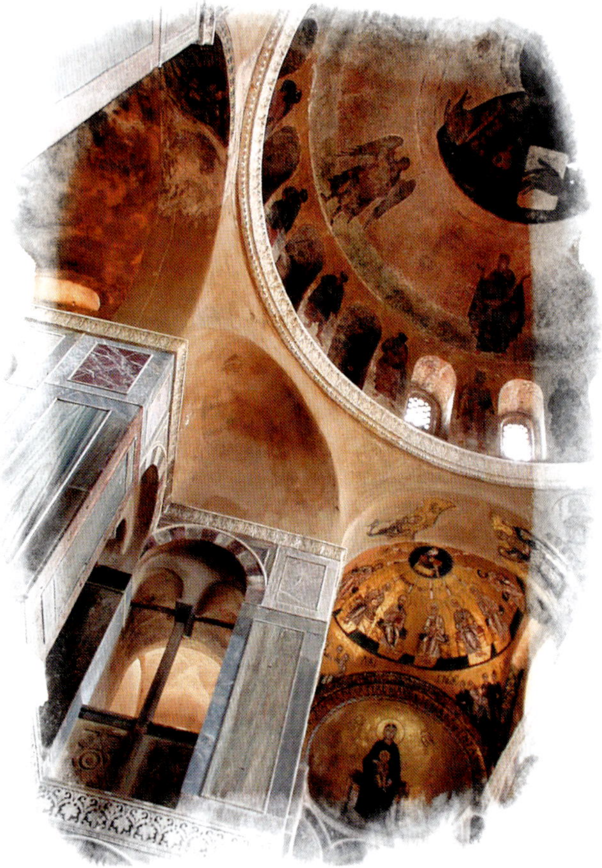

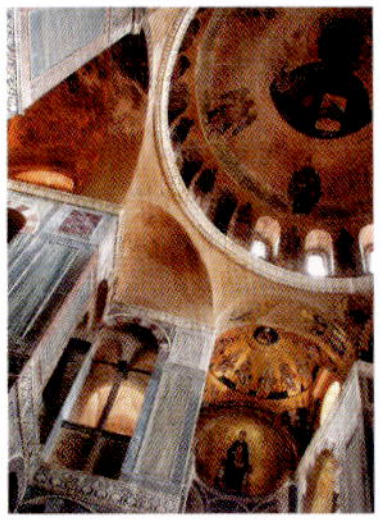

If you want your edge effect on a white background you need to invert the mask created in step 01 on the previous page and use Screen as the blending mode. In Screen mode any areas of the masking layer that are black will show through, and any that are white will be hidden.

## Vignette

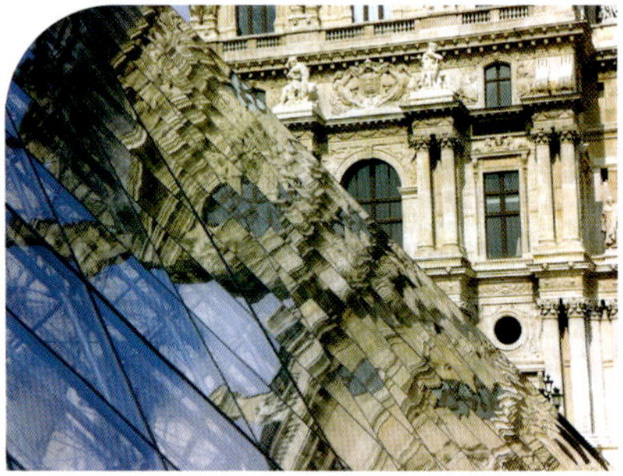

**01** The vignette, a fading shade framing the picture, is an old favourite. Start by opening your image. Here, I'm using a semi-abstract shot of the Louvre in Paris. Increase the canvas size by about 20% both horizontally and vertically.

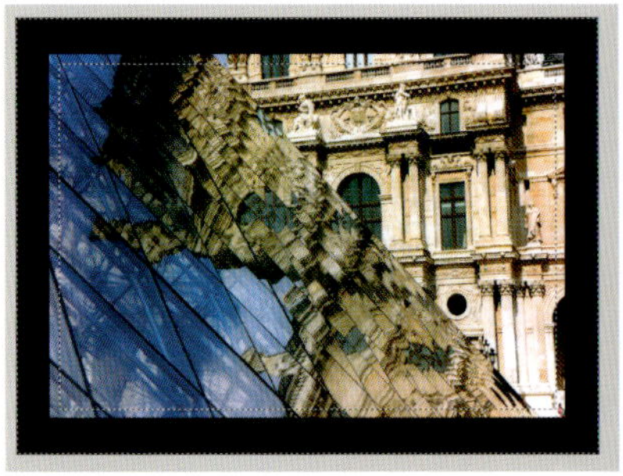

**02** Make a rectangular selection about a tenth of the way into your image on each side. Invert the selection (Select>Inverse).

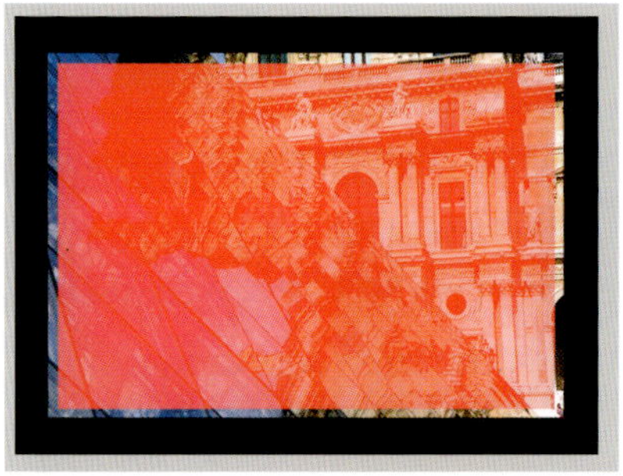

**03** There are several things you could do now: I'm going to use Photoshop's Quick Mask. Press Q to edit the mask.

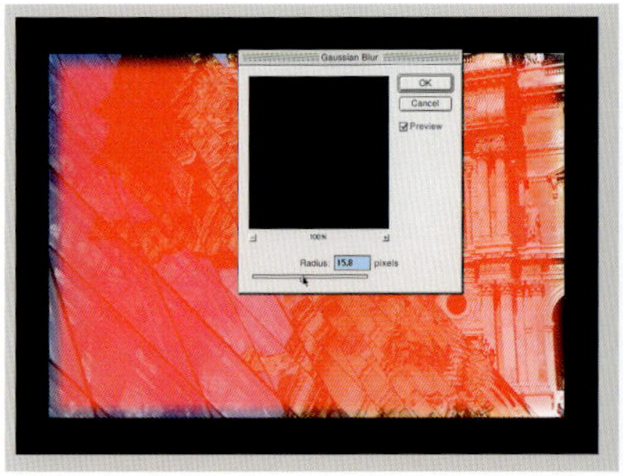

**04** Run the Gaussian Blur filter on the mask. The advantage of this method is that it is easy to see the extent of your vignette on the preview.

**Photoshop keyboard shortcuts**

| | |
|---|---|
| Enter Quick Mask mode | Q |
| Restore default colours (black foreground, white background) | D |
| Swap foreground/background colours | X |
| Transform layer | ctrl-T/⌘-T |

**tools**

Canvas Size
Rectangular Marquee
Layer Masks
Effects filters

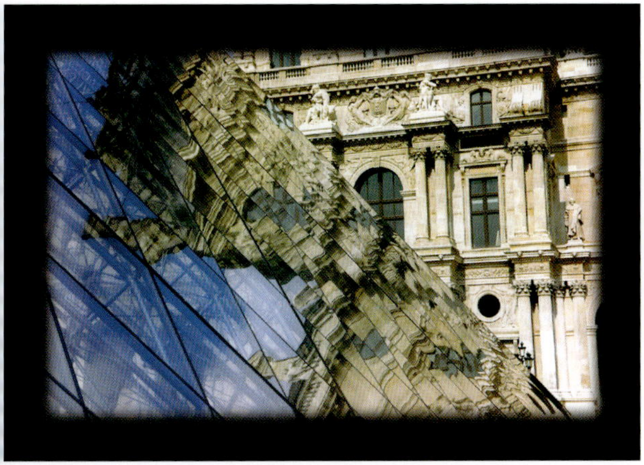

**05** Exit Quick Mask mode and (once you have the correct background color) press the delete key. Both white and black work well as backgrounds.

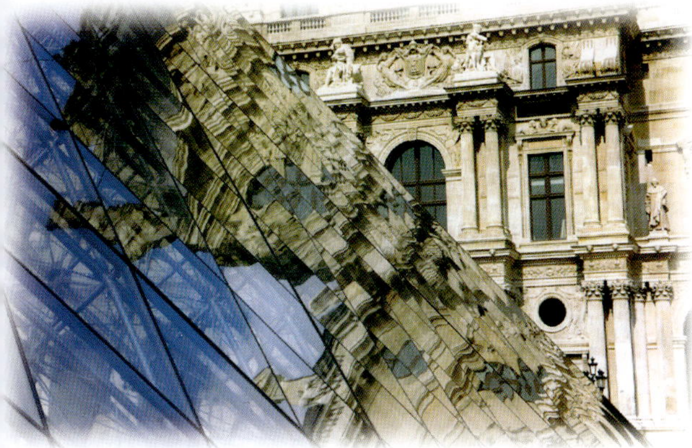

### Distressed edges tips

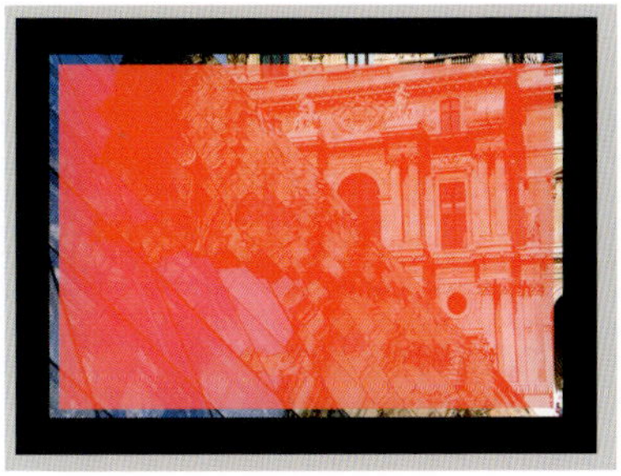

By distorting the mask created in step 03 on the opposite page you can make your own distressed edge.

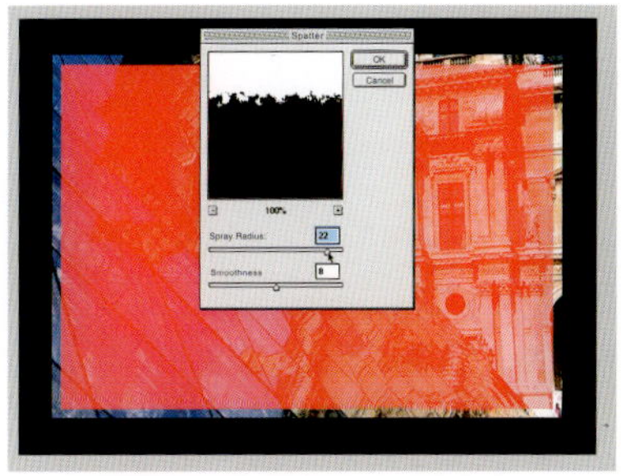

Here, I'm running the Spatter filter on the mask. As ever, the key here is experimentation.

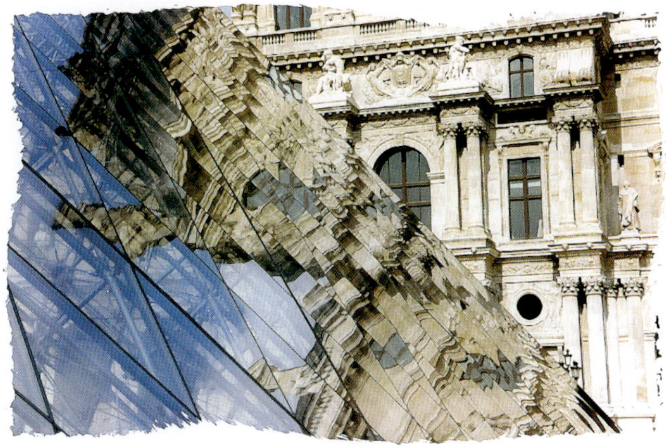

For the final image (above) I also used the wave filter to create a less rectangular mask.

**keep in mind**
An even quicker way to add a vignette is to simply feather a rectangular selection then delete (or flood-fill). The only problem is that the effect is impossible to preview and difficult to control. Don't forget that the Quick Mask technique described here can also be used with a normal Layer Mask, in which case you can tweak the effect to your heart's content.

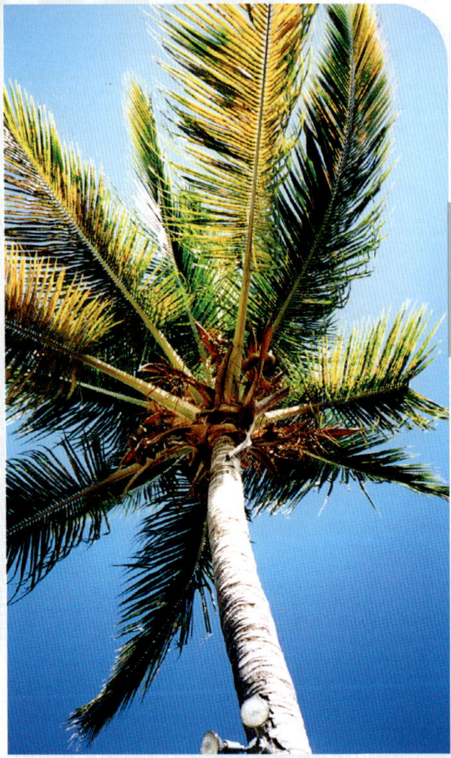

# Paint and texture

Although often overdone, paint and texture effects can transform an everyday photograph into a virtual work of art.

## input

**01** The best images for paint effects are those with strong, bold subjects, free of visual clutter and not too much detail (much of which will be lost in the process). The simple sky in this image also helps by not distracting from the main subject.

## process

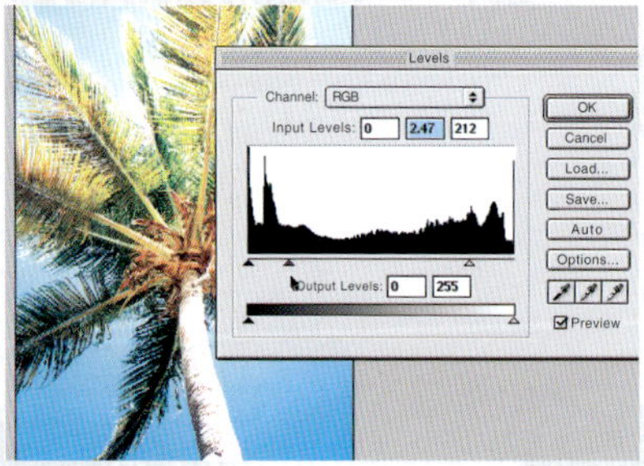


**02** To create a realistic watercolor, - and these tend to be quite 'washed-out' - let's lighten the image.

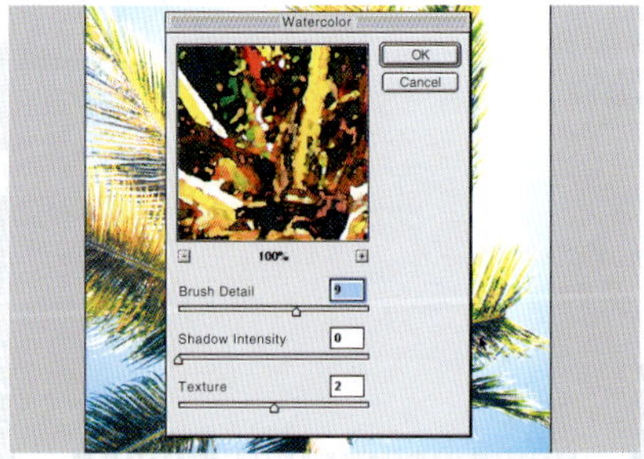


**03** Run the Watercolor filter - you'll need to experiment with the settings.

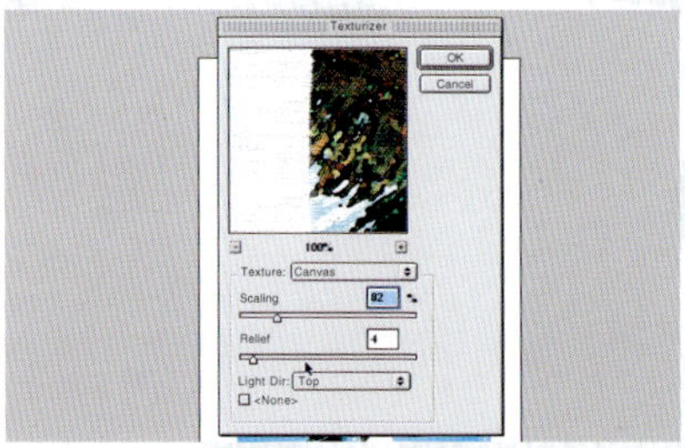


**04** Most paint effects are more convincing when they are combined with a paper texture. Here, I'm using Photoshop's texturizer and the 'canvas' preset.

**technical details**
Olympus C-2020 ZOOM digital camera
Adobe Photoshop 5.5

**tools**
Levels
Watercolor filter
Texturizer
Layer Masks

**keep in mind**
As an alternative to adding a texture digitally, experiment with different textured papers in your inkjet printer. With a little effort you can produce a very convincing 'painting'.

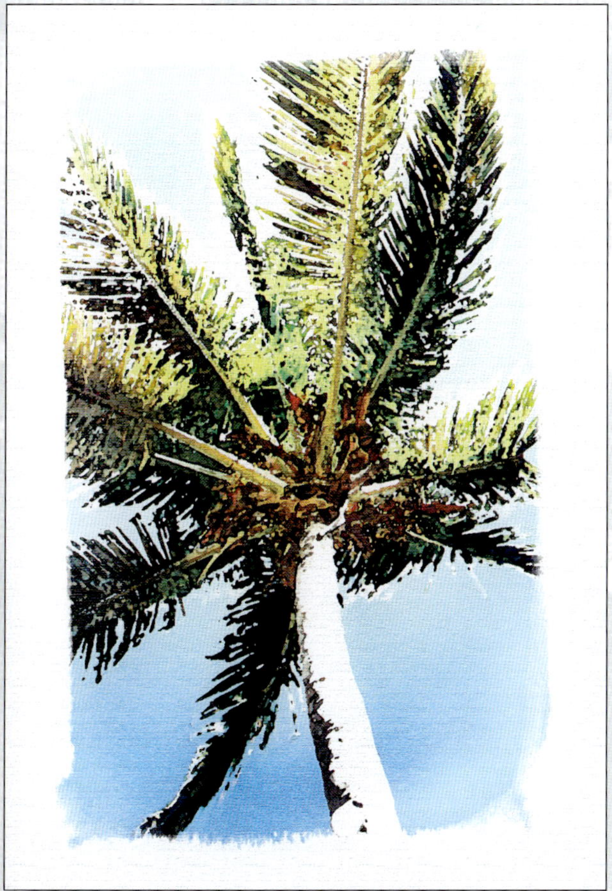

**05** The most convincing result was obtained using an edge created using the method described on page 105 (before the filters were applied).

## Paint effects tips

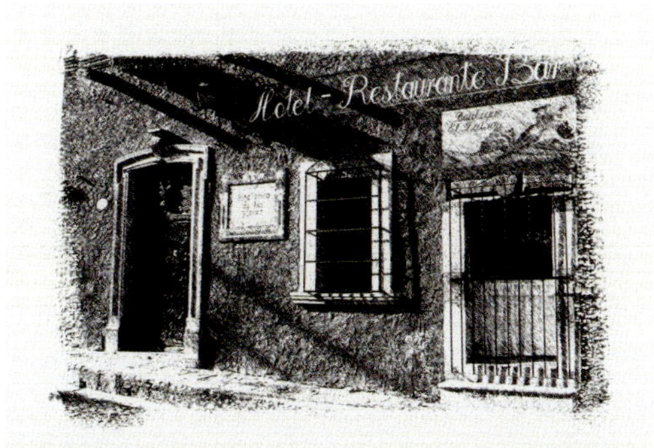


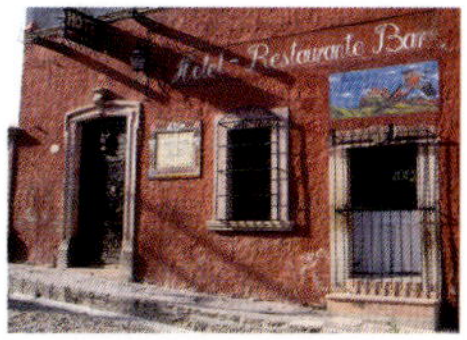


**Choose a non-white background color before running Pen filters and combine with a textured mask.**

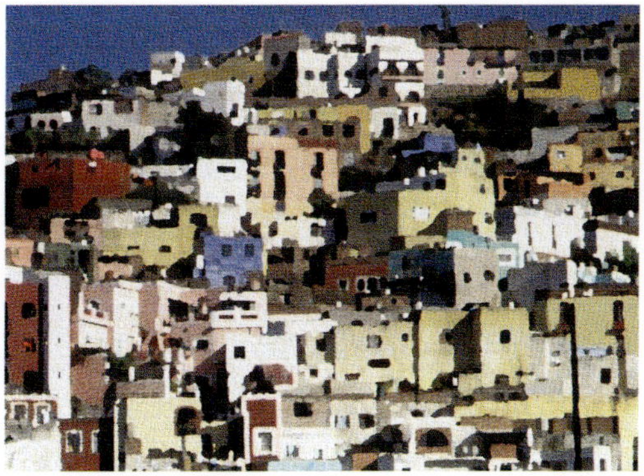

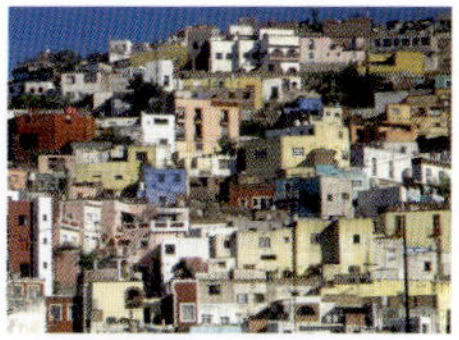

**The Palette Knife tool can, when used with a canvas texture, create a realistic oil painting.**

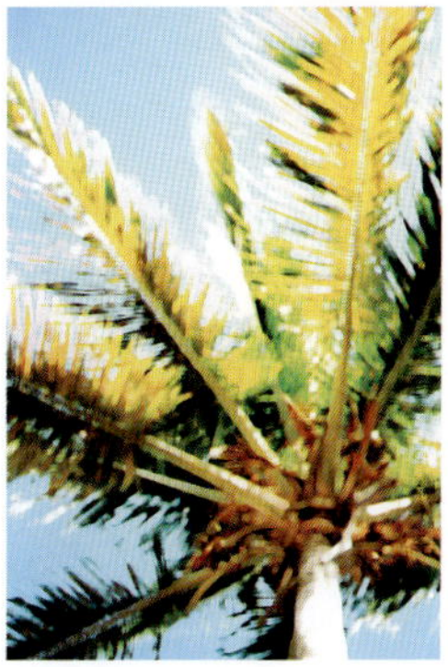

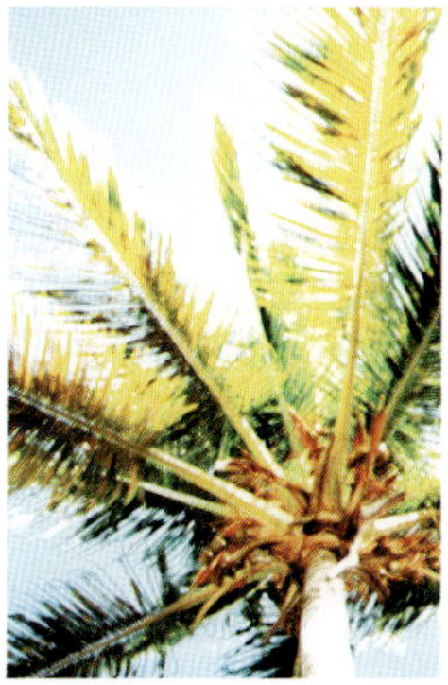

**Running Paint or Pen filters on a duplicate layer and changing the Blend mode can produce a subtle, soft effect. Here the Paint Daubs filter has been used on a Layer set to Screen Blend mode.**

**navigator**


Distressed edges p105
Using levels p64
Color printing p26

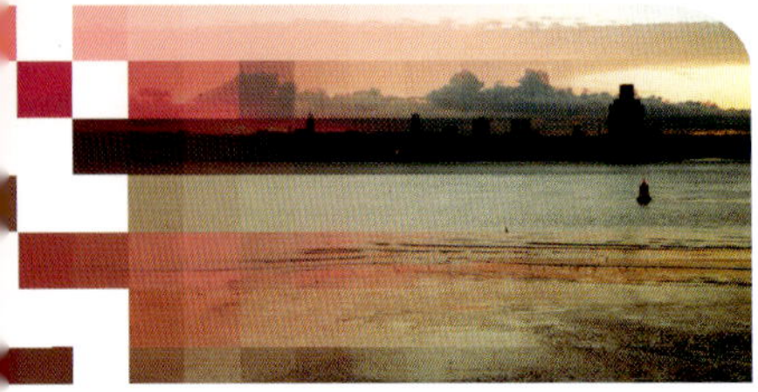

# Glossary

## A

**Aperture** • Variable opening that controls the amount of light that passes through the lens.

**Analogue** • Continuously variable.

**Anti-aliasing** • Smoothing the jagged edges of selection or paint tools in digital-imaging applications.

## B

**Bit** • A binary digit, basic digital quantity representing either 1 or 0. The smallest unit of computer information.

**Bitmap** • [1] An image made up of dots, or pixels. [2] A color mode in Photoshop where every pixel is either black or white (no grays or colors).

**Byte** • Standard computer file size measurement: contains eight bits. Other common units include Kilobyte (K: 1024 bytes), Megabyte (MB: 1024K) and Gigabyte (GB: 1024 MB).

## C

**CCD** • A Charged Coupled Device (CCD) converts light into electrical current. The digital camera equivalent of film.

**CMY, CMYK** • (Cyan, Magenta, Yellow) Color printing model used by dye-sub and low-end inkjet printers. CMYK adds black (Key) and is used for most professional printing. Most modern photo printers add pale Cyan and pale Magenta inks for improved pastel tones.

**Color bit depth** • The number of bits used to represent each pixel in an image; the higher the bit depth, the more colors appear in the image:

1-bit color = black-and-white image with no grays or colors;

8-bit color= 256 colors or grays;

24-bit color = 16.7 million colors ('photorealistic' color).

**Compact flash** • Type of removable media for digital cameras.

**Compression** • The 'squashing' of data to reduce file size for storage or to reduce transmission time. Compression can be 'lossy' (such as JPEG) or 'lossless' (such as TIFF LZW). Greater reduction is possible with lossy compression than with lossless schemes.

**Cropping tool** • A tool found in image-editing software that allows you to trim an image.

## D

**Data** • The generic name for any information used by a computer.

**Digital zoom** • Camera feature involving enlarging the central part of an image to give a similar effect to a telephoto lens (in fact, is simply a crop). This usually results in a drop in image quality.

**Dithering** • A method for simulating many colors or shades of gray with only a few.

**dpi** • (dots per inch) A measurement of the resolution of a printer or video monitor (see also **ppi**).

**Driver** • A software utility designed to tell a computer how to operate an external device (e.g. a printer).

## E

**Exposure** • The amount of light falling on the CCD of a digital camera or the film in a conventional camera. Exposure is determined by the combination of shutter speed (duration) and aperture (intensity).

**Exposure compensation** • The ability to increase or decrease the exposure set by the camera's automatic system.

## F

**Feathered edge** • Soft edge to a mask or selection. Allows seamless montage effects.

**File format** • The way that the information in a file is stored. In digital photography, common file formats include JPEG, TIFF and GIF.

**Filter** • Photo-editing software function that alters the appearance of the image being worked on, much like the physical filters that can be put on the front of camera lenses.

**Flash memory** • A type of fast memory chip that remembers all its data even when the power is turned off. Used in most digital camera cards.

**Focal length** • The attribute that determines the magnification and field of view of a lens.

**Focus** • Adjusting a lens so that the subject is recorded as a sharp image.

## G

**GIF** • A graphic file format developed for exchange of image files (only supports 256 colors).

**Grayscale** • What photographers would call a black-and-white image. It contains a range of gray tones as well as black-and-white.

## H

**Hue/Saturation** • An RGB image can also be defined by Hue, Saturation and Brightness, where Hue is the color and Saturation the 'strength'. Hue/Saturation controls are useful for altering colors without effecting overall brightness or contrast.

# I

**Image manipulation** • Once a digital image has been transferred into a computer, image-manipulation software allows the individual pixels to be altered in many ways. Color corrections, sharpening, photomontage and distortions are all forms of manipulation.

**Interpolation** • Increasing the number of pixels in an image or filling in missing color information by averaging the values of neighbouring pixels (basically using an educated guess). This 'upsampling' cannot add detail or information but is used by most digital cameras when recording images.

# J

**Jaggies** • The jagged stepped effect often seen in images whose resolutions are so low that individual pixels are visible.

**JPEG** • A file compression standard that is capable of very high level of compression, but is a 'lossy' method and so can degrade image quality. JPEG allows you to choose the level of compression (and thus the level of quality loss).

# L

**LCD monitor** • A small color screen found on many digital cameras that allows previewing/reviewing of images as they are taken.

# M

**Magic wand** • A selection tool that automatically selects areas of continuous color around the point where it is clicked. The tolerance setting defines how near a color must be to be included in the selection.

**Marquee** • Outline of dots created by an image-editing program to show areas selected for manipulation, masking or cropping.

**Mask** • In digital imaging an 8-bit overlay, which isolates areas of an image prior to processing. A mask is used to define an area of an image to which an effect will be applied. Often called a selection.

**Megapixel** • One million pixels; a measure of camera resolution.

# N

**Noise** • Unwanted electrical interference that degrades analogue electrical equipment. In digital cameras, this most often occurs in very low lighting or shadow areas in the form of pixels of the wrong color appearing at random in dark areas.

# O

**Optical resolution** • In scanners , the maximum resolution possible without resort to interpolation. Also used to describe a digital camera's true CCD resolution.

# P

**Photoshop plug-in** • A small piece of software that adds extra features or functions to Adobe Photoshop or other compatible applications.

**Photosite** • A single photosensitive element in a CCD that translates to one pixel in the resultant image. Also known as a CCD Element.

**Pixel** • (PICture ELement) The smallest element of a digitized image. Also, one of the tiny points of light that make up a picture on a computer screen.

**ppi** • Pixels/points per inch. A measure of the resolution of scanners, digital images and printers.

# R

**Removable media** • Small memory chips which store the captured images.

**Resample** • To change the number of pixels in an image. Upsampling uses interpolation to increase the number of pixels. Downsampling throws away pixels to reduce the size.

**Resize** • Changing the resolution or physical size of an image without changing the number of pixels. For example a 2x2" image at 300dpi becomes a 4x4" image at 150dpi. Often confused with **Resampling**.

**Resolution** • Measure of the amount of information in an image expressed in terms of the number of pixels per unit length (i.e. pixels per millimetre or pixels per inch). Camera resolution is usually defined as the actual number of pixels in an image (i.e. 640x480) (see **dpi** and **ppi**).

**RGB** • (Red, Green and Blue) TVs, monitors and digital cameras use a mix of R,G and B to represent all the colors in an image.

# S

**Saturation** • The amount of gray in a color. More gray means lower saturation. See also **Hue/Saturation**.

**Selection** • An area of an image isolated before applying an effect.

# T

**Telephoto lens** • Lens that has the effect of making subjects seem closer than they actually are.

**Thumbnail** • A small, low-resolution version of a larger image file that is used for quick identification and for displaying many images on a single screen.

**TIFF** • The standard file format for high-resolution bitmapped graphics.

# UVW

**Unsharp masking** • A software feature that selectively sharpens a digital image in areas of high contrast whilst having little effect on areas of solid color. The effect is to increase the apparent detail and sharpness.

# XYZ

**White-balance** • In digital camera terms, an adjustment to ensure that colors are captured accurately (without any 'color cast') whatever the lighting used. This can be set automatically, using presets for different lighting types, or measured manually.

**Wide-angle lens** • A lens of short focal length giving a wide-angle view, allowing more of a scene to be fitted into a photograph.

**Zoom lens** • Variable focal length lens that allows the user to adjust his field of view ('zoom in or out').

# Acknowledgments

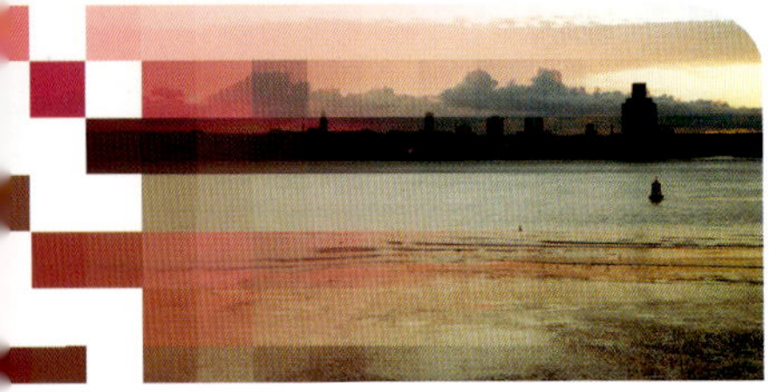

I would like to thank the photographers whose work appears throughout this book, especially Steve Davey, without whose wealth of travel-photography experience the first part of this book would have been considerably less authoratitive.

My thanks also go to Dave Edwards at S2 Creative Solutions for his help with the design and all the staff at RotoVision for the production of this book.

Thanks also to the many people working for manufacturers of digital imaging products who kindly loaned equipment for the production of this book, including Adobe UK, Fuji Photo Film UK, Nikon UK, Sony UK and Olympus UK.

Finally, I must thank Claire for her continuing support in everything I do.

**Simon Joinson**

PICTURE CREDITS

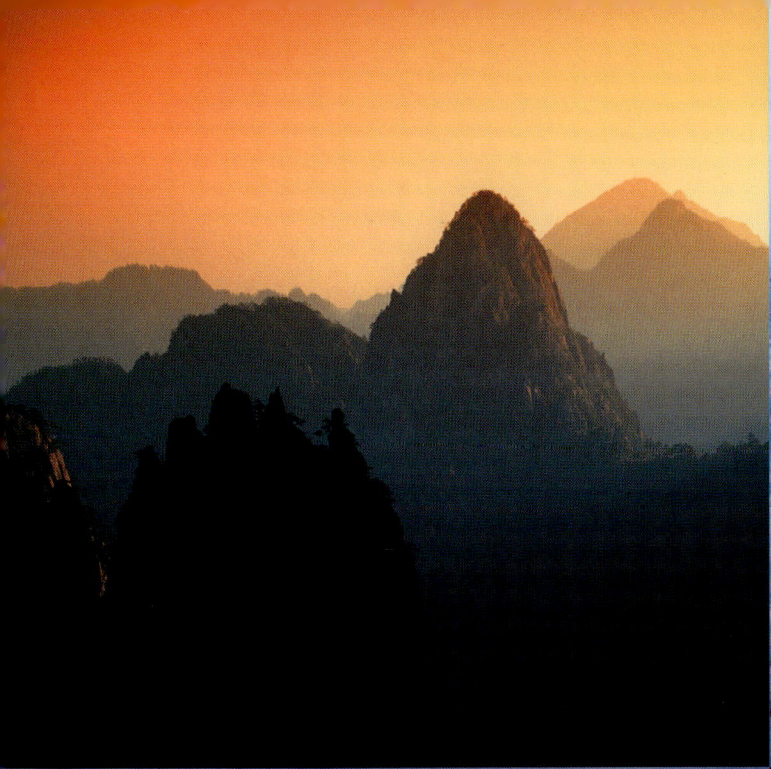
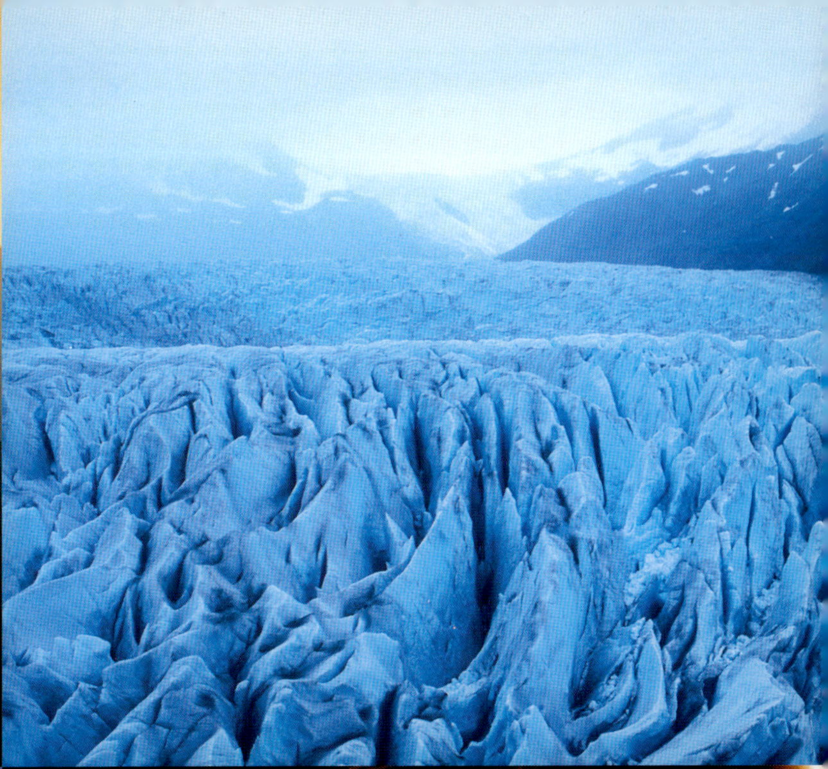
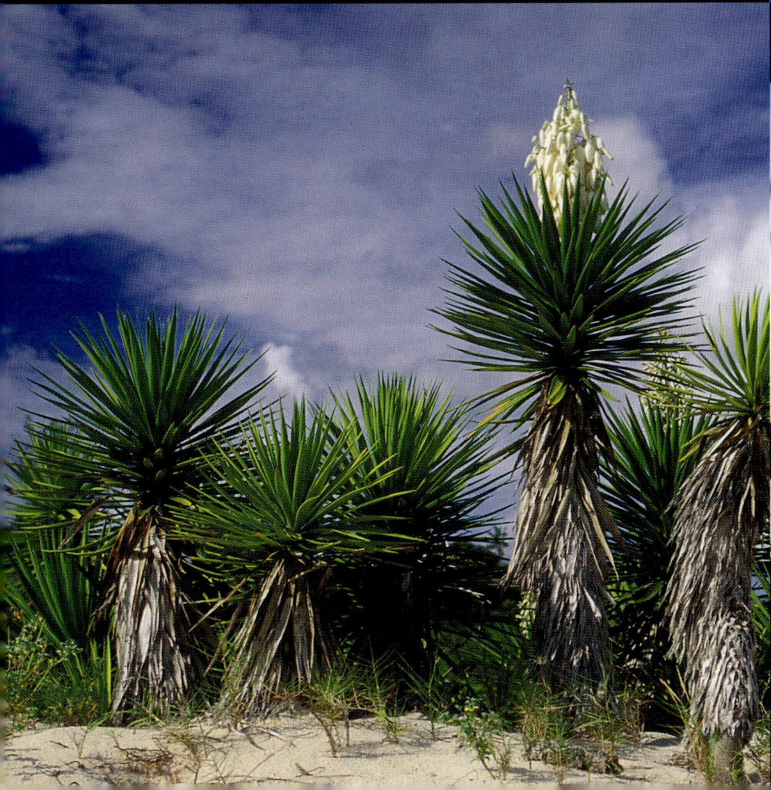
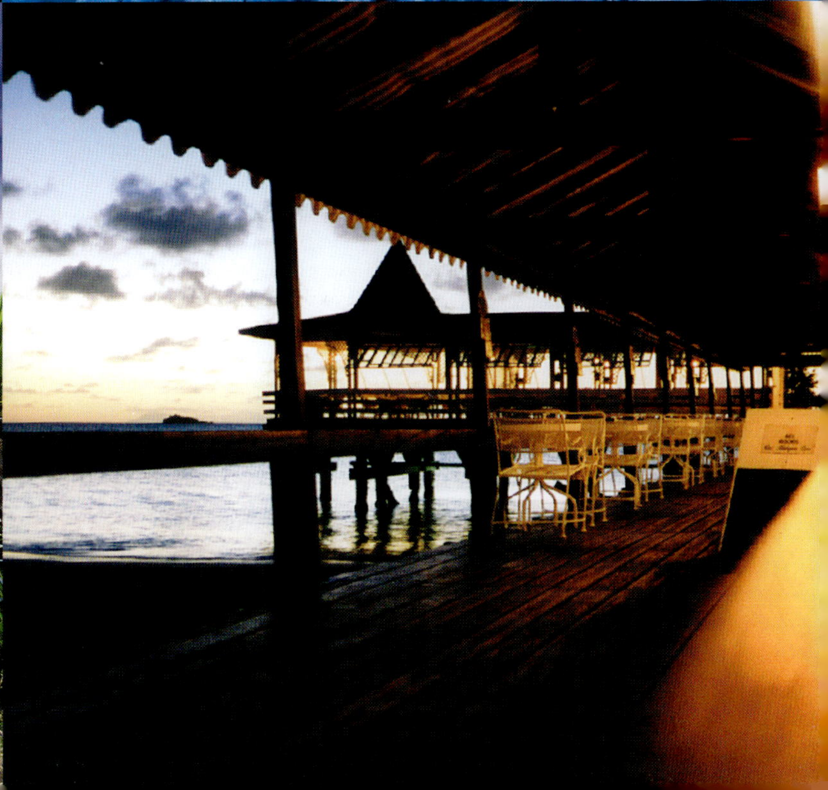

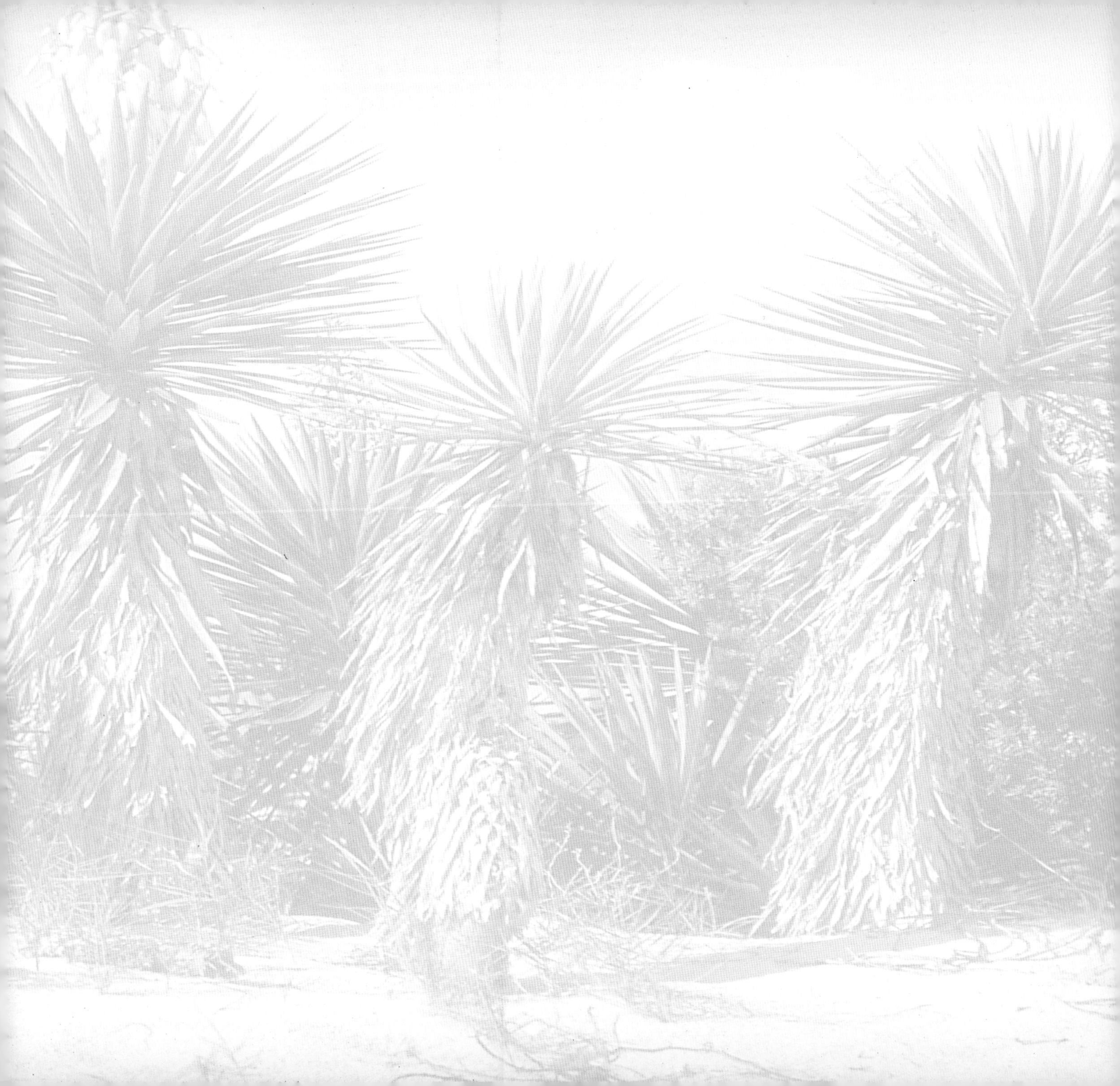